THE LION AND THE CHAKRA

Love, lies and loyalty in the last days of Anglo-India

OWEN THORPE

Matador
5 Weir Road
Kibworth Beauchamp
Leicester LE8 0LQ, UK
Tel: (+44) 116 279 2299
Fax: (+44) 116 279 2277
Email: books@troubador.co.uk
Web: www.troubador.co.uk/matador

ISBN 978-1848763-623

British Library Cataloguing in Publication Data.
A catalogue record for this book is available from the British Library.

Typeset in 11pt Book Antiqua by Troubador Publishing Ltd, Leicester, UK

Matador is an imprint of Troubador Publishing Ltd

Printed in Great Britain by the MPG Books Group, Bodmin and King's Lynn

For Maric and Paul

And in memory of Lt. O. E. Thorpe, 3/17th Dogra Regiment,

killed in the fall of Singapore on 15 February 1942

PRAISE FOR:

Paper Boats in the Monsoon –
Life in the Lost World of Anglo-India

Boyhood to manhood as an Anglo-Indian in post-independence India remembered in all its vibrant, hilarious detail.

'A prodigious memory helps the author to weave history and culture and the life and times of an Anglo-Indian family from 1940 to 1970 into a seamless narrative. The style is lucid and free flowing and makes for compulsive reading. I would certainly add this book to my collection on Anglo-India.'

Anglos in the Wind

'Paper Boats covers economic possibilities, the class struggle and the competing loyalties, some things that most of us did not dwell on while living in India. An ordinary story told in a breezy, whimsical style which is utterly enduring.'

Anglo-Indians.com

Available from:

Trafford Publishing - www.orders@trafford.com

Amazon, Waterstones and all good booksellers
– to order

Owen Thorpe – **www.owenthorpe.co.uk**

Where the mind is without fear and the head is held high;
Where knowledge is free;
Where the world has not been broken up into fragments by narrow
domestic walls;
Where words come out from the depth of truth;
Where tireless striving stretches its arms towards perfection;
Where the clear stream of reason has not lost its way into the dreary
desert sand of dead habit;
Where the mind is led forward by thee into ever-widening thought
and action –
Into that heaven of freedom, my Father, let my country awake.

Rabindranath Tagore
Gitanjali

CONTENTS

FOREWORD

This book is a work of fiction and no reference is intended in it to any person, living or dead, except for the few obvious historical characters mentioned. The story is set against the background of the disruptive Second World War in the Far East and the turbulent run-up to Indian and Pakistani independence which followed the Allied victory. Inevitably it refers to some of the significant events that took place.

The 3/17th Dogra Regiment is real – my uncle, Owen, fought in it through the battle for Malaya, only to die on the day of surrender – and the Dogras faced the Japanese at Kota Bharu, Sungei Choh and Singapore; but the officers and men I have portrayed are fictional. And, yes, Mrs Eleanor May does lie buried on a hilltop in Christ Church cemetery, Munnar, South India. Her story is real too.

It was a time when loyalties were wavering. The British, virtually bankrupt after WW II, were reluctantly forced to leave their rewarding, often indulgent life in India, the cornerstone of their Empire; the Indians were impatient to shake off a foreign occupier who had exerted influence and power over their country for nearly 300 years. Caught between them were the Anglo-Indians, people of mixed British-Indian race, the human by-product of the Raj; I have attempted to explain them, their culture and their aspirations through Ed Pierse, the central character in this book. Their hearts lay in Britain – a country most of them had never visited - but their lives were lived in India. Independence for them was a turning point and many left India and Pakistan to return to the land of their forefathers, convinced that they had no place in a new, independent India or Pakistan once their British protectors left.

In a way this was a pity. The first Anglo-Indians had been created in 1687 when the English East India Company encouraged its men to marry native women and so provide a ready stock of employees who spoke English and local languages, understood the Company culture and were resistant to tropical diseases. The Anglo-Indians were thus rooted in the history of British India. When Robert Clive arrived at Fort St. George, Madras in 1744, he found it garrisoned by 200 European soldiers and 100 'half-castes'.

Unfortunately, as a Christian hybrid race, the Anglo-Indians did not fit easily into caste-ordered Hindu society, or into Muslim society to whom they were 'infidels', nor did they fit into a European society that became riddled with Victorian prejudices; so they remained a race apart. The British used them to fill subordinate positions in the armed services and in public administration, which they did very successfully until Independence in 1947, when some went on to fill higher positions in independent India and Pakistan. But with the rush to emigrate, many of the Anglo-Indian community's best people left for the West.

I am indebted to my many British, Indian and Anglo-Indian friends for advice, guidance and support during the writing of this book. In particular, I am grateful to Ronnie and Peter Moore for their encyclopaedic information on the Calcutta

Police Force and the handling of the riots in 1946; to Mike Watson for the cover photograph and to Paul Thorpe at Brakeless Media for his help with the cover design.

I have drawn extensively on the works of others to ensure that the history has been correctly recorded:

The War in Malaya. Lieut. General A E Percival. Eyre & Spottiswoode 1949

Japan's Greatest Victory, Britain's Worst Defeat. Col Masanobu Tsuji. Sarpedon Publishers 1993

The Battle for Singapore. Peter Thompson. Portrait Books 2005

Singapore Burning. Colin Smith. Penguin 2005

Freedom at Midnight. Larry Collins and Dominique Lapierre. William Collins Sons & Co. Ltd. 1975

Raj. The Making and Unmaking of British India. Lawrence James. Little, Brown and Company 1997

The Forgotten Army. Peter Ward Fay. The University of Michigan Press 1993

The Indian National Army. K K Ghosh. Meenakshi Prakashan 1969

Owen Thorpe

CHAPTER 1

The Stranger

The sweet, swooping sound of a *shenai* playing an evening *raga*, ear-splittingly amplified from the park nearby, pierced the night. The man lying awkwardly, untidily across the stone steps, face down, didn't hear it. In the pewter light, of a clouded moon, a dark ooze was just visible, spreading under his face, another, more pungent, under his body, both slowly dripping their way down the steps. Father Sam regarded him with distaste. Dead, or worse, drunk, pissed himself, penniless, and on my doorstep.

He sighed dramatically and regarded the *mali* balefully. The *mali* stood there, jabbering in Tamil and air-washing his hands, uncertain of Father Sam's mood. The servants knew that he could, with little provocation, explode with irritability and rage. The *mali* had been on his way to buy *beedies*, cheap smokes, after an evening tending the vicarage plants, watering the garden and then making his meal; he had come upon the man collapsed on the steps under the church porch. His first instinct had been to rifle through the man's pockets but he had been too terrified to do so when he realized that this was a *sahib*. He had sprinted to Father Sam's bungalow shouting for Baldev, the bearer, to help. Father Sam himself, whisky in hand, had answered the door clad

1

in his thin cassock and had come immediately to see what was up. Of the bearer there was no sign.

Father Sam bent down and felt for a pulse in the neck. He couldn't feel anything except the pulsing of his own blood triggered by the exertion of trying to fold his considerable paunch in half. 'Shut up, shut up! *Choop rao!*' he roared at the jabbering *mali*. The *mali* didn't understand the English or the Hindi but he certainly understood the instruction. He stood as still as he could, shaking with fright and excitement. Father Sam felt again. The chap was still warm, so either recently dead or, unfortunately, probably not. He put his hand in front of the man's open mouth but he could not feel the exhalation of breath because of the warm breeze blowing through the porch. He tried the pulse again. Nothing at first, then a faint tremor – Father Sam wasn't completely sure. 'Bugger,' he thought. He turned to the *mali* and said urgently, 'Baldev, Baldev,' indicating with a wave of his hand that he wanted his manservant brought quickly. The mali ran towards the servants' quarters behind the bungalow. Father Sam shouted after him, 'Torch, torch – torrrrrch!'

In the light of the torch Father Sam and Baldev, a tall, angular Sikh who had served with him in Burma, noted that the dark ooze under the man's head was indeed blood and that the ooze elsewhere wasn't. 'Let's turn him over, Baldev,' he said, and they expertly turned the man face upwards. There was a wound on the side of his head; bloody, but it didn't look that bad. Father Sam gently slapped the man's cheeks but he remained unconscious. 'Let's see what we have here,' said Father Sam to no one in particular. An Anglo-Indian he thought, with his black hair and olive skin. He looked well groomed, broad forehead, even features, clean-shaven – though pale and ill, unsurprisingly. His clothes were of good quality, a dark short-sleeved shirt and buff coloured trousers. His feet were well shod in fashionable crepe-soled brown desert boots. His pockets were empty. He had indeed pissed himself – yet he didn't smell of alcohol. It was most odd – he didn't look like the usual down-and-outs who called at the church or his bungalow for help or handouts from the Friend in Need Society.

'He is breathing, Sahib,' volunteered Baldev and, as if on cue, the man uttered a small sigh and then a shiver went through his body.

They got him back to the bungalow and into the spare bedroom on a canvas camp cot. Father Sam sent Baldev to telephone the doctor and set about removing the soaked trousers to protect the cot while the man groaned and wheezed as he was pulled and pushed. Father Sam looked down in surprise at his left leg. 'Ah,' he thought, 'at least now I know something about you, my lad.'

Young Doctor Subramaniam arrived in a fluster, clutching a large and very worn black leather bag full of his pills, potions and instruments – many of them useless and out of date. The bag had belonged to Subramaniam Senior when he was in practice and the son had inherited the bag and contents which he lugged around as a sort of talisman, hoping something of his late father's genius would rub off on him.

'Good evening, Doctor,' nodded Father Sam, 'clout on the head that's laid him out, and a touch of malaria, I think.'

Subramaniam nervously went through the motions of lifting the man's eyelids, checking his pulse and trying to revive him – all under the watchful and critical eye of Father Sam, now clutching a refilled glass of whisky in his sawn-off fingers. He was terrified of this gruff old Englishman, a priest of a distinctly tough sort.

'Well?' enquired Father Sam. Subramaniam flinched at the question but with as much confidence as he could muster and, wobbling his head in the way that Tamils did, said, 'Yes, yes, yes, he is coming round. I think it is the head wound, as you say, that has made him unconscious – and he seems to have malaria fever, his temperature is high and he is shivering.'

'Ex prisoner of war, I'll bet,' offered Father Sam.

Subramaniam was startled. 'How you are knowing this?' he asked tentatively.

'See that scar on the calf of his left leg?' He pointed to a seven inch scar, still raised and livid, and relatively recent, 'I'll bet that is the result of jungle ulcers, and he is one of the lucky bastards. Many POWs lost their legs because of the ulcers; had to have them amputated under the crudest of conditions, and often didn't survive that.'

Subramaniam wobbled in acknowledgement – this was a new piece of medical information to digest.

'I wonder how he is getting bang on the head; must be that he is falling on the ground when he is fainting'.

The whispered reply startled them: 'Some buggers attacked me.'

The stranger struggled to open his eyes, taking in the dimly lit room, sparsely furnished, the tubby, round-faced Englishman in a cassock, whisky clutched in stubby fingers, a young, dark man wearing a stethoscope and, in the background, a tall Sikh, damp hair hanging loose, like a bearded lady at a circus.

'Pierse,' he said, 'Ed Pierse,' and then, automatically, 'Pierse with an S.'

'Well Pierse, what happened?' asked Father Sam, but the eyes closed again.

* * *

A short while later, revived and injected with atebrin and dosed with quinine for his malaria, head patched, some food in him and a glass of whisky in his hand, against Subramaniam's advice, he lay back on the pillows, head throbbing and still shaking with fever. His story emerged.

'I came off the train at Coialla station,' he said, 'I was feeling very, very ropey with the malaria and stopped to ask for directions to St. Peter's School as I had heard that one of my friends might be teaching there. A rather friendly and well dressed chap said he would give me a hand with my luggage and help me to get a horse-drawn *tonga* to take me there as it was a fair walk and I was in no fit state to do it. We went round the corner from the station and got a *tonga* and this chap spoke to the driver rapidly in Tamil, I presume to give him directions – I couldn't follow the conversation as my Tamil is poor, I'm from the North – can speak Urdu, Hindi and a touch of Bengali, but hardly any Tamil – and anyway I was feeling too ill to care. We went through the streets and byways and then stopped on a spacious road with big houses. My companion, who called himself Raju, said that it might be better for me to stay the night with his family as I was ill, and we could go to the school tomorrow. He appeared to be a decent fellow and this seemed sensible as I did not know if the person I was going to visit actually lived at the school and it was getting dark by now. This Raju went down a lane to check with his family that it was okay for me to stay, if not, he would take me to a hotel. He came back after a few minutes saying that everything was fine, asked me to pay for the *tonga*, which I did, and with him and the driver carrying my bag and holdall, we went down the lane. Raju dropped behind to light a *beedi*, and then suddenly attacked me and hit me across the side of the head with a brick or stone and I fell and must have been knocked out. That is the last I remember. I don't know how I got here. Was my luggage with me?' he asked plaintively.

'No,' replied Father Sam, 'those bastards robbed you because you were an easy target, sick and unable to fight back.' He felt rage at this, relief too, as Pierse was not turning out to be a 'ne'er do well' after all.

'I presume they got my money too?'

'Yes,' said Father Sam, 'all you've got is the clothes you're wearing. And you are lucky the bastards didn't take those too.'

Pierse contemplated the loss of his luggage and his money. He didn't care about the money and the clothing – all of that was replaceable. But some of his sentimental items were not – his photographs of Ellen, and the jackknife Uncle Derek had given him when he was a boy. He started up, but the exertion sent the room swirling and he fell back.

Father Sam and Baldev moved quickly to his aid. 'You'd better take it easy,' Father Sam said, 'we'll call the Police and get them to try to sort it out. Nothing you can do right now, so rest and get back on your feet.'

Pierse settled back into a fuggy sleep.

'How the hell did he get to the church?' Father Sam said to Baldev when they had left the room. 'He was not in a fit state to walk anywhere. Who brought him here, how – and why! This is all very peculiar.'

A police sergeant and a constable arrived an hour or so later and Pierse was roused and gave his story again. Descriptions of Raju and the *tonga* driver were given, but Pierse could not remember the street he had been taken to and the police sergeant's demeanor indicated that he thought the whole thing was a lost cause and a waste of his valuable time. But as he stepped outside the front door Baldev suddenly grasped his arm in a tight and unfriendly grip, 'Find them and get his luggage back,' he said in a threatening whisper, 'and do it soon – understand?' The sergeant was about to protest but something in Baldev's eyes didn't invite a riposte. He merely nodded, anxious to get away. But Baldev wasn't done. 'I'll come to the police station tomorrow and every day to check up on you,' he said.

* * *

Pierse was severely racked by his malaria for the next couple of days until, with the benefit of Doctor Subramaniam's medicine and Baldev's care, he was fit enough to leave his bed. Sitting in the vicarage garden for the first time, in the cool of the evening with the smell of jasmine in the air, a glass of whisky in his hand and the sunset colouring the sky, Pierse turned to Father Sam and said, 'I expect you will want to know a bit more about me and what I am doing here. You and Baldev have been very kind to help me, and I must be moving along so that I don't inconvenience you further. I will repay the costs of your hospitality as soon as I get back home to Calcutta.'

Uplifted by the news that his uninvited guest was moving on, Father Sam said jovially, 'Don't worry about any costs – good Samaritan and all that – though a donation to the church would help.' Then, smiling, 'Let me do a Sherlock Holmes, Pierse, and tell you what I have deduced from you so far!'

'Right ho,' said an amused Pierse.

'You are an Anglo-Indian – your hair and skin colour and your accent tell me that. You were a soldier in the war – that's the jungle ulcer and the penchant for desert boots; probably an officer in an Indian regiment from the way that Baldev has treated you with absolute respect, he's got a nose for these things,' he chuckled. 'You were a POW – I know that again because of the ulcer scar on your leg. You are searching for a lost love.'

Pierse looked startled. 'How did you get that?'

'You said you had come to see a teacher who might be teaching in the school – no names no pack drill. So I guessed,' replied Father Sam amiably. 'From your reaction I'd say I was correct.'

Pierse smiled.

CHAPTER 2

Invasion – 1941

In the closeness of the pillbox the smell of fear – that distinctively pungent, rancid odour of adrenalin-sparked sweat – overpowered the acrid smell of new, damp concrete. The atmosphere was slightly sweetened by the odours of coriander and cardamom seeds that the young, raw troops chewed as they strained hard to peer through the windy darkness at the beaches and the sea beyond, trembling hands and clumsiness betraying their agitation. There were Jap ships out there, closing in on the rough waves to discharge the vanguard of their invasion force. It had been talked about for weeks on the radio, in the government offices, the grand houses, whore houses, officers' messes, camps, bars and bazaars of Malaya – and it was now about to happen.

The Japanese were aiming for Kota Bharu, a small town on the rain-soaked coast in the north east corner of Malaya, set on the mouth of the Kelantan River and not far from the border with Thailand. Because of its strategic location it was blessed with an airfield manned by the Royal Air Force, flying somewhat obsolescent fighters. It was a bustling town, whose activity had gone up several gears in recent months as the preparations to repel an invasion had been completed. Lt.

Pierse and eleven of his men manned one of the pillboxes on the beach – linked by radio and field telephone to the troops in the defensive lines behind and to HQ. He had been in Kota Bharu for nearly a year with the 3/17th Dogra Regiment, helping to strengthen the defences and drilling his men to resist an enemy assault. It was his first time abroad and in his idle moments he had stood at the pillbox's firing slot, with its cinema screen view across the China Sea, imagining what he would be able to see directly ahead had he been blessed with Superman's X-Ray vision: probably the Philippines – about which he didn't know much – and beyond them the vast, undulating, intimidating blue of the Pacific Ocean, then jewel-like Hawaii with its volcanoes, ukuleles and dancing girls in grass skirts, then California, USA. He'd like to go to America one day with Ellen; Hollywood and New York – in the films everyone seemed so rich and confident, with their big cars, wide streets, well stocked shops and tall skyscrapers. Make a big change from the clanging trams, honking horns, beggars, dirt and noisy crowds of his home town, Calcutta.

It was the end of the first week of December 1941. Christmas preparations had begun in the Mess and had made him homesick for his family. He imagined them too preparing for Christmas: trips to Calcutta's New Market to buy material for the obligatory new clothes and ingredients for the cake, trips to the tailor to have the latest fashions copied, arranging early tickets for the popular 'shows', the dances and socials, before they sold out. Da would resurrect the old decorations from their leather suitcase above his almirah and the tree would soon be decorated with cotton wool 'snow' and crowned with an elderly porcelain fairy – a scuffed ancestral piece handed down by his Welsh grandmother. All of that could come to a juddering halt after tonight.

He looked round in the gloom at the scared young sepoys, all in their early to mid 20s, like himself, many of them new to the Regiment, recruited in the foothills of the Himalayas as Hindu Dogras were, though the wartime expansion of the Army had meant that the ranks had also been swelled with men from other areas and other religions. They were more used to farming than soldiering, hefting a hoe rather than cradling a Lee-Enfield rifle or sighting down a Bren light machine gun. Travel to Malaya had been a great adventure for them, as it had for him, and they had delighted in the differences they found. As farmers they were especially intrigued by the rice paddies and rubber plantations. They didn't believe him when he told them that the milky, sticky sap from the rubber trees would become big black tyres for cars and lorries; it didn't seem possible. He had got to know some of them well as they were enthusiastic recruits to the hockey teams that he ran for the Regiment. Few of them would have imagined that in the space of a year they would be facing the might of the Imperial Japanese Army, an enemy they barely knew, on a remote beach in Malaya, far from home. Pierse was unsure how they would behave under fire – in fact quite unsure of how he would react. He caught the eye of the experienced Havildar, Prem Singh; he looked alert but calm, nodded almost imperceptibly when he caught Pierse's gaze. Between the two of them they had to keep these young sepoys from panicking. His composure steadied Pierse.

Earlier that evening Prem Singh, a fatherly thirty year old, had talked reassuringly to the sepoys as they ate their meal. 'We are in a strong position,' he had said quietly. 'We are in a thick concrete pillbox, we have machine guns, the beaches are heavily mined, and the '*Japani*' will have to come off their boats in a rough sea and try to get through the mines and the barbed wire while you are firing on them and the artillery and aeroplanes are bombarding them. They are the ones who have to be afraid. Many of them will die and they do not stand a chance out there. All of us have the opportunity for a great victory – and you will be able to go home covered with medals, having won honour for your regiment and for yourselves.'

The sepoys knew the defences thoroughly as they had been involved in constructing them under the exacting eyes of British sapper officers and men. Four thousand land mines had been sown on the sandy beach a few yards up from the high water mark. They had a tendency to go off loudly in the night when coconuts fell off the palms or when pi-dogs ventured on to the beach. Pierse and his friends would laughingly turn to each other in the Mess and ask, 'Nut or mutt?' and take bets on what the morrow's inspection would bring. Farrell was convinced that he could tell if it was a dog because he swore that he could detect its last yelp as the mine went off! Quite often he was right, so there might have been something in it – and his ears did stick out more than most.

Up from the water's edge there were coils and tangles of barbed wire sloping upwards for six feet, with an identical slope falling the other way – a 'double apron fence' the tomato-faced sapper Major called it. It was already rusting to the ochre of congealed blood, as if in anticipation.

'Imagine the enemy trying to climb up the slope, that will be hard enough, but it will be even harder going down the other side, heads down and arses in the air, and all the time you boys will be popping away at them,' the Major said with satisfaction.

Behind more barbed wire stood the lines of reinforced concrete pillboxes, a hundred yards apart, in between which were L-shaped trenches with more troops. Each pillbox had a dozen men who had at least two or three Bren light machine guns as well as their rifles. There was plenty of ammunition, grenades and adequate food, water and medical supplies.

'If they get through that I'll eat my hat, what?' the Major barked.

'*When* they do Sir, would you like Worcestershire sauce and a coconut salad with it?' asked Mike Farrell faux innocently. The Major was outraged; Farrell's officer chums sniggered.

'You see, Sir, if I was them,' explained Farrell, 'I'd tunnel under the barbed wire – much safer, and the sand is soft enough. Or I'd blast my way through with a few Bangalore torpedoes.' The sapper Major stormed off – but he could see the point.

Behind the defensive positions was the 21st Mountain Battery providing artillery support. The venerable 18-pounder field pieces they used had for years fired the ceremonial salutes on grand occasions, but the gunners were untested in battle. The infantry officers joked that they probably couldn't hit a shithouse at a hundred yards though would certainly be able to fire a grand salute if a General was using it. The RAF stood ready at the airfield. Everything looked impregnable.

But as Farrell had indicated, he and his colleagues had their reservations. The Dogras and the rest of the 8th Brigade, who were part of the 9th Indian Division, were spread very thin. The Dogra Battalion was holding nine miles of beaches, the Baluchi Regiment, on their right flank, was spread even thinner – covering a twenty four mile front. Despite the elaborate defences, the river mouth was their weak point. It lay almost opposite the airfield and was the most likely landing spot an invader would choose. No money had been made available to put a chain across it, and the area was riddled with inlets which could easily be infiltrated. Farrell didn't doubt that the Japanese, with their local spies, were keenly aware of the situation and would exploit it fully.

* * *

Yesterday the RAF had spotted the seventy-vessel Jap convoy and raised the alert but in the bad weather and low cloud cover they lost sight of them and couldn't be certain of their destination or intent. The top brass and the 'box-wallahs' in Singapore were also uncertain about Japanese intentions and were scared rigid about doing anything to provoke them into war – the last thing Britain needed was to open another front. This morning an RAF plane had spotted one of the Jap ships with khaki-uniformed troops on board north of Kota Bharu and a second plane was fired on and had been hit by a Jap cruiser but was able to return. Then they had chanced upon four Jap destroyers heading for Malaya. The troops were placed on high alert and war appeared inevitable. Now, late at night, it was raining, with a strong wind blowing clouds of sand and spray and toppling the occasional coconut, the sea was rough. It was some comfort that the conditions were far from good for an invasion force to make a successful landing.

A rustle outside the back of the pillbox and Lt. Anil Chandra came through the entrance.

'Hello Piersey,' he said, smiling at Pierse and nodding to the Havildar and the other men. They sprang to attention and saluted. Chandra, along with Farrell, was one of Pierse's close friends. Short, confident and full of verve, with a shock of black curly hair and an Errol Flynn moustache, he was in charge of a platoon dug in on the sands at the rear of the pillbox.

'I've come to tell you that the landing is imminent so get ready. The RAF has scrambled to attack the convoy.'

Pierse was surprised they hadn't alerted him by radio or field telephone but was pleased to see Chandra. He looked at his watch, but couldn't quite tell the time in the gloom. A series of explosions startled him and his men, coming from the artillery positions behind; they were echoed by explosions out at sea. One of the sepoys began to retch, and Pierse's heart began to trip.

'Good timing Anil,' he said as nonchalantly as he could, 'everything out there okay?'

'Yes,' replied Chandra, then grinning and shouting above

the din, 'No. There are bloody bandy-legged Jap bastards on their way to attack.' Moving closer to Pierse he said quietly, 'May God be with you Ed and good luck,' and squeezed Pierse's hand.

'See you in Tokyo, and yours is the ugly Geisha,' shouted Pierse. 'Make sure your boys cover our arses Anil,' and, mimicking Farrell's English accent, 'we don't want those frightful Oriental fellows round our tradesmen's entrance.'

'Don't worry,' smiled Chandra, 'between us they won't even get off the beach'. With that he departed.

Havildar Prem Singh had calmed the retching sepoy and firmly pulled the others into line. Ed Pierse wondered again if he would set a good example to his men. His knees were trembling and he felt dizzy and sick with fear. Now was the time to do something.

'Boys,' he shouted in his best Dogri, trying to be heard above the racket, 'take courage and fight like the champions you are. Concentrate on doing your jobs. They will not get off the beach. We, the Dogras, will turn them back. *Jawala Mata* is with us. And,' he added trying to lift the tension, 'anyone who doesn't kill at least ten *Japani* will get fifty press-ups on the hockey field afterwards.' A few of the sepoys smiled thinly, Pierse was a mad keen hockey player. They watched and waited, straining to catch the first sight of the strangers who had now become their enemy.

The Japanese ships began a heavy bombardment and the night was filled with the flashes and sounds of an infernal Divali. Shortly after midnight the main landings began – and the launches with their cargoes of 'half-arsed, bandy-legged and short-sighted samurais' as one of the older British officers had dismissively described them in the mess, hit the beaches. In retaliation the Dogras returned a heavy and murderous fire that halted any advance by the invaders, forcing them to lie half in and half out of the water, heads well down and battered by the spray, burrowing into the sand like turtles for cover. Once the action had commenced, Pierse and his men pushed back their fears and concentrated on the task in hand, buoyed by the success of stranding the Japs on the open beaches taking casualties and unable to move forward. The air hummed and tore with explosions and the concrete walls of the pillbox vibrated and shrieked with thuds and ricochets.

The invaders were digging furiously, as Farrell had predicted, using their helmets to get into the sand and under the wire. The corpses were piling up, providing cover for the fellows who took their places and who dug desperately. They were making slow progress, but progress nevertheless, thought Pierse grimly. Then, with a muffled yell, one of the Bren gunners fell back, struck on the side of his helmet. He lay there dazed and bleeding, and Pierse sprang forward to man his gun, telling Havildar Prem Singh to check the casualty. Pierse fired like a madman at the shadowy figures struggling at the wire, his eyes running with sweat, his vision through the murk grey and useless. He wished he could see his targets better. They were just that – targets – he felt no compassion for them, he felt no disgust at the killing. He just wanted to stop them getting any closer.

Prem Singh, tapped him on the shoulder, and he stopped and looked round.

'Pierse Sahib, he is breathing okay, slight head wound.' The Havildar beckoned a sepoy to take over from Pierse and another to patch up the casualty.

Pierse radioed HQ to warn them that the attackers were gaining ground despite their heavy casualties. There were thunderous bangs as they negotiated the minefields but men just climbed over the bodies of fallen comrades. An incredible will seemed to possess them and the sheer force of numbers was beginning to get results. The wounded sepoy lay dazed in the corner and his replacement, Dina Nath, a new-comer to the regiment and a naturally talented hockey full-back, had manned the Bren enthusiastically – anxious to please Pierse, whom he admired greatly.

The fighting had been going on for some hours when Pierse became aware of shouting and screaming somewhere at the back of the pillbox and motioned the Havildar to investigate.

'They have broken through, Sahib,' he gasped as he reached for the pin on a grenade. 'We must go – now!' he shouted, lobbing the grenade through the rear entrance and reaching for another. Pierse's moment of uncertainty was ended swiftly when a stream of gun fire came through the slit and killed a Bren gunner and his loader, the ricochets striking sparks off the concrete walls.

'*Chalo Chalo!*' he roared at the men, bundling them out and firing wildly with his revolver at a face that showed itself at the slit. He knew that a grenade would surely follow and desperately made for the exit. The scene outside was a shock. The Japanese has infiltrated the inlets and got round the backs of some of the pillboxes, there was fierce hand-to-hand fighting going on in the rain, screaming sepoys were being bayoneted and others were fighting back, clubbing their attackers with their rifles. Pierse kept firing while running for the cover of the trenches at the rear. The Havildar was throwing grenades and Pierse noted with relief that most of his men had made it safely out of the pillbox and Dina Nath had recovered a Bren. Reaching cover he reloaded his revolver and shouted to the men to begin an orderly retreat, to the second line. Slowly they made their way back through the swampy ground and its watercourses, joined by others similarly dispossessed – including Anil Chandra and his men,

'God, Ed,' he said feelingly, 'I didn't think it would be like this. I've lost half my chaps and those Jap bastards have even bayoneted the wounded.'

'Let's keep going,' said Pierse grimly, 'we can't make a good defensive position here as they are still coming behind us through the inlets. We'll have to fall back to the next line.' He noted with some surprise that there were Japanese bodies this far to the rear, small men in khaki-brown uniforms and puttees, with round helmets and oversized rifles with large 20-inch fixed bayonets. Death wasn't clean, like it was in the films; the bodies were considerably mangled – limbs blown off, torsos torn apart by machine gun or mortar – and those were the lucky ones. The unlucky still lived, groaning and convulsing in their pain, half drowning on the swampy ground, unseeing, uncomprehending as they slowly gave up the ghost for their Emperor.

Confusion reigned as they fought their way through the swamps and inlets. The flashes of artillery explosions and the firefly flickering of small arms were now fading against a slowly lightening sky. They took up positions in a coconut grove. A constant stream of stragglers crisscrossed through them and Chandra suggested that they move further back as the enemy began to lob mortars in their direction.

* * *

Sunrise came bright and clear; overcast skies had given way to purest cobalt with cotton wool clouds. The mist burning off over the sea revealed a surprise – the Jap ships had gone! But numbers of small craft scuttled to and fro ferrying Jap troops and supplies to the river mouth and the creeks. With light came the air attacks: Japanese fighters and bombers targeting the airfield and the defences, the RAF planes struggling to attack these vastly superior enemy invaders. A Sikh officer came past with a muddy party of stragglers. Seeing Chandra and Pierse he exclaimed, 'We are beating them back at last – see, the ships have gone and our aeroplanes are destroying the invaders.'

'Then why are you retreating you stupid bugger,' shouted Chandra derisively, 'you should go forward and attack.'

The battle raged all day. The Japanese finally infiltrated the outer defences of the airfield. The panicked Australian ground crews withdrew in haste, effectively surrendering it and all its supplies to the enemy. Their departure was witnessed by the Hyderabad Regiment, the personal force of the Nizam of Hyderabad, on loan to the British Army, whose sepoys were disconcerted by the undisciplined and hasty retreat of these white *sahibs* whom everyone had said were fearless and invincible.

The following afternoon a combined force of Dogras and Sikhs was ordered to retake lost ground. Chandra and Pierse, each heading a motley band of troops, moved through the swamps and creeks attacking the enemy wherever they found them. After some initial success the attack became bogged down in the soggy terrain. Streams that were once easy to wade now ran like tea-coloured torrents, dangerously swollen by the monsoon rain. Men were struggling in the fast flowing waters and were at the mercy of the aircraft bombing and strafing them. The mud and ooze made rapid movement impossible – boots were sucked off, probably not too much of an inconvenience for Indian troops accustomed to going barefoot at home, but getting feet out of the mud was difficult and turned the men into easy, slow-motion targets.

As they began to cross a particularly swollen stream with the rain and the bullets rattling round them, Chandra lost his footing, tumbled into the water and was being swept away. He shouted for help as his heavy pack dragged him under and he was not a strong swimmer. The Havildar urgently tapped Pierse on the shoulder, 'Chandra Sahib!' he shouted. Pierse looked back to see his friend tumbling down the stream towards the Jap positions. He hesitated: should he risk his own life? Could he succeed in saving him? Wasn't he was the only other officer in the group and responsible for leading the men? But he launched himself towards Chandra.

Reaching him, he stretched out to grab the nearest bit of him he could find but Chandra, in his desperate struggle, grabbed out too and caught Pierse a blow on the nose which blanked out his vision and made him gasp, he took in a lungful of water and went under.

'Oh God, I could die here,' he thought as Chandra now had hold of him and in his terror to escape the water was clambering on top of him and forcing him deeper. Pierse tried to strike Chandra to get him off, the force of his blows random and dulled by the resistance of the water. Then he felt with his foot for Chandra's lower torso and kicked him sharply between the legs. Chandra curled over in pain and Pierse surfaced, turned him, ripped off his pack and got him in a headlock from behind.

'Keep still,' he yelled, 'or you'll kill us both! I've got you, don't struggle or we'll both go down.' He began to pull towards the bank, fighting the current and the dead weight of Chandra, who was doubled up and heaving with the pain of the kick. Dina Nath waded in to steady the pair and helped drag them to safety. They lay exhausted in the mud, soaking wet and covered in slime.

'How are you, old son?' gasped Pierse, 'sorry about the kick in the balls but it was the only way I could get you to keep still or you would have had us both.'

Chandra was still doubled up and coughing out the water in his lungs. 'Thanks Ed,' he eventually managed to splutter, 'I was shot and that's what dropped me in the water,' he showed Pierse his right upper arm where the sleeve was bloody from a graze that extended across the triceps. 'I don't know which hurts more, the pain in the arm or the pain in my goolies.'

'I think you may have broken my nose,' said Pierse, feeling it carefully and wiping off the blood. 'We could both have died in that stream,' he added unnecessarily. Chandra was clearly not fit to go forward so a sepoy remained with him to help him back to the lines.

Recovering from the effort, Pierse instinctively reached for the silver St. Christopher medal that Ellen had placed around his neck. It was gone, torn off in the struggle. He couldn't help but smile thinly. Ellen had insisted that he wear it even though she knew that he wasn't religious and didn't believe in it. 'I believe in it, and that's what matters,' she had said with finality. He imagined telling her the story. 'Seeeee,' she would say, 'St Christopher saved you – and your friend! You heathen! *Now* do you believe?'

A runner brought orders for them to join a company moving forward to try to retake the airfield. By now it was dark and raining again, the men were hungry, weary from lack of sleep and exhausted from fighting. They arrived at the airfield perimeter an hour later after threading their way with difficulty through the attacks going on round them only to find the Japs there in strength, machine guns playing into the shadows along the perimeter, aircraft burning and wild confusion all around. The bullets flew and the fuel barrels were exploding. As the melee continued, it became apparent that the airfield was now irretrievably lost and they didn't have the strength to take it and hold it against a determined enemy with more men and better air power. Orders were given to withdraw. Pierse, angry and frustrated, picked up a rifle off a dead sepoy and used the light given off by the burning fuel to snipe at the enemy, bringing them down one by one – like shooting duck on the Sunderbans outside Calcutta with Uncle Derek, he thought. It was a grim fit of petulance.

* * *

The days that followed were a recurring nightmare of air and ground attacks, retreat, rain, more rain, destruction, exhaustion, mutilation and death. Stragglers slowly returned, filtering through the coconut groves and paddy fields to rejoin the regiment. The Brigade's casualties had been fewer than feared and the men took heart. Pierse's company had lost a quarter of its men killed or wounded; but Havildar Prem Singh and the loyal Dina Nath remained comfortingly by his side.

A couple of days later, in the pre-dawn dark before they took up their positions for the day, Chandra and Pierse sought Mike Farrell at Divisional HQ, to find out how he had fared in the attacks. They found him in the back of a lorry, which he was using as an office, poring over a map by the light of a kerosene lantern.

'How are you Anil?' asked Farrell sympathetically as Chandra limped up to the tailgate.

'Still a little tender in the multiplication department, but the Doc says that I'm fit and should carry on. Better the pain than to have drowned, I suppose. Dying in battle is one thing, drowning in a ditch like a dog – well, it's not heroic, is it?'

'And very frightening,' interjected Pierse. 'Hope I don't get a permanent bloody bump on the nose,' he joked, feeling it ostentatiously.

'Oh, bugger off Pierse,' said Farrell laughing. 'Seriously chaps, did I not tell that damn fool of a Sapper Major that his defences were not impregnable?' Then, more reflectively, 'I think we completely underestimated this enemy y'know. We knew that he was cruel and callous from the reports we had from Manchuria and China. But he is so bloody determined, and so courageous dammit – death doesn't seem to bother these fellows.'

They agreed, remembering the figures burrowing industriously under the wire despite their appalling casualties.

'Aren't you chaps afraid of being killed?' Chandra asked.

'Everyone is Anil, we just try not to think about it,' replied Farrell

'But we have so much more to lose. I'm an only son in my family; they depend on me for the future, to run our family business. They didn't put me through La Martiniere School and St Stephen's College to die in a ditch!'

'Remember what Kipling wrote?' replied Farrell,

'A scrimmage in a Border Station –
A canter down some dark defile –
Two thousand pounds of education
Drops to a ten-rupee jezail.

It was ever thus. Some of the Japs we are fighting probably have just as much to lose.'

'I suppose it is *kismet*. When your time is up, you go,' declared Chandra fatalistically.

'I'd rather not trust in fate or divine intervention,' muttered Pierse. 'Better to rely on training and instincts to keep us alive. As for death, I'll do everything I can to make sure that he grabs the other bugger first.'

'How many Japs have each of you, you know, um, polished off?' asked Chandra tentatively.

'I didn't know this was a contest,' teased Pierse.

'No, no, just wondered. I've dispatched about five or ten, I think. Most when they were coming up the beach. What about you, Ed?'

'I've not been keeping count. Couldn't say,' replied Pierse.

'Well, I've only got one of the buggers so far,' declared Farrell, 'though I've slaughtered hundreds of bits of paper at HQ. May they Rest in Pieces!' He snorted at his own feeble joke. 'What I can tell you is that we Dogras have put paid to over five or six hundred Japs so far.' He smiled at Pierse and Chandra's astonishment.

'Didn't think it was that many,' said Pierse, 'we don't seem to have suffered as much.'

'So many grieving families: parents mourning their sons, wives their husbands, children their fathers.' Chandra spoke with feeling.

'You mustn't think like that,' said Pierse gruffly, 'to think like that is to hesitate for a fatal fraction of a second, and it will be your family grieving for you Anil.' Then, laughing, 'No, the way I see it, we are players in a big, important game, this is the All Malaya Cup Final against the Japs – and our task is to make sure we beat them.'

'Hockey! Hockey! Always bloody hockey!' exclaimed Chandra crossly.

'We tried to take some prisoners,' said Farrell, adroitly changing the subject, 'but not one Jap surrendered. They fought to the death – in one case the chap stabbed himself in the guts rather than be taken.'

'No, they don't seem keen on prisoners,' Chandra agreed. 'I saw them bayoneting our wounded sepoys, chaps who were barely conscious. I'll have to remind our men that they will need to fight just like the Japs – to the bitter bloody end. They'll get no mercy if they surrender.'

'And they travel very light,' revealed Farrell. 'We've turned over some of the Jap casualties to see if they were carrying any info we could use. All that the men have with them is a smallish bag of rice and some very smelly powdered fish. We, on the other hand, are burdened with field kitchens making different types of food for Sikhs, Hindus and Muslims. Your Jap seems set to travel light and move fast, living off the land.'

'In which case those buggers must have gorged themselves silly on the Christmas cake, food and booze that the Australians left behind when they abandoned the airfield,' replied Pierse bitterly.

'Our big concern just now,' said Farrell, 'is that we could be cut off if we are not reinforced or quickly evacuated. The Japs are already bringing in more troops and tanks by sea and flying planes into captured airfields, but the Generals and box-wallahs in Singapore don't want the Brigade to withdraw, saying it would give the enemy free run of the east coast.'

'So do we dig in and fight to the last man?' asked Pierse.

'That wouldn't be sensible as we face a massacre without proper air cover and without tanks. Discussions are taking place with the chaps in Singapore but the buggers can't make a decision!

'It doesn't look good,' agreed Pierse. 'We heard that the Japs have also attacked down the west coast, through Thailand – but in much greater strength. Apparently that now appears to be the main thrust of their invasion – is that right Mike?'

'Yes,' confirmed Farrell. 'The landings here seem to have been an elaborate diversion, but a clever one nevertheless, as they can now work their way down both sides of the country in a pincer movement. Oh, but one bit of good news, cloud with silver lining and all that! The Yanks are now in the war! With very calculated timing, while they were storming our beaches, the Japs were also launching an air attack on the American fleet at the naval base in somewhere called Pearl Harbor, Hawaii – sank many of their ships. They've also bombed Singapore and sunk two of our big ships, the Prince of Wales and the Repulse, which were coming to help us.'

'I tried my X-Ray vision but didn't see the Hawaiian attack coming,' Pierse joked to a mystified Farrell.

'You are a silly arse sometimes, Ed.'

CHAPTER 3

Retreat

Mike Farrell was having a hard time, up to his bloodshot blue eyes with infuriating HQ staff, officious company commanders and bureaucratic railway officials waving handful upon handful of forms. He had the hunched, hunted look of someone who was at the absolute end of his tether – cranky from lack of sleep, pissed-off by interfering senior officers, just wanting to get the job over and done with. He was trying to organise the urgent – and desperately secret – evacuation of the Brigade out of Kuala Krai, a small town south of Kota Bharu, on the rickety single line railway to the railhead at Kuala Lipis. Despite the extraordinary bravery that the Dogras, Sikhs, Baluchis and other 9th Indian Division troops had shown over the past ten days, they had to get out of here quickly or be in deep trouble if this fragile line of communication was cut. The list of dead and wounded was mounting as a consequence of the continuous enemy attacks by air and across the rice paddies and coconut groves. The local RAF airfields had been evacuated and the incompetent crews had left without destroying them. The RAF seemed quite unable to provide enough air cover to protect the troops from the marauding Japanese fighter and bomber planes. The east coast, with its sparse communications and rugged terrain should have made defence and delay of the Japanese easier if the local State forces had destroyed the airfields, passes, roads and bridges. It was too late now and the poor tactics were costing the Brigade dearly. The high-ups in Singapore had finally, but somewhat reluctantly, agreed to evacuate the troops to allow them to regroup and fight elsewhere. On the other side of the country, the Japanese advance continued steadily down the west coast. The Punjabis and Gurkhas of the 11th Indian Division had been overrun by a tank assault.

Farrell was pale, thin, tall and slightly stooped, almost patrician in his appearance – 'raw meat' they had nicknamed him at school. His face was dusted with freckles – 'like he'd looked out of the train when someone further up had crapped out of a carriage window' Chandra had joked. His reddish hair, beaky nose, upper class accent and tales of antics at his public school in England, Haileybury, a hothouse for generations of officials of the East India Company and then the Raj, set him apart from his fellows. He had joined up when the war began, having come out to India, he said, as an Assistant Collector, a cog in the Raj machine, working in the hills around Jammu and Kashmir. He had quickly learned more than a smattering of Urdu, a language similar to Dogri, enough to get accepted as an officer in the Dogras, and his quick intelligence and grasp of strategic detail had got him a place on the HQ staff of the Brigade.

Pierse and Chandra had met Farrell at the Indian Military Academy in Dehra Dun where they were officer cadets together, part of the emergency intake. It hadn't been the most propitious of beginnings; within days of arriving Pierse and Farrell were on the point of coming to blows on the cricket pitch. They had been drawn as members of the fielding side and Farrell, who was bowling, showed his annoyance with Pierse at cover point when the batsman, who happened to be

Chandra, hammered the ball past Pierse's ears and the latter's instinct had been to duck when Farrell thought he ought to have taken the catch. Farrell was unwise enough to call Pierse a 'sissy'. Chandra, found himself sandwiched between them struggling to prevent a punch-up. Pierse, angered, challenged Farrell to see how he would react if a cricket ball was flying past his head and Chandra slyly commented that it might make an interesting 'duel'. Inevitably, when stumps were drawn, Farrell and Pierse, with the stupidity and obstinacy of angry young men, had positioned themselves at either end of the wicket, Farrell with a cricket bat and Pierse with a hockey stick, with which he said he felt more at home, to whack balls at each other to test their mettle. It was an agreeable madness, and a crowd gathered to watch – with the outspoken, brash Chandra acting as Master of Ceremonies.

Pierse went first. He deftly scooped up the white hockey ball with his stick and struck it with full force at Farrell, who nonchalantly swung his bat to blast it to the boundary but misjudged the speed and the ball struck him in the ribs before he could make his stroke. The onlookers heard the hollow thud and saw Farrell fall. Chandra and Pierse anxiously ran to him and found him in severe pain and finding it difficult to breathe. They struggled to get him to his feet, but he was unable to continue – it seemed as though he had cracked his ribs, which indeed he had.

A profusely apologetic and worried Pierse, accompanied by Chandra, visited him in the infirmary. 'I'm sorry,' said Pierse uncomfortably, extending a hand. Farrell took it, the pain in his chest made him wince.

'No, I apologise Pierse. You were right to duck or you could have been lying here instead of me. It was stupid of me to say what I did, I'm sorry.' He smiled at Pierse, 'You'll have to teach me hockey so I can hit a ball as hard as that – and improve my batting.'

'I make no apology for the magnificent shot that started the whole thing off,' laughed Chandra. So began a friendship. But the incident had sowed the seeds of an absurd competition of 'duels and dares' between the three, which popped up whenever there was a dispute or difference of opinion to be settled – or just simply for the hell of it. Their bizarre dares became the talk of the College and its instructors: racing up the hills to see who could be the first to steal and bring back a cow – Chandra won that one, he simply bought the cow, but claimed that he had stolen it because he hadn't offered a fair price! Or dressing up as native women in saris to see who could go through the bazaar unnoticed: Farrell thought that he would win by wearing full purdah but, unfortunately, unable to see very well through the veil, stepped into a pool of something extremely unpleasant on the street and cursed and swore revealing his English accent and pink shins clad in brown canvas plimsolls. The people in the bazaar thought that he was a spy, or a pervert, and chased him all the way back to the Academy. One wag was unwise enough to refer to the three as 'the Liquorice Allsorts,' explaining that one was black, one was white, and one was khaki. When they found out, they strung him up from the college flagpole by his ankles – after he had been debagged and black and brown Cherry Blossom boot polish and white Blanco applied liberally to his genitals. When Farrell was assigned to what the others considered a cushy job in another Indian Army regiment he determinedly pulled strings to get posted to the Dogras a few months later to join his friends.

He looked at them now in the dim light of the hurricane lanterns, bedraggled, wet, muddy and exhausted, oblivious of the rain streaming down as they loaded their troops on to the waiting Federated Malay States Railway train. Pierse looked tired but remained ever the optimistic 'boy scout' they had so often joshed him about, hustling his men and their kit onto the wagons using a hockey stick like a shepherd's crook. An overgrown schoolboy, thought Farrell, soldiering was a sort of game to him; he was guileless, imbued with a strong sense of old-fashioned honour – the sort of chap the English public schools tried to turn out. Chandra, on the other hand, normally so cocky and full of jokes and bluster, looked very weary and low. The story of his kick in the balls had been greeted with uncharitable hilarity by his fellow officers and he had been cruelly ribbed. Given all that they had been through in the past few days, thought Farrell, it was the crude equivalent of light relief, though he felt that Chandra was beginning to tire of being the butt of the joke and the strain of the past days was beginning to tell. In his knapsack Farrell kept a photograph of his intake at the Academy, the cadets in rows, standing stiffly dressed in their red and grey striped blazers with the Star of India on the pocket. He had marked a small cross against those who had so far been killed in this war – the total now amounted to three. He wondered how many more would be crossed-out before the war ended, and whether he would be spared to do the crossing-out.

* * *

The railway line twisted and turned through wild country, wending its way over rivers and ravines to Kuala Lipis. The destruction of a single bridge by the enemy could scupper it, so Farrell and his HQ colleagues had spent days and nights organising rolling stock and systematically getting troops, vehicles and equipment away under cover of darkness before the enemy cottoned on.

Pierse sat in the bumping railway wagon gazing through the open door at the black beyond imagining the gullies and forests rolling by, lost in his thoughts. He felt bitter and depressed; defeat rankled and he hated having to slink away in the dark from the Japs. There was no moon. 'The moon will always join us together, wherever you are, wherever you can see it,' Ellen had said on his last leave. 'I will look at it every night and think of you and send you my love through it.' He had laughed at the time and teased her. But now he wanted the damn moon to appear, to slide from under the blanket of cloud to shine on him, to reassure him. He thought wistfully of Ellen. The photograph of her that he carried in his wallet in his top pocket had been thoroughly soaked and creased when he had dived in to save Chandra. He had carefully dried it and pressed it between sheets of paper to iron out the creases even though the image was burned into his brain: her long-lashed, flecked brown eyes set in a pale oval face framed with jet dark hair. He loved her, absolutely, completely, unquestionably. There had been many girls before her: convent girls, railway colony girls, boarding school girls from the hills, savvy Cal girls who liked fashion and dancing and going to the pictures. They were all, in their own way, pretty, intelligent and good company. But Ellen – she was different. She came to Calcutta from her home in Lucknow to train as a teacher at Loreto College. He had seen her playing in a netball match – he admired the new girl's skill on the pitch, and she was good looking too. By the end of the game he boldly asked her out – under urging from her friends she had said a somewhat reluctant yes. From then on they had spent almost every waking moment together until separated by the necessities of war, when Pierse went off to the Military Academy at Dehra Dun and from there to Jullundur in the Punjab, where the Dogra Regiment had its centre. Ellen planned to find a teaching post in Calcutta when her course was completed. He returned home to Calcutta and her at every opportunity and they planned to marry as soon as the war was over.

Pierse wondered how Ellen and his family would be reacting to the war in Malaya. They would know that the

Regiment had been in the thick of it at Kota Bharu. His father, Da, would worry openly – he wore his heart on his sleeve – his mother would try to maintain an aura of calm, she felt that she had to act as a counterpoint to her husband. Ellen? She would worry, of course, but try to keep herself busy. She would go to church and pray for his safety and for his soul, light candles, say a novena or two, put her trust in the Almighty to keep him from harm. Pierse was thankful that his brother, Kenny, was, at seventeen, too young to join up. He was the bright one, the one who was going to be a professor or a doctor or a lawyer, and already looked the spitting image of his father – pink-faced and thick set – 'like a pig on heat' one of his schoolmasters had described him. Pierse longed to be able to see them, even if just for an hour – it would give him a break from the rain and the fighting and the squalor of lying in muddy, waterlogged trenches trying to avoid death.

* * *

A week before Christmas the evacuation of the Brigade was complete. Farrell heaved a sigh of relief that the men and nearly all the stores and vehicles had been successfully recovered right from under the noses of the Japanese air force. Parties of engineers were now destroying the railway bridges to prevent the enemy using them. The battle for the east coast was over.

From Kuala Lipis they followed the road west to join with the troops fighting the main Japanese thrust down the west coast. The Dogras were placed in reserve to recover from their action at Kota Bharu and the other regiments of the Brigade bore the brunt of the constant harrying attacks. Enemy planes made movement difficult during the day and they were also attacked by ground troops pursuing them in requisitioned cars and lorries and on stolen bicycles down the expensive tarmac roads built by the British. The sepoys came to know well the distinctive 'tok, tok, tok' sound of the enemy's machine guns followed by the crash of mortars which signalled an attack – the Japanese seemed able to leapfrog them and appear where they were least expected. The days were spent fighting, the nights in retreating down the main road about seven or eight miles, cloaked in darkness and smothered by rain. Tiredness was becoming a big problem as nobody got enough sleep.

It was the 10th of January, just over a month since they had first faced the enemy. Outside the village of Serendah, and now attached to the remnants of the 11th Indian Division to bolster its strength after its earlier mauling, they were preparing to move out – part of a staged withdrawal of troops down the main trunk road that extended the length of Malaya, to make a stand against the Japanese at Fortress Singapore. The Gurkhas and the Punjabis were in the forward line facing the advancing Japanese, with orders to hold the enemy off for as long as possible and, more importantly, to prevent them from enveloping both flanks of the column. As the rearmost battalion, the Dogras now found themselves leading the move southwards. Just before dawn, under the shelter of the trees with the rain dripping through and the clatter and chatter of the regiment round them, Farrell, Pierse and Chandra sat sipping tea and smoking. Farrell was back in the front line after being released from his HQ post when the Dogras were loaned to the 11th.

'Another day, another horror', said Chandra, 'I could have been comfortably tucked up in a nice dry bed in Delhi, not waiting to be shot at by those Jap bastards.'

'Or better still, taking tiffin in the Raffles in Singapore, with a couple of gin-slings under the belt,' grinned Farrell. 'Nothing we learned at the Academy really prepared us for the reality of this war, did it? I've hardly been dry for a fortnight and I think I'm getting foot-rot.'

'Don't complain,' replied Pierse sarcastically, 'it's what you signed up for – the glamour of army life, the uniform, the girls, going to foreign places, getting foreign diseases.' The others smiled ruefully, looking at their wet, mud-encrusted uniforms and scratched legs where they had been bitten by mosquitoes and pricked by the undergrowth in which they had been forced to hide to avoid been seen by the Jap planes. 'And,' continued Pierse, 'look on the bright side. The foul weather and lack of sleep has unhinged us all so that nothing seems real anymore. It'll be like one of those stupid compositions we used to write in school, we'll wake up and it will all have been a dream!' He waved his arms theatrically.

'Unfortunately it's a regular bloody nightmare,' chipped in Farrell. 'Joking aside, it doesn't look good. We don't seem to be able to hold them back. They out-manoeuvre us and have the fire-power and the air-power. I feel frustrated and ashamed that we can't seem to deal the Japs a severe blow and halt them for once. And I don't like the idea of us Dogras today leading what looks like a wholesale retreat.'

'Why are we fighting for this God-forsaken place!' exclaimed Chandra tetchily. 'It is hot, there are too many insects and snakes, it rains all the time in the monsoon, and these wretched KD shorts offer no protection from the thorns and the insects. The natives are not exactly friendly to us now we are being driven back; have you noticed? The villagers have lost respect for us.'

'Part of our Empire, old chap,' replied Farrell. 'We can't just give it up. This is a rich country – rubber, tea, rice. We've built the railways and the roads...'

'Roads, down which the buggers move so quickly,' interjected Pierse. 'I hear that when we destroy the bridges they simply get their chaps into the river or stream carrying planks above their heads and the rest walk across. They're like a bloody ant colony, we can't slow them down!'

'That's your Jap for you,' replied Farrell primly, 'a cunning Oriental bastard.'

'I'd still rather be at home,' said Chandra. 'In a big, cool house, servants, cold drinks – and only getting wet when I take a bath. What about you, chaps?'

'Oh, probably a crisp, frosty winter morning in the English countryside,' said Farrell, 'away from this heat and rain, perhaps a shotgun tucked under my arm, doing a spot of rabbiting....'

'A shotgun?!' exclaimed Pierse in a Lady Bracknell voice, 'to kill a rabbit?! We'd have used a bloody catty!'

'Catapult,' explained Chandra to a nonplussed Farrell.

'You can't kill a rabbit with a bloody catapult Pierse,' said an exasperated Farrell.

'Perhaps not with the piddly ones you pansies use in England,' replied Pierse hotly, 'but we use vacuum rubbers on ours – rubbers pinched from the railway workshops. You need strength to draw them but, loaded with a steel ball bearing, also pinched, I might add, you could bring down a man, never mind a bloody rabbit.'

'And what would you like to be doing right now Ed,' said Farrell mockingly, 'I suppose a turn on the hockey field followed by a ride on Daddy's train.'

'Both sound wonderful,' said Pierse, not taking the bait, 'but my ideal would be a long walk with Ellen, then perhaps the pictures – then home to dinner with my folks and brother, Kenny. All those things I took for granted. Still, it will have to wait till I get back. Until then, it's back to business – here's the Havildar Sahib, come to get me. I hope the sepoys I've taken over from Bryce's reserve platoon to fill the gaps in mine will be up to the job.'

'Sahib,' said the Havildar, saluting Pierse, 'men are ready.'

'Havildar Sahib,' said Farrell, 'we were just talking about what we would like to be doing instead of waiting for the *Japani* to attack. What about you?'

Havildar Prem Singh looked uncomfortable and shot Pierse a look. Pierse gave an imperceptible nod to show it was okay to reply. 'The army is my life Sahib, so I am doing what I like.'

'But you must have a family Prem Singh,' said Chandra, 'wouldn't you rather be with them?'

'Sahib, I only see them once a year when I go on leave. The army is also my family.'

'Well said, Havildar Sahib,' said Pierse, frowning at Farrell. 'We are all one family here and it is good to be with them. I'll grab my kit and come in a moment.'

When the Havildar departed, Farrell said, scornfully, 'The Hyderabads weren't exactly one happy family, were they? Shooting their CO and British officers like that because they were too scared to obey orders and attack the airfield at Kota Bharu.'

'Look,' replied Pierse sharply, 'I was there and the place was a bloody mess. The officers could have been killed in cross-fire; there is no proof that they were killed by their men.' He jumped up, 'Must go,' picked up the rifle he had now become somewhat attached to and left to inspect his men.

Chandra turned to Farrell, 'They were just ceremonial soldiers belonging to the Nizam of Hyderabad and did not come to Malaya expecting to do any fighting. One of the Baluchi officers told me that they were rattled by seeing the Australians flee from the airfield. When the officers told them to advance they thought, 'Why should we do that and get killed when the white *sahibs* are running away and saving their lives?' So they declined, and when they were threatened by their officers, shot them in self defence.'

'Declined!' exclaimed Farrell. 'They were cowards with no loyalty to their officers or their regiment.'

'You heard Ed,' replied Chandra, 'he was there, and he and his men had to retreat because it was hopeless. These men are simple villagers Mike; they join the army to get a regular job.

Maybe they were loyal to the Nizam – more likely they felt a greater responsibility to their families and wanted to come home in one piece as they were the only breadwinners. Maybe they don't think that this is their war – fighting in a foreign country for someone who isn't their Maharajah, against someone with whom they have no quarrel.'

'But if the whole army thought like that where would we be?' demanded Farrell. 'If you take on a job, eat someone's salt and draw their pay, you owe them loyalty to do the job you were employed to do. Look at us three – we are from wholly different backgrounds, yet we are friends and loyal to each other! Look at our chaps – heroes to a man. They have fought hard and bravely, many have died and many more been wounded. Yet they obey without question. What's the difference between them and the Hyderabads?'

'Maybe we are better officers and they respect that and want to obey us and fight alongside us. We also have great regimental traditions to live up to,' mused Chandra.

'Don't think it is that simple,' replied Farrell. 'Our chaps are more disciplined, I agree. They have the right attitude: our enemy is their enemy. They see the benefits of being part of the Empire army and want to protect it too.'

'I don't know, I don't think so. I somehow feel sorry for the Hyderabads. It is a disgrace to have been disarmed and sent to be coolies. They must feel so ashamed,' said Chandra with feeling.

'The men despise them too,' said Farrell.

'I don't know,' said Chandra.

Their conversation was brought to a sudden end by a distant barrage of artillery and mortar fire and the drone of aircraft engines. The Japanese were launching what seemed to be a major attack on the column and there was a rush of officers and men to mount the 3-ton lorries and begin the move south down the main road.

* * *

Farrell, sitting next to his driver, leant out of the window and shouted to Pierse and Chandra, 'Race you down the road chaps. I intend to spend tonight in luxury – fed up of sleeping under the drip, drip of the bloody monsoon'. The driver clashed the gears and Farrell rode off in triumph only to be blocked about a hundred yards down the road by a group of sepoys who were loading ammunition cases. Pierse and Chandra were quick to respond to the challenge and ordered their drivers to turn briefly off the road and across the fields to skirt Farrell and his obstruction. As they passed in a cloud of mud and spray, Farrell ordered his driver to sound the horn and, shouting and gesticulating angrily to the sepoys on the road to move out of the way, set off in hot pursuit – as hot as a fully laden lorry could go, which was at a somewhat stately pace.

The sepoys in the back of the three lorries knew only too well the rivalry between their officers, and indeed had often been amused and willing participants in their dares and duels. Bets were being taken and there were cheers and jeers as the vehicles jostled for position, the drivers cursed or applauded as they either crashed their gears and lost position, or executed a passing manoeuvre – it was a welcome distraction from the business of war. Down the road they trundled, the Brigade strung out behind, some of the other officers goading their drivers to try to get ahead of the leading pack.

Farrell had regained the lead as a village came in sight after a couple of miles, tucked away under a dense covering of trees. Pierse, who was lying second, about fifty yards behind, suddenly saw Farrell's lorry swerve – flat tyre he thought triumphantly – but then he heard the chatter and realised that a machinegun firing from the village had smashed Farrell's windscreen, the shattering glass streaming off the driver's side of the cab.

'Pull off the road!' shouted Pierse to his driver as Farrell's lorry plunged drunkenly off the tarmac and crashed into the trees bordering the road amid the explosions of a pattern of mortar bombs. 'Oh Hell,' thought Pierse, as with squealing brakes his lorry also swerved off the road and cracked into a succession of stout saplings. He and his sepoys were vaulting from the truck as the 'tok, tok, tok' of the machine guns, the bang of mortars and the popping of rifles indicated that the Imperial Japanese Army had, once again, completely confounded its enemy and worked its way around the retreating troops to block their path south. The rest of the convoy strung out behind also ground to a stop and took cover.

With his sepoys under cover and returning fire, Pierse urgently turned to Havildar Prem Singh, already manning the Bren with his loader, Bela Ram, by his side.

'I'm going to see if Farrell Sahib's people are okay,' he said, revolver in hand, rifle slung across his back.

'Take Dina Nath and two others, Sahib,' suggested Prem Singh, 'they can give cover.'

Pierse and his small group moved forward, skirting the road through the thick undergrowth. 'We have to be very careful,' he said to the sepoys, 'we don't want Farrell Sahib's people to think we are *Japani* encircling them.' So he began to shout out to Farrell by name and Dina Nath called out in Dogri to Farrell's men. Pierse froze as he detected movement ahead coming his way. They crouched in silence, weapons aimed. Through the bushes came a crawling sepoy, leading Farrell, his face bloodied and behind them, the others, making an orderly retreat.

'Mike!' exclaimed Pierse.

'It's okay Ed,' replied Farrell, turning his head to the sound of Pierse's voice. 'Whacked the sodding windscreen, nothing serious, few cuts. Just got to get the sodding blood out of my eyes and the splinters out of my face.' Then, 'Driver's kaput;

bastards got him and got a couple of the others too – one kaput, the boys are bringing them.' He crouched low as bullets hissed overhead and the mortars continued to explode – one finally demolishing his lorry. 'How did the bastards get round us to the village!' It was not a question, but spat out in anger.

* * *

Assembled out of harm's way and under cover of the roadside ditches back down the road they had just travelled, Pierse, Chandra, and a cleaned up Farrell with a sizeable cut across his hairline and a face pocked with cuts from the flying glass, joined the other officers to decide on the next action.

'We have to get those Japs out,' said the Colonel, 'so our troops can continue southwards – and they are in the way. This is going to be a difficult one. They are dug in, we don't know the lie of this village – it is called Sungei Choh – and we don't know how many of the enemy are there and how heavily they are armed. Naturally all the villagers have disappeared, so we have no more information. We'll begin with an assault with mortars and machine guns to soften the bastards up, but then we will have to go in and clear what's left of them out, house to house if necessary with the bayonet. Sorry chaps, but it falls to us to get on with it – there's no artillery or any armoured support we can call as they are all busy on the front line, and time is getting short.'

So Chandra, Pierse and Farrell who, despite his injuries, insisted on being part of the assault force, found themselves and their men creeping cautiously forward in separate groups to attack. The sound of the rain through the trees, dripping into puddles and onto the hut roofs, cloaked the advance but also blunted their senses as they strained to peer through rain-stung eyes and hear through ears dulled by the hiss and drip of water. The village was a maze of huts, most constructed of bamboo and palm-leaf attap, many surrounded by creeper clad fences, with the detritus of village life – logs of wood, animal pens, building material, discarded pots and pans – scattered around. Criss-crossing the paths were drainage channels filled with running rainwater. It was every soldier's nightmare: an enemy well dug in and concealed within and under the huts having to be winkled out at bayonet point.

At the agreed moment, the Brens and heavy machine guns raked the village and mortars burst among the huts. A sudden lull and then, shouting their battle cry, the Dogras charged with fixed bayonets.......

It was a bloody day. The concealed Japanese poured heavy fire, mortars and grenades on to their attackers, who found their way blocked by the high and impenetrable creeper-entwined fences surrounding each hut – which provided concealment but no protection. It was, for the Dogras, a taste of the obstacles the Japs had faced at Kota Bharu. The attack soon stalled and the Dogras became pinned down.

Farrell was knocked sideways in the initial charge by a grenade blast. Lying dazed, he looked down to find his right side covered in blood. It was not his day. He lay behind a pile of logs and watched the blood slowly merge with the rain and dissolve into the sand leaving a rusty stain. His side burned with pain every time he moved and the cuts on his forehead and face were bleeding again, making it difficult for him to see.

Pierse, his Havildar giving covering fire, rushed the fence surrounding the hut ahead with Dina Nath and the other sepoys, revolver in hand, but the attack failed as the sepoys unsuccessfully tried to scale the fences and were repelled by machine gun and rifle fire. The Naik on Pierse's left was shot in the head and Dina Nath, on his right, fell, hit in the leg. Havildar Prem Singh, who was crouched against the trunk of a tree with his Bren, looked over at Pierse. Pierse shouted to his men that they were going to try again and signalled the

Havildar to continue firing into the hut to keep the Japs down.

'*Chalo! Chalo, jaldhi!*' screamed Pierse and the Bren opened up and he lobbed a grenade at the fence and another at the hut. Firing his revolver, he charged with his men but they fell back again as heavy fire claimed another two sepoys. On Pierse's order the sepoys rose from their positions and charged forward again and again, but fell back each time. The creeper fences were difficult to get over – getting through them was impossible. It was like a lethal childhood game of 'statues' – Grandmother's footsteps, his Da had said it was called in England – where children tried to rush up to touch a child, his back turned, who chanted, 'L-O-N-D-O-N London!' but must freeze in mid-action when he turned round or else be out of the game. Only here it was the 'statues' that wouldn't be playing anymore as they lay on the sodden ground. The chatter-chatter of enfilading fire from the surrounding jungle pinned them down. They were getting nowhere.

Eventually, a concerted attack with grenades dismantled the fences and they rushed the hut and killed its occupants. Then it was on to the next – and the next. It was a slow, bloody, painful process, leaving a trail of dead and wounded in their wake. Morning slipped unnoticed into afternoon and the fighting continued but the Dogras were not making much headway and the Japs were slowly but surely beginning to encircle them, drifting through the palm thickets that surrounded the village. Pierse realised that they had to try to extricate themselves or face being overrun and he began moving the men back in an orderly retreat. He wondered how Chandra and Farrell were faring; were they still alive? Littered all around he could hear wounded Dogras and Japanese, groaning and crying in their pain to their gods and their mothers. This was a disaster.

The Colonel realised that it was no longer a question of overcoming the Japanese lodged in the village – there were too many and they were too well dug in. It was now a mission to rescue what was left of his men who had taken part in the attack. The rain began to come down heavily and the sky was darkening – he had to move quickly as the darkness would be to the advantage of a jungle-trained enemy. He decided that the only way to extricate his men was to commit to a further attack to try to hold off the enemy for long enough so that they could be rescued. It was a risky gamble and he faced losing even more men in the process.

The first Pierse knew about it was an eruption of explosions as mortars, grenades, machine guns and rifles – even the distinctive crash of a Boys anti-tank rifle – opened up on the huts occupied by the Japs. Pierse understood and bundled his men back the way they had come, shouting at them to hurry. The attack, the Colonel's rescue mission, pinned the enemy down long enough for many of the men to pull back – yet it took much fighting, and more dead and wounded. Lying exhausted at the side of the road, Pierse realised that his uniform was bloody, but that the rain was washing out all but the worst of it – not mine, he thought with grim satisfaction.

* * *

'Havildar Sahib, what are our casualties? What happened to you and the others?'

'Sahib,' said Havildar Prem Singh contritely. I was pinned down when you charged the hut and Bela Ram, the loader, was hit. Then we ran out of ammunition. We managed to recover Dina Nath but he is in a serious condition as he lost a lot of blood from the wound on his leg. In all, Sahib, the *paltan* has lost five men killed – three of them the new ones – and eight wounded.'

'Have we recovered them all?'

'No Sahib,' replied Prem Singh, visibly distressed. 'We

have had to leave three of the dead behind, and two of the wounded are still there. I doubt now that we will be able to get them out.'

'Where are the rest of the wounded now? I would like to see them.'

'They were taken quickly by truck to a medical unit – I don't know where Sahib – but we will be able to find out.'

'Any news of Farrell and Chandra Sahibs?'

'Farrell Sahib was wounded, I don't know how badly. Chandra Sahib is missing.'

'Missing,' thought Pierse, a military euphemism for 'lying out there either dead or wounded and at the mercy of those Jap bastards.' He was too tired, too exhausted, to feel anything.

They were rapidly loaded on to lorries, packed in very tight as a number of the vehicles had been destroyed in the fight, and in the pouring rain driven round the enemy and made their way through Kuala Lumpur to a reserve area at Tampin. They came off the trucks, dropping in heaps, heedless of the rain – too tired to speak, some lying in the mud where they fell, lapsing into deep sleep. Most hadn't eaten since before dawn.

It was there that Pierse found Farrell. He was sitting up under a dripping canvas, in some pain and discomfort, with his ribs bandaged and his head blotched with iodine over his cuts.

'Grenade blast,' he said to Pierse, 'piece of debris whacked my ribs but the webbing straps stopped much of it going through – the ribs are cracked – and it hurts like hell. Could have been worse, I suppose......'

'Bad news about Anil,' said Pierse, 'poor bastard. I hope for his sake that he managed to escape. If he didn't I hope he had a clean death and is not lying there wounded and at the mercy of the Japs.'

'What's the story?' asked Farrell.

'Don't know that much. His Havildar said that Anil had led his platoon into the attack but that they had been pinned down and were taking casualties so they scattered and that is the last anyone saw of him. His lot lost four or five – most of them still out there. Bad business!'

'I think he knew it was coming,' said Farrell, 'the fight seemed to have gone out of him.'

'Don't speak like that about him,' replied Pierse sharply. He suddenly began to feel Chandra's loss deeply despite the exhaustion that overwhelmed him.

'He'll survive,' said Farrell consolingly, 'probably ensconced in some nice dry village somewhere.'

'And you, poor bugger,' said Pierse wryly, 'are still under dripping canvas. So much for the life of luxury you expected tonight.'

CHAPTER 4

Island Fortress

They crossed the causeway into Singapore at the end of January and it was blown a few days later after the last troops had straggled over. Not all had made it, many were still missing or in enemy hands. It was impossible to tell if any had accepted a provocative Japanese invitation to the Indian troops, conveyed through a member of an Indian medical unit who had been captured, to abandon their British officers and be welcomed by their 'loving Asiatic brethren'.

The Dogras were mere shadows of themselves after the losses they had taken over the past seven weeks. The men were weary in the extreme after fighting and withdrawing, and then fighting again. There were no reserves left to fill their depleted ranks and they had lost much of their effectiveness as a fighting force. The weather had not been kind and the enemy had been determined, strong, well armed and well supported by tanks and planes.

Singapore was now a fortress island crammed with over 80,000 troops – British, Australians, Malay and Indian – all digging in for the final assault. The troops who had retreated down Malaya felt that they might now have a chance for revenge against an enemy who had outmanoeuvred them in the jungle – this could be different. The units that had remained in the garrison at Singapore were fresh and confident that they would see off the Imperial Japanese Army. Hopes were resting on the Australians, who had inflicted defeats on the enemy in the retreat down Malaya and had shown that the Japs could be beaten. Would the Australians now be able to deal them a crushing blow and halt the invasion? The Aussies had swagger, a 'fighting spirit', and they were personally anxious to stop the Jap advance in its tracks to prevent it moving ever closer to their country. Reinforcements had arrived by sea in recent days and more troops and fighter aircraft were on their way. There were vast amounts of war material on the island – guns, vehicles, ammunition, mortars, mines, medical and food supplies. With the blowing up of the causeway the water pipeline from the mainland had been cut, but there was adequate water in the reservoirs in the centre of the island.

The Dogras were deployed as Corps reserves to defend the northern coast facing the Malay mainland, covering the area from Changi to the Causeway. They were thankful that they were not this time in the front line facing the strait but billeted in the barracks north of the village of Nee Soon. It was there that they waited.

* * *

Farrell was one of the first to hear. His Havildar came rushing up to him, breathless, saluting, 'Sahib, Sahib. Chandra Sahib is back.'

Farrell started, completely taken aback, 'What do you mean!' he exclaimed.

'He arrived just now with one of his sepoys who was also missing at Sungei Choh and has been taken to see the C.O.'

'Have you seen him?' asked Farrell.

'No Sahib. It was one of the orderlies who told me.'

Farrell rushed off to find Pierse, but word had already got around and there was a buzz of speculation among the officers gathered in the mess, Pierse in the thick of it. He was pleased that Chandra was back, but somewhat disconcerted. He looked down anxiously then turned to Farrell.

'Oh Lord, Mike,' he said quietly, 'after the action at Sungei Choh I wrote to Anil's parents to say he was missing. They will have been devastated.'

'It's okay,' replied Farrell after taking this in. 'Now both you and Anil can write to them to give them the good news. The wonderful news! It's just like a resurrection!' Then, seeing Pierse's tortured face, 'You did the right thing under the circumstances Ed. Don't torment yourself. It can all be sorted out,' he laughed.

When Chandra finally emerged from his debriefing with the CO, Pierse, Farrell and the other young officers surged around him shaking his hand and patting him on the back – very pleased to see him return from the dead and, of course, full of jokes and pithy comments about his absence. He looked scruffy and exhausted – like a *dhobi's* bundle, one of his fellow officers remarked. He was unshaven, his normally immaculate hair unkempt. He looked nervously around as his fellow officers crowded round him to hear his story.

'We became pinned down when we went in to attack the village and my men were taking casualties. I shouted to them to split up and move to where they could find some cover but, despite trying to, we could not move forward and so I thought I would try to skirt round the enemy to find a better way through, but those bastards had spotted me. I found myself under fire, so I moved further and further away to avoid being killed or captured. Then they started their usual tactics of trying to encircle so I went deeper into the trees. I couldn't get back as they were still moving about the area – there were too many of them for me to attack on my own and

I had lost my bearings in the rain and the confusion. I stayed there a long time and couldn't make my way back because they were in the area. When they finally moved back and the firing began to peter out, I started making my way to what I hoped would be the main road and came across one of my men who had found himself in the same situation. When we eventually got to the road in the early hours the next morning, we found that the Regiment had gone, but the Japs were still around us. So we had to get off the road into the fields and jungles and make our way south on bicycles that we pinched, until we came across a Sikh regiment, and got a lift with them. Unfortunately for us they were headed west rather than south, so we had to muck in with them until they finally joined the trail to Singapore. We were lucky to get across the causeway before they blew it up.'

'Anil,' said Pierse when they were finally alone, 'I wrote to your parents after you went missing at Sungei Choh, I felt that I had to let them know.' He looked apologetic.

Chandra looked shocked. 'Why?' he asked angrily, 'there was always the chance that I was okay or only wounded – that some of us would be trapped behind the enemy's lines and eventually make our way back – just as happened at Kota Bharu. My father is in poor health, this could kill him! What have you done! You had no right to do this.'

Pierse was taken aback by this reaction. 'I only said that you were missing. The Army would have done it anyway, and in an impersonal way by telegram, which I stopped,' replied Pierse, 'I thought they would welcome a letter from a friend of yours.'

Chandra shook his head vehemently, 'You shouldn't have done that! You shouldn't have done that! I've got to try to get a message to them immediately.' With that he walked off.

Pierse made to go after him but Farrell stopped him. 'He's tired and strained just now Ed, leave it for a while.'

* * *

That evening, Pierse sat honing the blade of his jack-knife, depressed and lost in thoughts of home and trying not to think of the upset that he had caused his friend Chandra. The door opened and a scar-faced Farrell came through and sat down gingerly on the camp bed opposite – his ribs still tender. He watched Pierse for a moment.

'You're always sharpening that thing Piersey,' said Farrell, 'I don't think a piddly little scratcher like that is going to help much in the coming attack. Why are you so attached to the bloody thing – get yourself a kukri, you can do a lot more with it, even kill a few Japs.' He grinned, while making swishing movements with his arm.

'Oh I don't know,' replied Pierse, hefting the knife with its strong six inch blade, 'this has got me out of a few scrapes. My Uncle Derek gave this to me as a confirmation present when I was eight years old. He said that if I looked after it properly, it could do more to save my life than all the religion and all the prayers in the world, especially those said by a fat bastard Bishop.' He smiled to himself.

'So he didn't like the Bishop?' asked Farrell.

'He was at school with him Mike, and couldn't stand the sight of the bastard, said he was a sneak and a whinger. When the bugger took holy orders that was it! No more religion for Uncle Derek.'

'Looks like a good one,' said Farrell, indicating the knife.

'Yes, he paid a lot of money for it. It is made of good Sheffield steel. As you can see, I've had it for years and it looks as good as new. Oh, and it also came in useful at Sungei – used it to cut through the floor of one of the huts and through some of those bloody fences.' He laughed, 'So Uncle Derek was right after all.'

'Don't do a Clive with it, will you,' said Farrell. Seeing the look of incomprehension on Pierse's face, 'Clive of India, cut his throat with his – committed suicide.'

'Not bloody likely!' snorted Pierse.

Farrell smiled then said, 'Ed, I think that Anil's got a problem.' Pierse looked up sharply.

'You know that the chaps have been making jokes about his going missing, mostly the usual banter, but now some of it is starting to get nasty and a bit out of hand.'

'Oh?' enquired Pierse, 'I've given him a wide berth after the dust up that we had over my writing to his people.'

'Well, it has gone from the usual jokey stuff about Anil bunking off to have a few days with a beautiful Chinese girl, to outright disbelief in his story. Our *favourite* Captain,' he said sarcastically, 'is being particularly off.'

'Does Anil know about this?'

'I'm not sure, I don't think so. He hasn't really emerged since the welcome in the mess. He was certainly beginning to tire of the jokes, just as when they ribbed him about his kick in the balls, but this is suggesting something that is no laughing matter.'

'You mean they think he funked the fight at Sungei?' Pierse mused for a moment. 'You and I have known Anil for some time now, and I have seen him in battle. He is as brave as the best of them – he and his chaps held the Japs off at Kota Bharu and helped my men and me to escape certain death in the pillbox. He nearly drowned in the stream after that, and wanted to continue but he was in such pain that it would have been impossible for him to walk, let alone trek through the inlets. Chaps are always being trapped behind enemy lines – look what happened at Kota Bharu, when the stragglers slowly returned. I think some of the officers are jealous because he comes from a well-to-do family. Anil is cocky and confident and doesn't kowtow to them; he doesn't have to depend on the Army for his future.'

'And he has a short fuse!' Farrell added.

'What do you suggest we do?' asked Pierse, though he felt he knew the answer.

'In his present state, and God knows what he has been through, he would be devastated if he found out. I noticed when we were loading up to move out on the railway to Kuala Lipis that he looked depressed and tired – I know we all were, but Anil seemed more weighed down. I don't think he likes to rough it in the jungle – prefers an ordered life. We've got to try to bring this nonsense to a stop.'

'Bit tricky. We can't charge in and accuse the Captain of spreading malicious lies without finding ourselves up before the CO. And you know how vicious our favourite Captain can be. Perhaps we can talk to some of the other chaps – making stupid allegations like this isn't going to help the Regiment's spirit when the Japs are breathing down our necks. We need to pull together. Anil will, in any case, be put to the test when the Japs attack, which is any day now.'

'Yup,' agreed Farrell. 'Softly, softly catchee monkey, eh?'

* * *

Pierse went off to try to talk to some of the other junior officers and sound them out, but Farrell went to Chandra's quarters, where he found him writing a letter.

'How are you Anil?'

'Still tired but I'm alright,' replied Chandra, pointedly checking his watch then continuing to write.

Farrell didn't take the hint. 'Look, old son,' he said, 'Pierse did what he thought was right. Maybe he should have waited longer, but I gather from him that he waited over a week and you hadn't turned up. We thought the worst had happened, all of us did.'

Chandra continued to write. Farrell was beginning to get exasperated.

'Look Anil,' he said quietly, 'we've all been through a difficult couple of months and we are not thinking straight. But what's done is done; you can put it right...'

'Are you implying that I am not thinking straight?' accused Chandra angrily, slapping down his pen. 'Do you know what I went through? Do you know how hard it has been for me, separated from the Regiment and trying to get back despite the difficulties out there? Do you think I don't know what some of you officers are thinking?'

'Now hold on,' said Farrell, his temper rising. 'Pierse and I are your friends, damn it, and we are just glad you are back. Bugger the other officers, they are just joshing. But Pierse is now really upset that he wrote to your people, he was not to know that you were okay and would turn up nearly three weeks later. It is unusual – that's all. Time for you to rejoin us Anil,' he said pointedly, 'we are going to need all the help we can get. Let's go and have a drink.' Chandra shook his head. Annoyed, Farrell left.

He found Pierse in the mess, beaming. 'Okay, what's the secret?' asked Farrell.

Pierse waved a couple of pieces of paper, 'Passes,' he laughed, 'the Old Man is letting a few of us go into the City tomorrow and you, Mike, are one of the lucky chaps!' He savoured the look of incredulity on Farrell's face. 'Not all fun though,' he said mock seriously.

'Oh? What's the catch?'

'We are going to call in on our casualties in the General Hospital to see if any will be fit enough to rejoin us over the next few days.'

'Ah.' Farrell's face fell.

'Cheer up! We are then free to take in the delights of the city for the rest of the day – but back at 6 o'clock.'

Farrell chuckled. They had been angling to get a day out in Singapore since they arrived but had been too busy setting up camp and organising the men. With the Japs massing across the strait, they thought that there would be little chance of anyone being allowed to leave the camp.

* * *

They had known the city well before going up to Kota Bharu, but the war had made its presence felt across this pearl of Empire. The main streets were khaki rivers of troops, mainly Australian and British, drunk and boisterous, all in search of a good time and partying as though it was the end of the world, which in a way for them it was. Threading their way through the mayhem were the tight-lipped European residents, determined to maintain their standards and behaving with calm, studied indifference as though life continued as before. Houseboys and amahs went about their duties, dodging the uniformed crowds on the pavements, amazed at the bad behaviour of these new *tuans*. The Chinese and Malay shopkeepers were agitatedly trying to squeeze as much trade out of the new customers as they could, wincing at their wilder excesses yet determined to drive hard bargains to maximise profits. Sometimes the hard bargaining of the shopkeepers and the drunken belligerence of the customers came close to boiling over – but the shopkeepers were too skilled in the bargaining game, too schooled in human nature, and mollified customers were soon sent on their way with what they believed were bargains – but the truth was that they were being robbed blind.

The evidence of the Japanese air raids and the shelling lay everywhere – burnt and damaged buildings, splintered trees, rubble in the streets, mangled remains of vehicles – buses, cars and rickshaws. The empty eyes of the windows looked down at it all, their crystalline tears showered on the pavements. It was like a Wild West town on a Saturday night – but set in the South China Sea.

As they came out of the hospital after visiting the men, Farrell said, 'They were really pleased to see us, Piersey, but probably more pleased to see the grub!' The Regimental cooks had pulled out all the stops to cook favourite meals for their wounded comrades. 'I was surprised though that most of the chaps seem genuinely keen to come back into the line rather than enjoy the rest and care – and the nurses. Oh, the nurses!'

'It was nice to see Dina Nath getting about,' replied Pierse. 'I really thought he was finished after he went down in Sungei. The Doc says that he could be back in a few days, though I don't know if he will make it back to the hockey field.' Pierse had been touched by the warmth with which Dina Nath had welcomed him. 'It was so sad to see Ragunath in such a bad state.' Ragunath was one of Pierse's protégées. 'He could have played hockey for India you know, such a rare talent. He was so shy and almost inarticulate when he joined the Regiment. He had never played hockey before but took to it naturally. Don't know where the skill came from. But now it's gone. Hope he survives.'

'Hockey,' said Farrell, 'is not the most immediate thing on my mind just now.' He looked at his watch, 'Time for a drink or three in the bar of the Raffles and then a spot of tiffin in the dining room. Are you game?'

'Lead on,' grinned Pierse. 'But that reminds me – after lunch I need to get myself a new watch; mine went kaput when I dived in after Anil at Kota Bharu.'

'You really know how to live it up, don't you,' mocked Farrell. 'Wouldn't you prefer an afternoon filled with girls?' He looked at Pierse, 'No, you wouldn't,' he smiled, 'saving yourself for Ellen, eh? You miserable, lucky bugger!'

Alas, the crowd of uniforms waiting outside the Raffles indicated that it was going to be impossible to get into the bar or to take tiffin that day. Too many had the same idea. They eventually fetched up at an Indian eating place off Orchard

Road. After a leisurely lunch of fragrant curry and rice and bottles of cold beer, a meal that they gamely pronounced was just as good as the tiffin at the Raffles, though perhaps the restaurant lacked that hotel's style and ambience, Pierse asked the manager if he could recommend somewhere to buy a watch. This being Singapore, the manager had a cousin who ran just such a place, so Pierse set off to buy a watch while Farrell went in search of 'an old friend'.

Farrell disappeared with an expectant urgency towards the cramped, narrow, bustling lanes of Bugis with its higgledy-piggeldy wooden shops, eating places and tea houses all wrapped in a cloud of dust, spices, steam, the scent of food and the stinks of sewage. In the lanes surged a colourful cast of customers, shouting, touting shopkeepers and sweaty half-naked Chinese and Malay labourers struggling under loads, children scuttling through the throng, passers-by and rickshaw pullers striving to work their way through to their destinations. Behind the shutters lay another, darker world of opium, gambling, girls, boys and gangsters. It was a world far removed from the one Farrell usually inhabited.

* * *

Expecting a small, somewhat shady establishment, Pierse was surprised to find a large, well-stocked and swanky shop with cases of elaborate gold and silver jewellery. Feeling a little intimidated, he introduced himself to the Tamil manager, a dark, dapper man, with a wide, toothy smile over the heavy gold chain around his neck, and explained that his cousin had recommended his business. At the mention of his cousin, the manager, Mr Naidu, welcomed Pierse like a long lost friend – especially when he recognised that Pierse was an Anglo-Indian and soon established that he came from Calcutta but had travelled in South India. As is the Indian custom, family histories were soon being exchanged and mutual connections established before they got down to business. Noting that he was from the Dogras, Mr Naidu, moustache twitching mischievously, said that he had sold a very good watch to a Dogra officer only the week before and that Pierse might like to buy an identical one. Pierse was bemused by this claim.

'You must be mistaken, Mr Naidu,' he laughed at this blatant bazaar salesmanship. 'We only came across the Causeway two days ago.'

But Mr Naidu was insistent. 'He was in mufti,' he said. 'I cannot remember his name, but his father is a big zamindar.'

'Are you sure it was a week ago?'

'I am positive.' Naidu riffled through his receipt book, looked up and nodded, 'Yes, last Tuesday.'

'What's his name, I may know him.'

'Mr Pierse, sir, we are not giving that type of information,' he said, shaking his head emphatically and firmly closing the receipt book. He turned on his beaming smile: 'Let me show you the watch.' He produced a handsome steel watch with a black leather band, 'Here, this is identical model. It is waterproof, and has radium dial so you can tell the time in the dark. It will last you long time. Best for army!' He saw Pierse looking somewhat sceptical and, not wanting to lose the sale, offered a sizeable discount.

* * *

On their way back to camp Pierse and Farrell animatedly discussed the delights of the day and an amused Pierse described to Farrell the conversation in the shop and how the shopkeeper had claimed that he had sold a watch to someone in the Regiment, but had been caught out when Pierse had pointed out that they hadn't been in Singapore then.

'Of course,' said Pierse, 'there could have been a real

customer who had lied to Mr Naidu and pretended to be an Indian Army officer to get a better discount. And Naidu was not to know that an Army officer would not have been dressed in mufti with a war round the corner.'

'Or, more likely, he didn't want you to see the exorbitant price he had charged! Lying bastard,' laughed Farrell, 'an outrageous piece of salesmanship. You can't trust the buggers, even if it looked a respectable shop. Oh,' he added slyly, 'you'd better remember to shove your shiny new watch up your arse when the Japs get here, Ed, or they'll have it off you in a flash.'

Back at camp, Pierse and Farrell headed for the mess and a beer. 'You get them in Mike,' grinned Pierse, 'I'm going to drag Anil out of his quarters, by the scruff of his neck if I have to, and get him to come and have a drink with us. It's time to make our peace, I think. He'll want to know about the chaps we visited in hospital today.'

But the room was empty, Anil Chandra's cot stripped bare and unoccupied. Seeing one of the other Lieutenants, Pierse asked if he knew where Chandra was as he seemed to have moved rooms.

'Left the camp,' said the Lieutenant, 'went this morning, sent to the General Hospital. I think he had a touch of appendicitis, he was in pain and feeling ill.' Pierse felt deflated. Knowing Chandra, he would have kept his pain to himself, he thought. Perhaps this accounted for his overreaction. God knows what the poor chap had been through. He went back to the mess to tell Farrell and found him drinking with a couple of the other young officers. They confirmed the news.

'Thought you knew and that you might have seen him at the hospital today,' said one. 'I sometimes think that you three chaps are invisibly joined, Ha Ha.'

Pierse later confided to Farrell that he was worried. 'Hospital isn't the best place to be with the Japs about to attack.

Those bastards have shown no compassion towards the sick and wounded so far and they can't fight back.'

Farrell disagreed. 'At least he won't have the pleasure of the front line, Ed, and if the Japs do get through all of us and reach the City I think by then the whole show will be over. Anil may actually stand a better chance than we do and he's in the best place to be as a burst appendix can be fatal.'

* * *

The Japanese air raids and the bombardment from the mainland intensified in preparation for their assault. Plumes of dense, black smoke rose from hits in Singapore City, rubber stocks were burning in Kepple Harbour and fuel tanks had been set ablaze at the naval base at Changi in the north. A grey, malodorous cloud rose over the island and began to settle in an oily film on the buildings, trees and the people as it came down with the rain. Then, on the 8th of February, exactly two months after they had first landed in Malaya, following a day of ceaseless bombing and shelling, the Imperial Japanese Army began its invasion of Singapore, the great prize, at thirty minutes to midnight. Thirteen thousand men landed on a front of four miles on the north west coast of the island, in the dark, having come across the narrowest part of the strait in a flotilla of boats and improvised rafts under cover of mortar and shell fire – right into the path of the Australian Imperial Force defending a difficult, bleak area of swamp and stunted rubber trees. The 'wily oriental bastards' had come via the tradesman's entrance. Ten thousand more came after dawn.

Pierse, waiting in the rubber groves with his men, grateful once again for the reassuring presence of Havildar Prem Singh, could hear the noise of the battle away to his left. He noticed with surprise that he no longer felt afraid before the battle;

there was no sense of nervous, sweaty anticipation and foreboding – perhaps this was what being 'battle-hardened' meant. It seemed like 'just another day at the office', Japs in the In Tray to be dealt with and shifted, dead or wounded, to the Out Tray. No pauses, no mistakes – no time to think of anything else. As the night passed, reports came through that the Australians were being pushed back and that their line was being infiltrated. Reserve troops were pressed into place to shore up the defences but by dawn the Australians were withdrawing under the ferocity of the attack. The Dogras and the rest of the 11th Indian Division were concerned that if the Australians withdrew too far and too fast, their left flank would be wholly exposed.

The naval base had been hit repeatedly and the many ruptured fuel tanks were pouring blazing oil down the creeks, making the air dense with even more choking, acrid smoke and oily soot. After dark the Japanese Imperial Guards, ultra-fanatical elite troops, 'not a man under four foot two,' Farrell had disparagingly joked, began their assault in the causeway area, supported by a heavy artillery bombardment. They were to be the Dogras' nemesis. To try to stop them, and to deny them the remaining fuel, the valves of the oil storage tanks were opened and blazing oil flowed into the Kranji River. The tide coming up the creeks spread the fire and took a heavy toll of the Guards as they crossed the river. Pinned down and taking heavy losses, they suddenly got lucky. First, the Australian troops opposing them, filled with many new and untrained replacements, cracked and fled, abandoning their weapons. A Sikh sepoy turned to his British officer: 'Why are they running away, they are all Sahibs!' The frustrated officer retorted angrily, 'They are not Sahibs – they are Australians!' Some of those fleeing went straight to Singapore City, where they tried to embark on boats to take them home. Then the Australian Brigade holding the Causeway withdrew in the early hours of 10th February, allowing the Guards to consolidate their landing but exposing a huge gap in the defensive line – the very thing that Pierse and his colleagues had feared. They were ordered forward to plug the gap.

Confusion and chaos were everywhere and Pierse lay in a muddy ditch trying to make sense of the battle. He couldn't see far forward because of the thick vegetation, and he couldn't see the enemy but they were there, pressing, always pressing. The fighting was intense: machine gun and rifle fire and the explosions of the mortars uprooting the thickets, splintering the trees. The raw teenagers of the Punjabi Regiment bolted, but the line was quickly steadied by the other, more experienced, Indian troops supported by anti-tank guns and heavy machine guns. The Geordie anti-tank gunners knocked out the advancing Jap tanks and with their loss the Guards' advance was halted yet again. Pierse continued to lie there firing at an enemy he couldn't see until the order was given to withdraw and other troops came forward to plug the gap.

Day and night the fighting continued unabated. The noise of the aerial and artillery bombardments reverberated round the island. Japanese heavy guns were firing across the strait in support of the Guards' advance. The British naval guns, the pride of Singapore, swivelled 180 degrees to return fire across the island, their heavy shells moving overhead with the sound of express trains to crash onto the main road, blasting huge craters into it to prevent the enemy from using it to move forward. By the afternoon the Guards, attacking ferociously, were gaining ground and the 11th Indian Division had fallen back to dig in outside Nee Soon village.

Pierse and Farrell were in separate positions along the line, gradually retreating under the fury of the assault. The Division was slowly, inexorably, being squeezed into a retreat. Farrell's unit found itself being encircled by a group of Japanese infantrymen and he was only saved by the intervention of an experienced Baluchi section equipped with two Brens. Pierse came face to face with a Japanese officer who sprang forward from the bushes as though in a dance, with sword held high in both hands to attack. Pierse fired his rifle from the hip and watched the Jap fall backwards and finish his dance in a series of juddering twitches, his sightless eyes rolling towards heaven, his grip still tight on his sword. The son of a respected Professor of Haiku shot down by a 'ten Rupee jezail' wielded by the hockey-mad son of an Indian railway man.

'A Spring sacrifice
For the red sun of Fuji.
The black rain weeps on.'

The protection of the water supply was becoming a serious concern. The Dogras were ordered to defend the pumping station at Woodleigh near the MacRitchie reservoir in the centre of the island. The fighting there soon became fragmented, with intense personal battles taking place as both sides fought for position. It was close quarter stuff; grenades, rifles and bayonets, soldiers fighting through the gullies and ditches, the enemy lying concealed in the pipelines. Pierse knew in his heart that the battle was all but lost. The much vaunted garrison troops had crumbled; the lessons from the retreat down Malaya had not been learned. Without air cover the British-Indian Army was unable to cope with an enemy who popped up like a jack-in-the-box from the undergrowth or who rained down bombs from the air or shells from across the strait. There was confusion, cowardice, calamity, incompetence. Our team is permanently on the defensive, he thought, and a winning goal by the Japs is inevitable.

By the 14th of February the Japanese had ingeniously repaired the causeway and most of their troops and heavy guns were brought on to the island to press home their attacks. The

Dogras found themselves facing the Guards at Paya Lebar, to the east of the pumping station. Other Japanese troops were now beating at the outskirts of Singapore City. It seemed clear that the island was irretrievably lost.

* * *

A day later Singapore surrendered. Pierse and Farrell heard the news through their Company Commander. He stood wearily before his officers.

'General Percival has informed the Japanese commander, Lt. Gen. Yamashita, of his intention to surrender. The formal surrender will take place this evening in the Ford Factory near Bukit Timah.'

'Why are we surrendering, Sir? We can fight on.'

'They are driving us back and we can't stop them,' the Major replied, 'and there is only enough water for another twenty four hours as the bombardments have severely damaged the pipelines around the City. The priority now is to prevent unnecessary civilian loss of life and hardship. We must, however, continue to defend ourselves and to remain vigilant until the cease fire is announced this evening.'

Wise words, for there was no let up in the fighting; heavy artillery and air attacks continued for most of the day until news of the surrender permeated both sides and an eerie silence settled over the city as night fell; for the first time in days they could hear the hissing tinnitus of insects and the chirping of crickets in the undergrowth.

In the quiet of the night, Pierse went to speak to his men. They looked at him dully, uncomprehendingly. They were wet and filthy with mud and soot, eyes red with tiredness and strain. Pierse was angry, and choked with emotion.

'We have surrendered. We could not hold out against the *Japani* despite your bravery. We had no air cover, and no tanks to help us. You fought like heroes and we could have carried on fighting but it would have resulted in great loss of life to soldiers and civilians – none of us wants to see women and children killed in the cause of war. I thank you for standing with me in the fighting from Kota Bharu right down to Singapore. I am proud to have served with you and I will always remember our comrades who lost their lives. We do not know what tomorrow will bring under the *Japani*, but we must continue to be brave, continue to remember that we are Dogras and that one day we will get the chance to rise again and drive out our enemy – just as we have done so often in the past. *Jawala Mata* will protect us. *Jawala Mata ki jai!*' He turned away, tears in his eyes. His men said nothing.

All along the line officers and men were numbed and despondent at their failure to prevent the disastrous loss of Singapore and Malaya. Pierse wondered how Chandra was faring in hospital and if he would ever see him again. His thoughts turned to his own uncertain future – and the loved ones he would not see again for a long time, if ever. The barbarity of their victors was well known and life over the coming months, even years, was going to be harsh. But, for now, the guns were silent, and that night he and those around him slept the deep, narcotic sleep of exhausted men.

* * *

The next day, under a sun veiled by clouds of smoke, all British and Australian officers and men were ordered to march off to Changi Cantonment as prisoners of war. The Indian officers and men were separated from them and ordered to report to Farrer Park. As a fair-skinned Anglo-Indian, Pierse did not have a moment's hesitation in deciding to which group he belonged. He said goodbye to his men, thanked Havildar Prem Singh for his support and joined Farrell and went to

Changi. As instructed, they tore off their 9th Indian Division badges – the blue nine-pointed star that they had worn since Kota Bharu – in order to prevent the Japanese from taking reprisals for the heavy casualties they had suffered at their hands. They marched through the steamy heat carrying all that they could salvage from their baggage. Defeat lay everywhere: the stench of corpses rapidly decomposing in the tropical heat, the pall of choking, grimy smoke from burning buildings and fuel tanks and the destruction of war all around. The roads to Changi were lined with sullen, silent locals, watching the humiliation of their former colonial masters trudging grimly into captivity and wondering what their own future was going to be like under their new colonial masters.

Singapore was now 'Syonan' – a new Japanese name for a new Japanese territory. This corner of the British Empire had been overrun by the 'half-arsed, bandy-legged and short-sighted samurais' in just nine weeks.

Pierse pulled off his new watch and tucked it into his underpants, Farrell laughed – then suddenly turned to Pierse in surprise. 'Bugger me! I've just remembered. When I went to see Anil in his tent he checked his watch and it was one just like yours!'

'Couldn't have been,' replied Pierse uncertainly, 'he didn't have one because his went kaput at the same time as mine.'

CHAPTER 5

Homecoming –1945

The welcoming crowd, intermingled with the general confusion of coolies, dockworkers, lorries and bullock carts at Calcutta docks, watched the rust-ridden troopship secure its moorings before disembarking its cargo of men returning from captivity in Malaya. Most of them were going on to regimental depots or being trucked elsewhere to meet their sweethearts, wives and families. But Pierse was coming home to Calcutta. On the eve of the Regiment's departure he had fallen ill, too sick with dysentery and malaria, compounded by years of malnutrition as a prisoner, to travel home with the rest of his comrades. He had lain critically ill in hospital in Singapore while his brother officers departed for India; ironically it was the same hospital he and Farrell had visited before the battle for the island. Some of the Regiment's Indian officers and many of the sepoys would have returned to cashiering or courts-martial for their part in collaborating with the Japanese in the renegade Indian National Army. Anil Chandra was one of them, accused of being one of the leaders of the INA. The senior British officers of the regiment had been shocked and ashamed at the scale of the desertion of their Indian officers and men to the INA.

65

Pierse scanned the faces of the people waiting on the dockside and caught sight of his father and mother in the crowd talking to a white uniformed and Wolseley-helmeted traffic police sergeant, his silver chevrons flashing in the sun. No sign of Ellen! The disappointment choked him. Why wasn't she there? He had imagined this moment every day in captivity: the absolute joy of seeing her again and being together forever. It had sustained him through the darkest of times when it seemed as if he would slip this earth – the thought of staying alive to be with her once more had held him fast. He felt confused and crushed. He looked intently at his parents, hoping and willing her to appear. Then the police sergeant looked up.

'Good God!' exclaimed Pierse under his breath; it was the 'randy pig', Kenny! What on earth was he doing in police uniform? What dented ambitions that conveyed. Kenny a policeman! Pierse felt his heart sink even lower with disappointment – this was not what he was expecting. Then he reminded himself: he had been away since 1941, four and a half years. He must not jump to conclusions. They would have a lot to tell each other, it would all be explained. He could see Kenny and his parents anxiously looking up at the crowds of yelling soldiers lining the ships railings. He waved frantically and shouted too, but they didn't seem able to hear him or spot him.

He eventually took his turn and limped down the gangplank towards his family, kitbag over his shoulder. He waved and called out – they looked quizzically at him and he could see a flutter of horror dance across their faces as recognition kicked in. They ran towards him and he was solidly enveloped in a three-way hug. Tears flowed among the smiles and Pierse's father broke down; the big, tough ex-engine driver, who commanded great respect now as a loco supervisor, sobbing like a child.

'I never thought I would see you again, son,' he said

between sobs, 'you have come back from the dead. It is a miracle – an absolute bloody miracle. St. Anthony be praised!'

His mother, normally so composed, was crying too, clutching her son tight and shaking her head in disbelief. Pierse was caught up in the emotion of the moment and he felt the pain of all those years begin to leave him through his tears. Even the 'randy pig', so solid in his white uniform, was smiling awkwardly, his topee tilted awry about his head in the family crush, his eyes red, his face tracked with tears.

'Where's Ellen?' asked Pierse. He could feel the family scrum tense.

'She's teaching down South,' said Kenny quickly, 'we haven't been able to get a message to her as we don't quite know where, so she can't be here.' He looked affectionately at his brother. 'We were told you were dead, dammit! But here you are. It is a bloody miracle.' He enfolded Pierse in a bear hug, patting him gently on the back as if to check that he was real.

'Dead?' repeated Pierse incredulously.

'Yes, dead. We got a telegram,' said his mother, 'in '42. You look so thin – you're all skin and bone. And what has happened to your leg! Oh, you poor boy, you must have had a terrible time.' Her tears began to flow again.

'I'm okay,' said a confused Pierse, hugging her, 'just thin – nothing that a few good feeds can't put right. The limp is from an ulcer on my leg that I got in the jungle a couple of years ago, that's all. But who told you that I was dead?'

'I'll show you the official telegram when we get home,' said his father, 'don't worry about it now, son. This is a time to celebrate and enjoy being back at home safe and sound. We want to hear all about you, about everything that happened. We got very little news. Nobody knew what was happening until we got a letter from you last month. It was like Lazarus returning from the dead. We were shocked and so overjoyed. So, so overjoyed!'

As they drove home, Pierse took in the familiar and the new in his city. He told them briefly of his war, of captivity in Changi and then being selected to go and work on the Burma – Siam railway as slave labour for the Japanese. He left out the gory details – this wasn't the time and he really didn't want to talk about them; to do so would only distress his parents and turn over painful memories. He described the joy and relief when, recovering from malaria and malnutrition, he didn't call it starvation, back at Changi, the Japanese finally surrendered after the atom bombs of Hiroshima and Nagasaki. He told them bitterly, and somewhat ashamedly, of the bewilderment and anger he felt when he learned that many of the Indian troops, including those of his regiment, those of his platoon even, had traitorously switched allegiance after the fall of Singapore and joined the Japanese-backed INA. His father and Kenny nodded, they had heard of it too. And he told of his sadness that the traitors had been cashiered and that the ringleaders, Chandra among them, were now imprisoned in the Red Fort in Delhi. But above all, he wanted *them* to tell him about Ellen – how was she, how did she look, when was she returning to Calcutta, when would he see her again.

* * *

Back home, they sat him down with a cup of tea and then told him.

'This telegram informed us that you had been killed in February '42 in the battle for Singapore,' said his mother, voice shaking nervously. 'We were all shattered. Ellen went completely to pieces. She couldn't stop crying, she was depressed, she didn't eat, she became very, very ill and very thin. She couldn't teach and we thought she would lose her job. We were so worried for her.'

'After a few months she couldn't even bear to visit us,'

continued his father, unable to meet his son's eyes, 'it was too painful, you see. The Loreto nuns in the school were very good. They were very patient and helped her gradually to come to terms with it. We heard that she was spending so much time with them that we began to wonder whether she would join the order herself.'

'Then, at the beginning of '44 we heard that she had got a teaching job in a school in South India. Apparently she had decided to move away and start again. And later that year we heard that she had got married,' said his mother quietly, voice choking, clutching her son's hand, feeling helpless in the face of his obvious distress.

Pierse felt destroyed. He got up, face expressionless, and went into the garden. The shock and the pain were tearing him apart. His one reason for living, for surviving, had been taken away. He felt sick. He sat there under the jacaranda tree for a long time, alone in his thoughts, scarcely hearing the sounds of the city round him and the raucous cawing of the crows as they prepared to roost in the lengthening shadows and the gathering veils of darkness. Then he broke down.

Observing him quietly from the house, his distressed family let him try to come to terms with his grief, uncertain what to do. Then Kenny came out with two whiskies.

'They wanted me to bring you another cup of tea Ed, but I said that you needed more than that. I'm sorry. This is not how it should have been for you – and you have been through hell for the last four years.'

'You don't know the half of it Kenny,' said Pierse, closing his eyes, 'you would not believe me if I told you what it was really like. You don't know the half of it.'

'Question is, how did the Army get it so wrong and tell us that you had been killed? I've been thinking about this ever since we heard that you were alive. Did the Japs allow them to get information out from Singapore? How did they muck it up?' asked Kenny.

'I don't know,' said Pierse. 'I've got to report to the Regimental depot in Jullundur in three weeks and I'll try and find out when I get there. When I find the bastard who did it his life won't be worth living, I tell you.'

'Come back inside,' said Kenny. 'I know the news about Ellen has been awful for you Ed, but think of Ma and Da. They too have been through hell for the past few years, believing they had lost you to the war. Ma came close to breakdown for a few months and it certainly affected Da deeply. This was to be a day of joy for them, though they were dreading it too because they would have to tell you about Ellen. Please – can we be back as a family for today and just celebrate your homecoming? Tomorrow we will try to find Ellen – I'm a policeman after all – I have my sources,' he said archly. He put his arm around his brother.

Pierse smiled through his tears, 'Of course, Kenny. As you can imagine, I'm not thinking straight.' He clinked glasses with his brother and they downed their whiskies in one. Then, with forced jollity, '*Chalo*, let's go! A policeman, eh? Why?'

'They didn't want to lose another son to the war, and I wanted to do something useful after university rather than sit in an office,' replied Kenny. 'I wanted to go into the Armed Police but Da said no. So now I chase round inspecting the traffic police, but I also get to police the demonstrations and help out when there are riots – and they can get quite dangerous. The 'Quit India' buggers have been very active, so this policeman's lot has been quite a tricky one. I've had to wave this a few times,' he said proudly, patting his revolver holster.

'But there's nothing in it,' smiled Ed.

'Oh, we get issued with them when we go on duty, either Webley .45s, or Smith & Wesson .38s. One of these days I hope I get to use them on one of those buggers.'

'I hope you don't have to,' replied Ed. 'People who are shot don't seem to die neatly, Kenny. It is bloody, untidy and smelly – and the wounded scream like you've never heard before.' He smiled and put his arm around his brother's shoulders.

* * *

The Pierses marked their son's return to the land of the living that evening with a dinner of all Ed's favourites – potato cutlets, yellow rice and ball curry, fried brinjals. 'We have to feed you up,' said Mrs Pierse ladling rice onto Ed's plate as he protested. He did not have an appetite for the food, but forced himself to eat it as he didn't want to upset his parents or the cook shyly watching from the kitchen. He drank a lot, sinking his father's precious Scotch whisky as fast as he could to try to numb the hollow feeling inside. He put on a great act, but his parents were not fooled and their hearts ached for him, as parents' do when they are helpless to make things better for their child.

That night, as he lay awake in his bedroom under the cranking electric fan, Kenny came in, silently closed the bedroom door, and sat on his bed. 'I'll find her for you Eddie, if it's the last thing I do,' he whispered, patting his brother's forearm.

'What's the use Kenny if she's married,' replied Pierse. 'She didn't wait that long after I was reported dead, did she?' he said bitterly.

'That's not true and you know it. She was completely grief stricken, absolutely finished when we got the news. But what could she do? She's young; she has to look to the future, to go on living. She was told that you were gone, we all were. What was she to do?'

There was a long silence. 'I understand all of that, Ken, but it is hard to accept that she is out there somewhere with someone else, she doesn't even know I'm alive, she needs to know that she made a mistake.'

'What then?' asked Kenny, 'do you expect her to get divorced, to come back to you? What if she can't – or won't? None of us can know how difficult it is for you, but you need to accept that Ellen has gone from your life. There is a whole world out there for you.'

'Not much of a world, is it? I've lost my girl, I'll probably get de-mobbed or a medical discharge from the regiment, I've buggered my leg so I can't even play hockey to the standard I used to. I've lost trust in my closest friends. I can't forgive Anil Chandra for turning traitor and Mike Farrell – the bastard generously recommended me to go to 'help the Japs with their railway' because I was a 'railway boy' and he thought I would enjoy it. He wasn't there to be tortured, starved and worked almost to death. I nearly didn't come back from there, Kenny, while he sat smug and safe back at Changi. I suppose I should at least be grateful I didn't get cholera, which finished off hundreds of our fellows.'

Kenny sat silently. 'Listen Eddie,' he said eventually, 'I promise you that tomorrow morning I'm going to start the search for Ellen. When I find her, you go and see her. I don't know what will happen, but that is for the two of you to sort out.'

This seemed to mollify Pierse. 'Thanks Kenny,' he said, glad that Kenny could not see his tears in the dark. 'I'm sorry I'm such a wet rag but it has been a hell of a shock – not the way I expected my homecoming to be.'

'You're going to have to put up with the homecoming celebrations for a week or two, Ed, Ma has invited most of the clan round after church on Sunday. They know about Ellen so I don't think they will put their collective feet in it.'

'Collective feet!' exclaimed Pierse, 'is that any way for a policeman to talk!' He hugged Kenny. 'Thanks Ken, thanks for

the help. Don't forget, you promised to find out where Ellen is
– in turn I promise that I'll just go to see her to let her know that
I'm alive. We'll take it from there.'

* * *

Pierse had returned from Malaya with nothing other than a
change of uniform. Convinced that he was dead, his family had
got rid of his clothes except for his scout and hockey shirts and
his Dehra Dun blazer – the almirah was bare! He set off in the
morning for the New Market to buy some clothes. The city
seemed different: the usual chaos, bustle and noise was there
and probably would be in Calcutta till the end of time, but there
were reminders of the years of war; noisy, exuberant American
troops in unfamiliar jungle green, who must have been
preparing to go home, Indian troops in army trucks, cars and
lorries with their bumpers and mudguards outlined in white
paint to make them visible in a blackout – the docks had been
bombed by the Japs in December '42 his father had said. And
there was a new mood among the people, somewhat less
deferential, more strident, more confident. And along the walls
and the sides of buildings were 'Quit India' slogans challenging
the British and a number of Indian National Congress and
Muslim League flags: the horizontal saffron, white and green
stripes with a blue stylised spinning wheel of the Indian
National Congress, and the green of the Muslim League. There
were pro-INA slogans too, often accompanied by a portrait of
the INA founder, Subhas Chandra Bose, uniformed and
peering through round-rimmed specs, and there were posters
bearing pictures of Nehru, Gandhi and Jinnah, some splattered
with a stream of red betel nut spittle, a casual yet calculated
insult from Hindu or Muslim. These were visible and
disturbing signs that there was a growing pressure for a more
equal say in the governance of India.

As his rickshaw turned off Chowringhee, Pierse had to smile at the white-uniformed traffic policeman with his red turban, standing on a platform made out of the top of half an oil drum, blowing his whistle shrilly and waving his arms fretfully to try to make some sense of the honking traffic milling around him. The New Market looked familiar, but its Victorian clock tower, under which he and Ellen had often met, perfumed by the wares of the flower sellers who surrounded it, was an uncomfortable reminder of the past. The coolies, rickshaw-wallahs and shopkeepers still hassled for trade and the beggars for pice. The limbless beggar was still there, he noted with some satisfaction. The youth Pierse remembered had grown to manhood and he patrolled his patch, dashing up to potential benefactors on his crude, rumbling wheeled platform, one leprous stump outstretched. For the first time Pierse felt that he could understand his desperation – everything in his life reduced to the bare necessities to ensure he stayed alive – money, food, shelter, staying mobile. Pierse gave him a silver Rupee. The generous gift was simply taken, briefly acknowledged, the roaming eyes searching for the next benefactor. Far from being affronted, Pierse understood.

Walking into the busy market, Pierse recognised faces among the traders and shoppers down the crowded aisles though few recognised or acknowledged him as he had become so thin in captivity.

But someone did. 'Piersey, you bugger!' a voice called and he turned to find Mickey D'Cruz, an old hockey team-mate from the Rangers Club. Greeting him with an enthusiastic handshake, Mickey said with his usual lack of candour, 'Bloody hell Piersey, men, you look terrible! Isn't the army feeding you?'

Pierse was pleased to see Mickey, a superlative left-winger. 'No Mickey, I've just come back from Malaya – POW and all that.'

'Yes I know,' replied Mickey. 'We heard that you had been killed some years ago, you bugger, and think how shocked we were to be told recently that you were alive. You were always a fly swine Piersey.' He laughed; then his face darkened, 'Those Jap bastards, did they mistreat you? We heard terrible, terrible stories, men.'

'No more than usual,' replied Pierse affably, he wanted to change the subject. 'Are Rangers still playing? How's the hockey going?'

Mickey was only too happy to give Pierse all the hockey gossip. As they were parting, Pierse said casually, 'Do you hear anything about Ellen Lewis? Apparently she married and went down south.'

Mickey looked shifty. 'Ah, you heard that she was married – I thought that you two were engaged!' Then seeing the look on Pierse's face, 'Oh, the war eh? I tell you who will know, men, try Hubie O'Connor, he is teaching at St. Xavier's School now, and he is very pally with this girl, Pammy, er, Pam Francis, who was a close chum of Ellen's and used to play basketball with her on the maidan for Bird and Company. Hubie or Pammy will know.'

Pierse went to the cloth shop, selected his material and was measured for new clothes which the tailor, having being told that it was something of an emergency, promised to let him have before Sunday. On a whim, Pierse decided to pay Hubie O'Connor a visit at St Xavier's School.

* * *

St Xavier's School and College sat as solidly as ever on Park Street. Next door to it was the Archbishop's palatial House – fortuitously close-by perhaps as many a Jesuit priest had made the short hop from priest in the College to Archbishop of Calcutta; the Society of Jesus seemed to have a monopoly on the job. Pierse walked through St Xavier's entrance gates and across the paved quadrangle surrounded by the buildings through which he had so often passed on his way to school and then to college before joining the army. Taking the entrance on the left he passed on in to the school building behind. The school seemed quiet, its pupils at their lessons. There was a game of football taking place on the scrubby playing field. College students thought Pierse, as he watched the game briefly. He saw a familiar figure come down the corridor in his long white cassock, slightly misshapen head cocked to one side as though he had a permanent crick in the neck. He bore the signs of a large scar along his scalp so, with all the sensitivity of young boys, was appropriately nicknamed 'Scab head'.

'Hullo Father Lawrence,' said Pierse with a smile. Father Lawrence S.J. had taught him English in school, a reserved and strict teacher, regarded as very eccentric because of his habit of stopping in mid-sentence and staring into space for a long.... long.... long.... pause as though suddenly remembering something more important, before continuing with whatever he was saying. The boys did not particularly like him as he was terribly aloof and not as friendly as the other staff, but he was undeniably a good teacher and Pierse had relished his no nonsense approach. Father Lawrence was a cuckoo in the nest – an English Jesuit among the Belgians and the French.

The Father peered peevishly through his steel-rimmed glasses. He had taught English to hundreds of boys in his time and could not be expected to remember all of them years later. He looked at this thin young man in khaki army uniform, the man did not look well and Father Lawrence taxed his brain to try to establish a connection.

Pierse could see him struggling. 'Edwin Pierse, Father, it was a long time ago and you probably won't remember me.' The reply surprised him.

'Edwin Pierse!' exclaimed Father Lawrence. 'We heard

that you had been killed in the war – but clearly the report of your death was greatly exaggerated.' Seeing Pierse's quizzical look, 'Mark Twain,' he said, 'I'm referring to his famous quotation'.

Pierse shook Father Lawrence's hand. 'Surprised that you remembered me Father,' he said, pleased.

'You were a good student, Edwin, you once wrote an essay supporting atheism, I remember. I was impressed by the arguments from one so young.'

'But you gave me a caning for it!'

'Ah yes, but it was heretical, and you are supposed to be a good Catholic,' replied Father Lawrence, 'we Jesuits cannot allow such a thing.' Then he surprised Pierse by laughing, an unfamiliar dry, cracked sound. 'I think I may still have your essay somewhere – just in case.'

'I'm looking for Hubie, er, Mr Hubert O'Connor, Father. I believe that he is a teacher here.'

'Yes, he teaches here, but he is away just now visiting a relative in Bandel, I think it is an aunt and she is very sick. I don't know when he will be back, but you could try his house and see if his family can tell you.'

'Thanks Father, do you know where he lives?'

'No.' Then, looking closely at Pierse, 'Have you just come back from the war? Malaya wasn't it? Yes, yes, I remember, Malaya – we said a mass for you when they told us you had been killed. Is there anyone else who can help you as Mr O'Connor is away?'

'I am trying to find someone and Mr O'Connor may know where she is,' he said, but the catch in his voice was not lost on Father Lawrence. Those pebble-hard blue eyes softened.

'Come up to the office, I will see if we can find an address for Hubert O'Connor. If you have time, I'd like to know a bit more about the war in Malaya – we get so little news, only what the Viceroy and his Government chooses to tell us.'

Pierse found himself in a lounge used by the Fathers for entertaining. A cup of tea was pressed into his hand while a clerk went to find Hubie O'Connor's address. He told Father Lawrence about the battle for Malaya. Father Lawrence was particularly interested in the role of the Royal Air Force.

'They were never there when we needed cover,' said Pierse bitterly, 'things might have been different if the Air Force had supported us better. I heard that they were betrayed by a British Army officer, someone told me that his name was Captain Heenan, who was spying for the Japs; this enabled them to obliterate much of our Air Force. They say that Heenan got his come-uppance though; executed in Singapore during the Japanese attack.'

Under Father Lawrence's questioning he told of the Japanese Zero fighter planes and the bombers, the incessant air attacks. He had never known anyone to have such a long and detailed conversation with Father Lawrence, on so peculiar a subject, and it felt like talking to a confessor as the Father gently drew out of him the horrors of life in captivity and on the Burma Siam Railway. Finally, Pierse found himself telling Father Lawrence about his homecoming yesterday and what had happened about Ellen.

'Father,' he said finally, 'the war has destroyed my life – I've lost Ellen, I can't return to top level hockey and I had hopes of one day representing India in the Olympics. My army career is over – I doubt they would pass me medically fit and in any case they are demobbing hundreds of soldiers and officers. I find it hard just now to see how I am going to continue.' Though he was dejected, there were no tears – this really was like a confessional, he needed to talk.

Father Lawrence contemplated all of this in silence – lost in one of his abstract moments. Finally, 'I understand, my son,' he began, but Pierse interrupted.

'How could you understand,' he snapped, then regretted

his anger. Before he could apologise, Father Lawrence began to speak.

'War is shit! Absolute bloody shit!' he said vehemently, the crude language shocking Pierse. 'The country that destroys the most wins. But the winners face destruction too, in the thousands of lives lost, the families devastated, the economy ruined. But even those who return victorious are not without damage. I joined the Royal Flying Corps in England in 1917, to fight in the 1914-18 War – so I know what I'm talking about, my son.' Pierse nodded. 'The death rate for pilots was so high that they were shipping us out to France with a minimum of training and I was sent to a front line squadron in September 1917 flying a biplane, an SE5A, very rugged and fast, equipped with two machine guns. We didn't call them fighter planes in those days, you know, we called them scouts.'

'It was not the glamorous life that is often portrayed. We lived in crude accommodation, the older and more experienced pilots were very cliquey and many were bordering on the insane or very mentally disturbed by their experiences in combat. We drank ourselves into oblivion each evening to try to escape the terror of starting every day at 4 am for the dawn patrol, finding our lives under threat from the other fellow. You flew frightened because you had a good chance of being shot down, or burnt – our life expectancy was estimated at about three weeks. When you gain the upper hand and are sitting on the tail of the enemy, there is little difference in the relative speeds of your aircraft so that everything is in close up. You are a hundred or two hundred yards behind him, you can see him in your sights, you aim and squeeze the trigger and you see him and his aircraft jerk as they are hit and fall to the ground spinning or in a vertical or over-vertical dive. You have killed a man and his deadly butterfly. Your mind is changed forever. I regret that I did it, twice.' Father Lawrence was sweating now, his breath rasping with effort. He continued.

'One early morning on patrol we saw a German plane below, an Albatros – did you know that the plural of Albatros is Albatri? Not Albatrosses,' he said, reverting to being a schoolmaster. 'Anyway, I was ordered to investigate in case it was a trap to lure our aircraft down. I dived on him and followed closely as he skidded and swerved, diving and spinning to get away. A sixth sense made me aware that someone was behind me, followed by bullets hitting my plane from behind and to the right. I had been lured into a classic ambush and then I was struck in the thigh. I desperately dived away and became aware of a fellow pilot in an SE5A following a similar path down, his aircraft in flames and hotly pursued by another Albatros. I could see him screaming as the flames burnt him – couldn't hear him of course because of the noise of the engine and the wind in the wires. I couldn't use my right leg to operate my rudder so my plane also went into a slow spin, my pursuer was still firing at me and I could feel myself beginning to faint. Than the most extraordinary thing happened which startled me back into consciousness and saved my life.'

'The burning pilot, still pursued, climbed to the top of his fuselage to get away from the streaming flames. Then he extended his arms sideways, just as you would on a diving board, and jumped to his death rather than burn.'

'Didn't you have parachutes?' asked Pierse.

'No, only the men in the observation balloons had them. Our High Command thought parachutes would encourage us to abandon our aircraft at the slightest sign of difficulty. Anyway, I was so shocked by the pilot jumping to his death – a flaming crucifix – my senses cleared. I could see the ground coming up and I put my hand on the knee of my useless leg and pushed with all my strength to operate the rudder. I do not know how, but I brought the aircraft out of the spin about five hundred feet above the ground and aimed it at a field – my pursuer had given up the chase thinking I was finished. I didn't have sufficient control and the aircraft crash landed and fell on to its nose. I was knocked unconscious.' He gingerly felt his scar. 'Apparently some German soldiers pulled me out, it is a miracle they didn't kill me, but I think they had been fascinated watching my comrade and I descend to earth in our separate ways. I ended up in one of their field hospitals where my leg and a cut on my head were treated, but, more than the physical damage, my mind had also undergone a total collapse because of the experience. Lying in that enemy hospital and seeing the horrific results of what our side was doing to their soldiers was a very uncomfortable feeling and I used to have nightmares – still do. After weeks of this I recovered enough and began to try to help the nurses and the patients learn a few English phrases in return for their improving my German. I think they knew by then that the war was lost and used to joke bitterly that they had better learn English quickly. I realised, very starkly, that we were just men and women together with the same hopes, failings and desire for peace. None of us wanted the war – it was the politicians in charge. I resolved that I would spend my life helping people, helping the other patients to learn English triggered a desire to teach. My mind was affected; it is still not healed, so I understand what you have been through.'

'It was quite different with the Japs,' said Pierse quietly. 'There was no humanity. Surviving and coming intact out of captivity was a struggle, but I set myself the task of returning home and did everything in my power to make it happen. It made me mentally stronger, I had a goal to aim for – Ellen. But I cannot deal with the knock-back from finding that the fiancée I had thought about constantly, the light that kept me going through those dark years, had gone – and with it my hopes and dreams for the future.'

Father Lawrence looked at him directly. 'You have to rely on that mental toughness to pull you through again Edwin. You have had a wound to the spirit – the worst kind of hurt, and it is harder to heal. But sometimes fate throws you a lifeline – out of darkness comes light. For me it was devoting my life to helping others, to seeing my old pupils succeed in life. In this way I know that my life has been worth it and that I have overridden, but not overcome, my fears. So Edwin, you must look for a guiding light, something to lead you away from the pain, to make your resurrection worthwhile – for that is what both of us have had.'

The clerk, who had been hovering, came forward with a piece of paper on which he had written Hubie O'Connor's address. Father Lawrence took it from him and passed it to Pierse.

'May God go with you my son,' he said, getting up to indicate that the interview was over.

'But I'm an atheist Father, remember?' joked Pierse. Then, taking Father Lawrence's hand he shook it warmly, intrigued by the priest's story, his mind turning over what the Father had said. 'Thank you, Father,' he said feelingly.

'You'll find the guiding light Edwin, start looking for it.'

CHAPTER 6

Farrell's Folly

Farrell sat in the cool of Firpo's Restaurant on Chowringhee, Calcutta's great road fronting the green of the *maidan*, tucking into a well cooked steak with béarnaise sauce and sipping a tall, cold glass of Muree beer. He thought of this morning's interview – he had applied for a tea plantation manager's job knowing that he was soon to be demobbed from the army. It had been a tough interrogation; there were many candidates like him coming out of the army and looking for well paid interesting jobs that would keep them in India, so the competition for these jobs was fierce. It wasn't that Farrell was particularly in love with the country – though he found it very agreeable. No, he had sussed out the possibilities for enormous wealth and influence. If he could secure a manager's position in tea or jute, or one of the other commodities with which India supplied the world, he could, before long, ascend the ladder as other British managers took fright at the coming of Indian independence and scarpered for home. This would open the door for chancers like him, men on the make, to fill their boots. The Indians, he thought, were not yet ready – nor experienced, or confident enough to take on these jobs. A few years at the helm was all he needed, then he could retire enriched by *baksheesh* and by granting favours – a modern day Clive of India, to live out his life in wealth and comfort. What an opportunity India offered to live well, to have servants, to ride and shoot, maybe to have a young, lithe native companion or two for the dark evenings – just like the Nabobs of old. *Carpe diem* – seize the day! No, bugger that, *carpe dolce* – grab the bloody pudding!

He looked around. In London a restaurant of this quality and the fine meal he was eating would have cost a fortune. Here he could afford it – indeed, this standard of living was expected of him. He liked being a *burra sahib*! He certainly didn't want to go back to cold, grey England – probably colder and greyer now that the war was ended – and he didn't want to return to his old life of grind and dreariness. He'd seen pictures and heard tales of the destruction of England's cities and how people were still on rationing and that there were shortages everywhere including a desperate shortage of work for men returning from the war. No chance of a Firpo's lunch there! No, he intended to stay here in India and make his fortune like so many of his compatriots before him; he wanted nothing more than to end his days here as 'Farrell *sahib*'!

Unfortunately, the morning's interview hadn't gone particularly well. It had begun happily enough and the English Chairman of the interview panel had been impressed by Farrell's pedigree, his reference to his public school education, previous employment in India and his account of the way he had organised the evacuation of the troops out of Kota Bharu under the noses of the Japanese – a good enough tale, but one which improved with his embroidery of it. The Chairman, his eyes turning hard, pressed Farrell on why he thought he was suited to the work he was applying for, and Farrell had pulled out all the stops to give him the answers to his tricky questions. In the end, 'Just the sort of background, initiative and managerial skills we are looking for, old boy,' the Chairman had said. The second member of the panel, another Englishman, rather louche and lounging fit to fall off his chair, had asked him about his sporting activities, which had given Farrell a chance to tell him about his high standard of cricket, and that he played polo – though he omitted to mention that he had only played it once and that his poor horsemanship had caused great hilarity among the officers watching the game. Then the third member of the panel, an Indian, Farrell understood that he was a tea-taster, had begun to ask him about bloody tea! What did he know about growing it? Farrell had scrabbled about in his memory for everything he might know about tea – it had come from China – that should keep the bastard happy; it grew on hills, only the topmost two leaves and a bud were picked, that sort of thing. Then the Indian had asked him to name as many types of tea as he could. He said 'China, Ceylon and Darjeeling'. That was a far as he could take it.

But the crunch came when the Indian asked him what he thought about the Quit India movement and what it might mean for the future of the tea plantations *when* the British were no longer in control. Farrell reflected ruefully that the panel must have seen him go crimson with indignation, a scarlet to match his hair. He recalled using the word 'buggers' in relation to the Indian National Congress, and declaring that the British were not going to be pushed out of India by 'this Gandhi fellow' and that the Raj was here to stay. They had thanked him politely, but he had seen from the shiftiness in their eyes that he had blotted his copybook, and not just blotted it but emptied the whole bloody inkpot over it. Ah well, he thought, he would learn from this and next time he would make sure the buggers got the mealy-mouthed answers they were hoping for. He had another interview this afternoon, arranged through Morton, a well-connected officer he had sought out and befriended in Changi with an eye to the future. Morton had promised that this would not be an interview but more of a chat really with the manager of a jute mill on the Hoogly River near Dum Dum. On offer was a managerial job which, though not so well paid, had promise. So he had better eat up and get along to it.

The Dum Dum 'chat' was conducted by a young Englishman and an older Scot. The Englishman, a stocky man with a thin moustache, was the more junior of the two, he had been in the Army, involved in the Chindit campaign in Burma, and had been invalided out and returned to his old job in the jute mill. He seemed more interested in swapping anecdotes about the war. The Scot, who seemed to be the mill's manager, asked the occasional question in a cultivated Edinburgh Morningside accent – he seemed interested in Farrell's ability to handle people. This was more like it thought Farrell. No awkward bloody questions, certainly not about jute – about which he knew absolutely nothing – just a chat to see if one was *compos mentis* and would 'fit in'. Dealing with native workers wasn't really that difficult, it was just like dealing with sepoys: let them know you were the boss, be fair and firm with them, don't take sides – and severely punish the buggers who transgressed. At the end of the interview the Scot asked if he would like to join them for a drink and they repaired to a sort of club in the grounds of the mill where they drank good malt whisky and told tales. Farrell was offered the job – he accepted, thinking that he would really prefer to have a tea plantation manager job in the cool of the hills but, bird in hand and all that, this would have to do until he could get one – and it was close enough to the delights of Calcutta to compensate for the lower pay.

* * *

That evening, starved of company, he found himself in Jeremiah's Bar, not far from his hotel, a dive frequented mainly by sailors and servicemen, mostly Americans, in search of a drink and female company. It was noisy and smoky, there was a band playing – piano, saxophone, double bass and drums – and couples dancing close on the small dance floor. Farrell wasn't there too long before a pretty, dark haired woman, a bit older than the others, she must have been in her mid thirties, in a tight yellow satin dress, asked him if he would like to buy her a drink. Farrell looked her over suspiciously.

'C'mon, I won't bite you,' she laughed.

Her name was Irene, and she liked to talk. Farrell listened, amused, as she chattered on in her sing-song voice about nothing in particular. She asked him about himself and he gave her the full pedigree – but didn't mention that he expected to be working in Calcutta very soon. He thought it best to be cagey as he didn't want a floozy to know where he would be employed, so he told her that he was on leave. Irene told him that she had been engaged to a serviceman, he had been killed in the war and this had made her realise that nothing was permanent and that life had to be lived as it came. Farrell asked if she would like to have dinner and then perhaps come back to his hotel for a drink – 'The Grand Hotel,' he said proudly to impress her.

'Okay dear,' she said matter of factly, 'but we'll have to be careful as the doormen in the Grand know me and they don't like us girls going up to the rooms.' Farrell felt deflated; Irene had obviously been to see her pick-ups there before. They went to a restaurant in Park Street for a meal and later, at the Grand, she steered him into the bar, crowded with the ubiquitous American servicemen, where she downed a couple of expensive cocktails. Farrell was beginning to worry that this was going to be a very costly night.

'Okay,' said Irene, 'tell me your room number and you go there and wait for me to knock on the door. I'll have to go up another way to avoid the security men on Reception. Oh, and since you are a rich public school boy you can give me five Rupees to bribe the man at the back door.' Farrell reluctantly handed the money over, wondering what he had got himself into and whether he would see her again – from the number of glances cast in her direction, many of the Americans seemed interested in her too.

He opened his door to her soft knock. She smiled and said, 'You thought I'd done a bunk, didn't you.' She came in through the door and took him in her arms. 'Don't be afraid,' she said as he tensed, 'is this the first time?'

'No, no,' Farrell exclaimed, he was finding this very uncomfortable and even a little frightening. 'Before we go any further Irene, what is this going to cost me? And, er, I don't have any er, prophylactics.'

She laughed. 'You have given me dinner, so I'll only charge twenty rupees. And don't worry about the French letters – I have some.' She kissed him.

They undressed and lay on the bed and Farrell tried his best to enjoy Irene's lithe body but something held him back. In the end she sat up. 'What's the matter dear? Don't you like me? This is your first time isn't it?' she teased.

'Shut up you stupid half-caste bitch!' shouted an angry Farrell and he shook her roughly in his frustration.

Irene regarded him calmly. 'There's no need for bad language dear,' she said quietly. 'And don't throw me around, I don't like that. I won't take that from anyone. Just because you are paying me to sleep with you doesn't mean you can treat me like muck. I think I'll go.'

'No, no please stay,' said a chastened Farrell. 'I'm sorry.' He smiled.

'Your first time?' she asked again.

'With a woman,' nodded Farrell miserably.

Irene digested this interestingly ambiguous answer. It was a challenge. She went to her handbag and got out a hip flask and gave it to Farrell. He gratefully drank the whisky – it wasn't scotch, probably the Indian stuff by the taste of it.

'As it is your first time,' she said and launched herself vigorously at him, using all the wiles and techniques she had learned in her trade. Then – success at last. A contented Farrell fell into a deep sleep, exhausted by the day's events.

* * *

When he woke in the morning Irene had gone, and so had his clothes and his wallet.

Farrell panicked. He searched the room, looked under the bed, behind the curtains. But everything had gone. She had put his clothes back into his small valise, pocketed his wallet and taken the lot.

'The Goddam bitch,' repeated Farrell over and over. Then he wondered what he was going to do. He had no clothes, no money to pay his hotel bill, his cheque book and his railway warrant had gone so he couldn't return to the regiment. He was naked, friendless and penniless. Desperate!

The Bengali Assistant Hotel Manager arrived in response to Farrell's frantic phone call. He surveyed Farrell, just about managing to keep the amusement out of his eyes. He had seen it all before.

'Sir,' he said, shaking his head, 'you should not have brought the bad lady up to your room. That is against the Hotel rules. We will have to charge you for a double room.'

'Bugger that,' shouted Farrell, 'get the police. I want that woman found. I want my stuff back!'

This outburst barely raised a flicker on the Assistant Manager's face. 'The police will not come here Sir. There has been no breaking and entering of your room, and no force has been used on you. Your friend has taken your things – maybe she has taken them to the *dhobi* and will bring them back. Do you know where she lives?' He was enjoying this hugely, winding up this panicky red-faced and red-headed Englishman wrapped only in a bed sheet.

Farrell was apoplectic with rage, but sensible enough to realise that he was at the mercy of the Assistant Manager. The bugger was enjoying this and there was the not inconsiderable matter of the bill yet to be negotiated.

'Manager Sahib,' he said with all the charm he could muster under the circumstances, 'could you please arrange to get me a spare set of clothes and shoes so that I can go down to the police station to report the theft. Put the cost on my bill – I'll telephone my Regiment to arrange the necessary funds.'

They kept him waiting for a couple of hours. Then, attired in a white shirt and a white pair of trousers from the hotel's staff laundry plus a new pair of cheap shoes from the market, Farrell went to Taltolla Police Station, running the gauntlet of the smirking staff in the hotel lobby. Everyone seemed to know what had happened and the sight of a red-faced *burra sahib* dressed in waiters' uniform with trousers flapping half way up his ankles was something to savour.

* * *

The beefy, florid-faced Inspector, dressed in a sweaty khaki uniform and scratching his crotch under his 'Bombay bloomer' shorts, regarded him balefully across the desk. He was annoyed because his Bengali Sub-Inspector hadn't turned up for duty and he had to take this case. These stupid, pompous army officer buggers didn't learn; they were always falling for the easiest of tricks. They had expensive public school educations but little knowledge of the ways of the world. They were too used to 'commanding' but had little understanding of human nature. No wonder the Raj was going to pot.

'You look like a waiter,' was his smirking opening remark to Farrell, designed to put him in his place.

Farrell bristled. 'I've come to report a robbery,' he began but the Inspector interrupted him.

'Yes, yes, we know all about it, the Grand's Assistant Manager telephoned. What was her name and where did you pick her up?'

'Irene, I met her at Jeremiah's Bar.'

'Irene, eh? Irene what?'

'Don't know, she never said.'

'Well, I've never heard of her and we know all the girls who tout in Jeremiah's. Didn't your mother tell you never to go into seedy dives in search of naughty women?'

'Can't you get your chaps round to Jeremiah's to ask the people there,' said Farrell testily, 'she was dark haired, wearing a yellow dress.'

'Then what?' replied the Inspector, leaning back, 'she will deny being in your room, nobody saw her going there – your word against hers. Do you want it all aired in court and in the papers?'

'You can search her house for my stuff, that's your evidence. I just want my things back.'

'You know nothing about girls like this, do you? If she took your stuff it will hardly be kept at her home, will it? Most of the girls are honest and this sort of case is rare, but it happens. Did you upset her or treat her badly in any way? Some of you chaps haven't had female company for a long time and can be a bit eager, eh?'

Farrell thought about it, ignoring the insult. 'I lost my rag with her briefly.' He wondered where this was going.

'Tell me what happened.'

'I got annoyed with her. I called her a half-caste bitch and just shook her, that's all. I didn't hurt her. We made up and it was all okay. She got a little upset, but then she was okay.'

'Half-caste, eh? That was probably worse than the shaking. I'm Anglo-Indian myself you know, I wouldn't like to be called that. Bloody insulting!' He looked coolly at Farrell.

Farrell tensed his jaw, this wasn't going well. He had thought the damned Inspector was Welsh because of the colour of his skin and his sing-song lilt. He suddenly remembered the strange-tasting whisky she had given him. 'I think she slipped me a Mickey Finn,' he said lamely.

'Ah! The girls like to be treated properly,' said the Inspector. 'All the robbery cases we have come across have happened because the gent, and I use the term very loosely in your case, has been insulting or violent. They get their own back, you see, they are smart like that. I think you can kiss goodbye to your stuff, sir. Do you know anyone in Cal who can lend you some money to pay your hotel bill and get you home to your regiment?' He had taken a strong dislike to this beaky, supercilious, red-headed Englishman.

Farrell thought. He didn't know anyone in Calcutta and could hardly contact the people at the tea company or the jute mill for help – it was too bloody embarrassing. He thought of Pierse – didn't expect he would be back from Malaya yet as he had been hospitalised, might even have died of his illness. And he was certainly not in Pierse's good books, not after jokingly recommending him for work on the Jap railway. He thought he was doing Pierse a good turn and was horror-struck when he returned nine months later to see what the Japs had done to him and to the other survivors. Blessing in a way – a fit Pierse would have torn him apart.

'I'm hoping that the hotel will advance me the cash to get back to my regiment and I can then repay them and settle the bill.'

'I think you'll find, sir, that the hotel will do nothing of the sort. It will want its bill paid now and we may have to detain you if you can't pay it.' The Inspector was enjoying this game.

'Look, it is a long shot, but I know a fellow officer called Pierse who was with me in Malaya, Pierse with an S, whose family comes from Calcutta. Perhaps you can find them in the telephone book and they may be able to help me.' He was desperate.

'Pierse,' mused the Inspector, 'we have a Sergeant Pierse in the traffic police. Unusual spelling of the name, perhaps he's related.'

* * *

A couple of weary hours later, the Inspector summoned Farrell from the crowded and noisy waiting area. In the room was a stocky, fair, belligerent-looking traffic police sergeant, dressed immaculately in white tunic, white cavalry pattern breeches, polished black leather gaiters and boots, Wolesley-pattern pith helmet in hand.

'Sergeant Pierse – with an S', announced the Inspector. Farrell looked confused. This chap didn't look anything like Pierse.

'Do you know Ed Pierse?' asked Farrell.

'Yes, he's my brother,' replied Kenny. 'And you're the bugger who, for a laugh, sent him off to the Jap railway!'

Farrell was startled. Then, not daring to meet Kenny's eyes, 'It was innocently meant,' he blustered. 'We were told that the prisoners of war were going to the countryside, to the hills where the climate was better, to do some light work – to get healthy. None of us knew that those lying Jap bastards were deceiving us.'

'Well then, why didn't you go?' was the harsh reply.

Farrell considered the question. Did he tell the truth, that the British officers had decided that they would send away many of the non-British officers – move the 'half-castes' out. He had gone along with it as he didn't want to upset them or to fall out with this crowd of influential men who could be useful to him when the war ended and he was looking to stay on in India.

Instead he said, 'It wasn't my decision.'

'If Ed gets hold of you he'll probably kill you,' replied Kenny.

'Is he back in Calcutta? Is he okay?' asked Farrell quickly.

'Yes, he's back, no thanks to you. Look, Farrell, why should we help you, you son of a bitch?' Kenny was turning a nice crimson with rage.

'Ed and I were friends, I hope we can still be,' said Farrell imploringly. 'Just let me talk to him, let him know I'm here.'

'No!' snapped Kenny. 'He has enough on his mind just now without buggering about with a whoring, back-stabbing son of a bitch who let him down. If I had my way, I'd shoot you, you bastard.' Kenny patted his holster threateningly, turned and walked out.

The Inspector regarded Farrell. He didn't want this lanky bugger hanging around like a ten day old curry. Finally he said, 'Look, I'll telephone one of the Army liaison chaps at Fort William and see if they will come and sort you out. You go back to your hotel and wait.'

* * *

Back at the hotel, there was a message waiting for Farrell. The tea company sent its regrets, but the job had gone to someone else. Well, wasn't that a bloody surprise! He sat dejectedly in his room awaiting the contact from Fort William. It had been an awful time. Everything had gone wrong. He felt very vulnerable; everything that was Mike Farrell had been taken away from him. He felt like a 'nobody' dressed in these waiters' clothes, stripped of all his money, his possessions, his identity, his dignity. Then he thought about Pierse and the Jap railway. He began to understand.

There was a knock on the door. Must be the Army liaison chap. 'Who is it?' he called. There was no answer, so he went to the door and opened it. Kenny Pierse stood there.

'Compliments of Irene,' he said, handing over Farrell's wallet and cheque book, 'less her fee of course. Your clothes she threw into Wellesley tank so you can forget about them.' Before Farrell could say anything he went on, 'She wanted to teach you a lesson. I think she's been a bloody good teacher, don't you?' He laughed heartily and left.

CHAPTER 7

Taking Leave

Pierse's three weeks' leave was up. He'd been to see Hubie O'Connor and his girlfriend, Pammy, but she had denied knowing Ellen's whereabouts, though Pierse was unconvinced by her protestations. He in turn had pleaded, even nearly shed a tear, but to no avail. The best he could get from her was that Ellen Lewis was now Mrs Taylor and that she had married a history teacher called Alec. Pammy said that Ellen had gone to a school – near Madras, she thought – but she had no details and had lost touch. Kenny too had come up with a blank – so much for his 'sources'. Pierse had even written two letters to Ellen's parents in Lucknow but they had gone unanswered. In his desperation and paranoia Pierse had one evening accused his parents and Kenny of deliberately lying about not knowing Ellen's whereabouts. It had led to a row, his father angry, his mother nearly in tears and Kenny in a sulk for a couple of days. Either they did not know – or were very good at concealing the truth.

The INA trials began on the 5th of November and the newspapers were full of them. Pierse scanned the pages of The Statesman for news of Chandra, but his name was not among those in the first batch of trials. Later that month, Calcutta's college students decided to celebrate an 'INA Day' and marched in procession to Dalhousie Square only to be thwarted by a police barricade across Dhurumtollah Street. The confrontation erupted into three days and nights of rioting; cars, buses and lorries were set on fire, Europeans who ventured out had bricks and stones chucked at them, Indians in western dress had their hats and ties torn off. The whole city came to a standstill as workers went on strike – a *hartal* – refusing to open businesses or run public services. Kenny was busy, arriving home at odd hours exhausted and nervous. Rioters were killed when the police fired on them; the situation seemed to be getting out of control and was spreading elsewhere in the country. Then, inexplicably, it stopped as suddenly as it had begun.

Pierse and Santosh sat on the *maidan* in the cool of the evening after their hockey practice a week after the riots. Around them Calcutta's green lung, originally kept free from buildings and obstructions to give the guns of Fort William an open field of fire on its landward sides, was filled with the people of Calcutta anxious to escape the noise and pollution for a while and breathe in the gentle evening breezes – *hawa khana*, 'eating the wind' was the expression for taking the air. Numerous games of cricket, hockey and football were underway, kites were being flown, lovers shyly walked and talked, small family picnics were tucking into their spicy, fragrant food and the *puchkawallas*, *ting-ting wallahs* and other vendors were busy peddling their wares. Over in one corner, a group of turbaned and bearded Afghan 'Kabuliwallahs', moneylenders, sat in a circle, notebooks out, comparing debtors. It was as if the disturbances of a few days ago had never taken place.

Santosh Chatterjee, 'Sunny' to his well-to-do family and to his friends, had been a close friend of Pierse's from school. They had a shared love of hockey but Sunny had now developed a greater interest in coffee house politics and the family business – much to the detriment of his hockey, Pierse felt. He had been one of the first visitors to the Pierse household to welcome Ed back to Cal and they had spent many afternoons going to the cinema, drinking coffee and playing hockey on the *maidan* in a move to get Pierse fit again. Home cooking and hard physical activity was filling out Pierse's frame and, as his leg muscles strengthened, his limp was less pronounced. He felt ready to return to the Regiment – he was looking forward to going back and to meeting his old comrades and catching up with the news, though dreading the inevitable medical and the looming threat of demobilisation. He tried hard to come to terms with the gnawing hurt over Ellen, but told himself that he would find her come what may, and at least get a chance to see her again and to let her know that he still felt the same about her.

Sunny lay back on the grass and talked of the riots and of India – of the change in its psyche. 'You know, Ed, the fact that the British lost so completely and collapsed so quickly in Malaya is a severe blow to the Empire; a catastrophic blow! I think it was the sign for us that the Empire's days were numbered. The invincibility of the British Army was wiped out and people began to believe that it was time for the British to go. They sensed that the British had been seriously weakened by the war here and in Europe – Gandhi-ji had seen it coming a long time ago. And even though Britain won in the end, that was only possible because of the help from other nations – the Americans mostly – but other countries in the Empire like India, Africa, Australia, New Zealand and Canada. Of course we Indians have been agitating for some time for the British to leave – we feel more than ever that the time has now come for us to be independent.'

'But, Sunny, without the British, India would not have the railways, the roads, the factories – all the benefits of the modern world. Surely we need the British to keep them running until Indians can be trained to take them over. And, as you know, any Indian Government will quickly disintegrate into chaos because of the factions in it – Hindus against Muslims – the Congress and Muslim League can't stand each other. The local Rajas and Princes will resume their squabbling to the point where nothing will get done and the *Babus* will bugger everything up in a maze of bureaucracy and corruption.'

'I freely accept that some good has come out of British rule, including a good system of justice. But the fact remains that British rule has itself perpetuated a deeper injustice where the people of one country have been made subservient to the people of another. Ed, this is the very thing the British were fighting Germany for. We Indians are not free to carve our own destiny, our *dharma*. Much of our wealth goes to London and a lot of decisions about India are made thousands of miles away by people who don't know our country. Britain is bankrupt after the war Ed; they will now suck our wealth up like leeches. And what about chaps like you? You Anglo-Indians, you are not permitted, in the nicest possible way of course, to get the top jobs. Despite your British ancestry the British don't really accept you as one of them, or trust you, and yet at least fifty per cent of each of you is British. What hope for chaps like me – one hundred per cent Indian?' He laughed.

Pierse bridled at this. 'What rot, Sunny, if I was good enough I could work my way to the top – look at our hockey players, Olympic champions.'

'Ed, I am not talking about hockey. They are happy for Indians or Anglo-Indians, or anyone to be sportsmen or entertainers or writers. But they will not tolerate them in jobs with power, the jobs that matter. The British are obsessed with their class system.'

'And Indians with caste!' interjected Pierse.

'Exactly – and I don't condone that either, but it has evolved over thousands of years and it will not disappear overnight. The British have their class system, which condemns anyone who is not British to a sub-caste of their own – it has always been like this.'

'Then explain to me, Sunny, how chaps like Nehru and Jinnah, London educated lawyers from wealthy Indian families, hold so much power and influence and are pally with the Viceroy and his people in Government?'

'And the princes also,' agreed Sunny. 'But they do not have an equal relationship. They are the 'Westernised Oriental Gentlemen' – WOGs – in the eyes of the British. The princes appear to be treated well, but the real power in their territories is exercised by a British administrator. And explain to me why they have to swear loyalty to the King Emperor?'

'So are you saying that I should support you in the Quit India movement, Sunny?' laughed Pierse.

'Most definitely! This is your country, you were born here; you have fought for it, nearly died for it, why should you not have the opportunity to run it?'

'Steady on, Sunny,' exclaimed Pierse in amusement, 'we've got enough trouble with the officers and men who went over to the INA without yet another serving officer preaching sedition. When I go back tomorrow I'll find out what exactly is happening to the INA chaps from my Regiment. I'm particularly worried about my friend, Anil Chandra, who, God knows how, got mixed up with them. I don't approve of what he did, but I hope it all turns out okay for him. Are you arguing that I should have joined the INA and supported the Japs?'

'The Indian National Army, the *Azad Hind Fauj*, is an interesting phenomenon,' mused Sunny. 'I am not sure of my feelings about it. Subash Chandra Bose, the founder, was trying to use Britain's enemies as a lever to get independence for India – you know the expression, 'my enemy's enemy is my friend'. I don't think that Bose supported Hitler's ideals or those of Japan. But you know, Ed, you must seriously ask yourself why so many of your sepoys, and their officers, went over to join the Japanese, and went so willingly. Perhaps you should ask that question when you go back.'

'I imagine it offered a better opportunity to stay alive than being locked up, tortured and starved in a POW camp. Many of them quit the INA within a year and came back to us.'

'But many didn't. And there were senior Indian officers, educated and Dehra Dun trained men like yourself, who joined the INA with the express purpose of liberating India from the British.'

'If I listen to you any more Sunny, I'll be wearing homespun *kadhi* and a Congress cap and throwing stones at Kenny!' laughed Pierse.

'And he might even pat his revolver holster at you,' riposted Sunny and they laughed at the shared joke.

* * *

That night there was a farewell party for Pierse. He hadn't been keen to take up the invitations he had received from friends since his return to attend house parties, dances and 'shows' at the big Anglo-Indian clubs. He had reluctantly gone to a dance with his old hockey team mates, but had left after a short while, feeling alienated from the post-war gaiety and out of touch with the frivolous gossip after his years away. He missed Ellen terribly and wanted her to be there – she loved to dance. He had tried to persuade his parents and Kenny not to have a party at home to celebrate his return to the land of the living, but they thought that he needed something to lift his spirits. As he would not be home for Christmas, his farewell was also a pre-Christmas party and Uncle Derek, large, loud and ruddy from long exposure to the heat of the engine firebox in his job as a fireman on the railway, had arranged for a Christmas tree and had dressed up as Father Christmas to give Ed his Christmas presents in advance. Ed's mother had been busy too and there was a home-made and potently alcoholic Christmas cake and *kul kuls,* cakes, sweets and curry puffs from Nahoum's in the New Market and plenty of strong drink. Uncle Derek sank his tots of rum, sang his songs and fussed over his nephew. Aunty Philly, his wife, was equally extrovert and took over the piano for a sing-song of carols and sentimental old familiar tunes. Sunny and his sister, Suchitra, were there too, mingling with the cousins and great aunts and uncles, with Kenny taking a keen interest in her. Towards the end of the evening she came and sat down next to Ed in a rustle of silk sari and a hint of perfume.

'Have you been avoiding me?' he teased, 'you haven't come to talk to me all evening.'

She smiled. 'Your family comes first, they haven't seen you for so long and I didn't want to intrude. I didn't think you would remember me.' Her voice was deeper than he remembered, silkier. The fifteen year old schoolgirl he had known before the war had certainly changed; she had grown into a very attractive woman.

'I'd know you anywhere, Suchi,' he laughed, 'though you have changed – for the better, much better! It's a good thing that you didn't inherit Sunny's looks.' He glanced at her, she was stunning. Wide, lustrous brown eyes lined with kohl looked boldly back at him and their eyes locked for more than a moment.

'Sunny says that your parents are searching for a husband for you,' he said quickly. She nodded glumly. 'You don't seem keen.'

'Well, what's the hurry,' she replied, 'I've just finished my B.A. degree and I don't want to go straight from studying into marriage. I've been studying since I was five years old.' She sounded like the petulant schoolgirl Pierse had known.

'Well, your days of climbing trees, messing up our hockey games and getting us to sneak you into the Eden Gardens after dark to go on the boating lake are over,' he laughed, 'you have to be a good Bengali lady now. Get yourself a rich, fat, old husband and use his money to have a good time, or a young, good-looking poor one – there never seems to be anything in-between.'

She looked at him scornfully. 'It is not that funny Eddie. They will marry me off to someone I have never met just because he is the right caste and the right social class. I don't get a say in the matter. It's just so... so... old fashioned.' She looked away and he could see her shoulders drop slightly.

'Surely you must be able to choose,' he said, anxious not to see her upset. 'This is the modern world, for God's sake, it's your life, you must have a say in who you marry.'

She turned back to him. 'I know who I want to marry!' Her retort surprised and amused him.

'Aah ha!' exclaimed Pierse, 'who is this lucky chap? Good looking and poor? Wrong caste? Do I know him?'

'Yes to all of those,' her smile had returned.

'It's not Kenny, the randy pig, is it?' asked Pierse in mock seriousness.

'He's like a brother to me!' she retorted with a laugh.

'Well he *is* a brother to me,' said Pierse, 'and just now he is proving to be a useless bloody detective.'

'Ah, Ellen,' she said quietly. 'Are you still looking for her even thought she is married? You should let her go Ed – there is someone else out there for you.'

'Thanks, Suchi,' he said, brushing her hand, 'I hope things turn out alright for you. If you love this chap, do everything you can to get Sunny on your side, he's a progressive chap. And don't forget to invite me to the wedding.'

'If it all works out, you'll be there,' she replied enigmatically.

Sunny had come up to get his sister to take her home. He shook Ed's hand, patted him on the back and thanked him for the evening and said he would catch up again when Ed returned home on leave. Suchi looked at Ed uncertainly for a moment, then stepped forward and hugged him tightly, her hair brushing against his cheek. She turned away quickly and was gone.

'What a *patarker*,' said Uncle Derek appreciatively as he passed by on his way to get another drink, both he and his Santa costume looking the worse for wear.

* * *

Starved of sleep and with a bad hangover, Pierse sat in the gharry with his parents on his way to Howrah Station across the Hoogly River. They had insisted on accompanying him to catch his train and he knew that it was useless to protest. Mercifully, Kenny had said his goodbyes at home as he had to go on duty and had roared off on his big red Harley Davidson police motorcycle.

'Are you okay, son?' asked his father.

'Okay?' enquired Pierse.

'About going back to Jullundur and the Army.'

'Yes, looking forward to it. Be nice to catch up with the chaps. I'm dreading the medical though as I'd like to stay on if possible.'

'Plenty of jobs now in civvy street, son. You could always come into the Railway but, with your degree and background, there are better paying jobs in the big tobacco companies or in the jute mills or tea estates.'

'Ummm.'

'Look,' said his father pointing, 'we are coming to the new Howrah Bridge!'

'When did they finish that?' said Pierse as he surveyed the impressive steel girders and wide roadway.

'Couple of years ago – wonder why the Japs never bombed it. Remember the old pontoon bridge Ed?'

'Yes. And when the tide was in and the hinged pontoons rose the bloody bullock carts and handcarts couldn't get up the slope,' smiled Ed. 'Traffic chaos – it was like a circus sideshow. Thank God we're not relying on that today or I could miss the train."

'Cal's much the same as it was,' said his mother, 'the Americans and the other troops will soon be gone and we can all go back to being normal.'

'Yes, but the bloody Quit India wallahs are causing more and more trouble,' said her husband, 'the rioting last month was really very bad, Ed. There was also big trouble on the Esplanade before you came back. I was really worried for Kenny because the crowd were throwing brickbats, bottles and home-made bombs at the police. I don't know whether the British will cling on here or pull back to Blighty now that the war's over and Britain has almost been made bankrupt.'

* * *

They stood awkwardly at the door of the railway carriage to say their goodbyes; around them the normal chaos of the station. Red-shirted porters hefting towers of luggage on their heads, pushing and shoving to get it on to the train, their sweaty and almost hysterical passengers close behind; hawkers crying their wares, shouts, streams of blood-like betel juice being expectorated onto the railway line and, above the din of people and announcements, the sharp hiss and clouds of steam from the giant locomotive gathering its breath before its rush to Delhi. Then its whistle cut deafeningly through the racket, followed by the shriller, more urgent staccato whistle of the stationmaster as he waved his flag.

Pierse reached to hug his parents. There was a sudden

flurry of pushing and shoving around him and Kenny burst through the crowd his face ruddy with excitement and effort.

'I've found her!' he shouted, 'I've found her!' He thrust a scrap of paper into Pierse's hands. 'The school she's at!' The train creaked and slowly began to move.

'How?' Pierse shouted, clambering into the carriage doorway. But Kenny's yelled answer was lost in the noise of the crowd and the hiss and rumble of the train.

CHAPTER 8

Return to Arms

Every half hour or so throughout the train journey to Jullundur Pierse retrieved from his pocket the scrap of paper Kenny had given to him at Howrah Station and looked at the three words written on it. They were now burned into his brain. They had become a magic spell, an alchemist's formula, co-ordinates for buried treasure. He held it gingerly and looked at it for the umpteenth time. 'St. Peter's, Coialla' it said in Kenny's hurried scrawl. That's all. But he now knew where he could find Ellen – tell her he was back and that his love for her was as constant as ever. He couldn't contemplate the possibility that she would reject him, their bond was too strong. He was back from the dead! Her marriage could be undone; it was based on a mistake. He didn't care if the Catholic Church refused to condone divorce; he just wanted to be back with Ellen. He was sure she would feel the same emotional pull.

So it was with spirits raised that he arrived at Jullundur and entered the gates of the Dogra Regimental depot to the crashing rifles and salutes of the guard. He was back among friends, comrades in arms, back in the ordered life of the Regiment. He made straight for the officers' mess.

There were lots of new faces there, mostly Indian officers, and they looked at him curiously.

'You'll have to take that insignia off,' one said by way of welcome, pointing at his cap badge, a large number 17 surmounted by a crown, the insignia of the 3/17th.

'I've got more right to it than you have, you insolent bugger,' said Pierse aggressively, 'where were you when the fucking Japs came to call?'

'I didn't mean to be insulting....' stuttered the offender but the rest of his apology was drowned by a shout from the bar.

'Pierse, old chap! Welcome back!' shouted Connell, an officer Pierse had known from the 2/17th.

'What are you doing here, Connell?' Pierse demanded with a grin.

'Part of the reorganisation, old chap. The 3/17th and the 2/17th are no more – we are all Dogras now – we are just The Dogra Regiment. That's why Kumar there was pulling your leg.'

'I'm sorry,' said Kumar, chastened, 'I didn't know you were Lt. Pierse,' he offered his hand. Pierse took it with a smile.

'Colonel wants to see you when you arrive,' cautioned Connell, 'we didn't think you'd make it back,' he chuckled.

'I need a stiff drink first,' said Pierse nodding to the Mess Bearer, 'whisky soda please.' Then, turning to Connell, he asked, 'Is Mike Farrell here?'

Connell nodded. 'He's got his demob papers and goes in a couple of weeks. Got some sort of job in Calcutta, I understand.'

Five minutes later Pierse was in the Colonel's office.

'Sit down Pierse,' said the Colonel kindly. 'Have you fully recovered from your illness?'

'I'm making good progress, Sir.'

'There have been a lot of changes here Pierse. We are now re-badged and amalgamated together as The Dogra Regiment.'

'Yes, I just heard, Sir. Why?'

'It is mostly to do with bringing the numbers down now the war has ended, we don't need so many battalions – Government can't afford 'em for a start. But, between ourselves, I think it is also to do with the stain on the reputation of the 3/17ᵗʰ of so many of our men going over to the INA in Singapore. Some have been cashiered, others reduced in seniority or dismissed, and we have filled a lot of the gaps with men from the other battalions as well as recruited new ones. India is changing, Pierse. The 'box-wallahs' want to remove the traces of the Empire from our regiments in preparation for handing over the show to the Indians. Chaps like me are on borrowed time.'

'And chaps like me, Sir?'

'Well, Pierse, you're on an Emergency Commission so you will be in line to be de-mobbed. You've done your stuff, you deserve a well-earned rest.'

'But I was hoping to stay on in the Army, Sir.'

The Colonel looked uncomfortable. 'The good news, Pierse, is that you have been promoted Captain. So congratulations. The reason we have done this is so that you can continue in the Army for a little longer to help train the new chaps. The young Subalterns in particular could benefit from your experience. I'll see what I can do about a more permanent posting, but I can't hold out much hope as the pressure is on us to reduce our numbers not keep people on. Your medical record doesn't look too clever though I think you'll get by. The C-in-C is keen that we should have Indian officers.'

'But I'm Anglo-Indian, Sir. I was born in this country. My parents have worked here all their lives. This is my country too!'

'I'm sorry, Pierse.' Softening his tone, the Colonel continued, 'The problem is that you hold an Emergency Commission, and now that the war is over there is no longer a place for Emergency Commissioned officers. It isn't fair and it isn't sensible as chaps like you have the battle experience and skills that the Regiment needs. But I can't go against the 'box-wallahs' who write the rules.'

'Yes, Sir,' said Pierse stiffly. He saluted and left.

He went straight to the Adjutant's office.

'Ah! *Captain* Pierse!' exclaimed the Adjutant pointedly, welcoming Pierse with an enthusiastic handshake. 'Piersey, how are you?'

'I'm fine John. Just a bit shocked having met the Old Man and been told that my services are at an end.'

'The same for all of us Ed; the Colonel too. New world and all that. There's more treachery in peacetime than there is in war.'

'John, I've a favour to ask.'

'Fire away.'

'When I got home from Malaya I was shocked to find out that my family had received a telegram from the Regiment after Singapore fell to say that I had been killed.'

'What!' exclaimed the Adjutant. 'That's not possible. We were all POWs and there wasn't a means to communicate with the people in the Depot here. We eventually sent lists to the Red Cross, but you were probably not on ours as you had gone to work on the Burma Railway by then. I'll check with the Depot clerks but I'd be very surprised if any telegram came from here. They certainly didn't send anything to the families of those who had been killed. What a curious to-do!'

'It had a devastating effect on my family,' said Pierse.

'Of course it must have, dear chap. I'll look into it right away. How curious.'

* * *

As he left the mess for his billet, Pierse saw a familiar figure walking back from the parade ground, swinging a swagger stick and clipping stones in the dust.

'Mike! Hey, Mike!' he shouted, waving.

Mike Farrell looked up. He went pale with apprehension. 'Hello, Ed,' he said guardedly.

Pierse came up and clapped him on the shoulder.

'Mike, it's good to see you after all this time. Nice to spot a familiar face around here.'

Farrell realised with great relief that Kenny didn't seem to have told his brother about the incident with the girl in the Grand Hotel.

'Good to see you too, Ed,' he smiled tightly. 'Look, I hope that you are fully recovered from your malaria and dysentery – and that you have forgiven me for my stupidity in suggesting your name for the Jap Railway. I had absolutely no idea what those Jap bastards were really going to do.'

'It's okay Mike. Let's let bygones be bygones, eh? You thought you were doing me a favour. I was bitter about it when I got back from Songkurai but you are my friend, so just let's let it go.'

Farrell nodded, much relieved, but remaining wary.

'I hear that you are being de-mobbed and are moving to a job in Cal,' said Pierse.

'Yes, only two weeks to go and then I'm off to work for a jute company in Dum Dum. Pay's not wonderful but it will do as a stop-gap until something better comes along.'

'So you're not going back to England and your family?'

'No, Ed. I quite like India. It suits me. I want to stay on.'

'That's splendid, Mike. I expect that I'll be de-mobbed soon too and we can meet up in Cal. There are lots of interesting places in which to dine and drink. And I'll teach you to play hockey.'

Farrell concealed his discomfort. 'That will be wonderful,' he said. 'Ellen will have to find me a nice friend so we can go out in a foursome.'

'Ellen's not in Calcutta,' said Pierse quietly. Something in his voice made Farrell realise that all was not well.

'Oh?'

'Long story Mike, tell you later. I'm going to drop my stuff at my quarters and then go and see Havildar Prem Singh. Is he around?'

'Yes, but he's not a Havildar anymore. He's been promoted to Jemadar. He too had a hard time under the Japs, Ed, but remained loyal and didn't join those cowardly INA buggers.'

* * *

Jemadar Prem Singh, now a Viceroy's Commissioned Officer, was supervising the drilling of a platoon of recruits. His face split into a big grin when he saw Pierse and he marched over and saluted his former officer, still smiling. Pierse returned the salute and noted that he looked older and thinner, his face was deeply lined, the nose broken and the moustache now more grey than black. The two men regarded each other for a while, saying nothing, holding tight to their emotions. They had not seen each other since the surrender of Singapore in February 1942, nearly four years ago. Pierse had looked on the older, more experienced Prem Singh almost as a father. Prem Singh too held Pierse in high regard. Much had happened since then. Many had died; many had turned against the Regiment. They had remained constant. But their lives had been irretrievably altered by the cruelty and horror of it all.

In the shade of a tree bordering the parade ground they sat and talked. Prem Singh, his voice unsteady, recalled the events following the defeat at Singapore.

'The *Japani* wanted us to join with them when they gathered us at Farrer Park, Sahib, two days after the surrender. We were surprised to see Mr. Chandra there, on the platform among a group of other Indian officers, when he was supposed to be in hospital. There was a British officer there, and he said, 'You belong to the *Japani* now, so do as they say'. Some of our own Army officers, the ones with whom Mr. Chandra was standing, told us that we must join a new Indian National Army and, with the help of the *Japani*, we would march back into India and liberate it from the British. I told our men that we must not believe the *Japani*. Had they not seen what these *shaitans* had done to their colleagues? Did they not remember their cruelty in bayoneting men who had been wounded and were trying to surrender? Did they not hear that the *Japani* had killed the Englishmen lying in hospital beds in Singapore – and their nurses too? How could we trust such people! We had eaten the salt of the British *sarkar*, we were men of the Dogra Regiment, not of any new National Army. But many did not listen. Some said, at least if we join the *Japani* we have a chance of living and returning home to our families. Others said, is it not time that we freed ourselves from the British Raj – here is our chance.'

'But I refused, Pierse Sahib. So those of us who refused were imprisoned, we were beaten and treated badly – and none of those officers who had asked us to join the INA did anything to help us, their fellow Indians. In fact, some of our Indian brothers who joined the INA and became our prison guards treated us just as badly as the *Japani*. We were first put in prison in Singapore then later the *Japani* sent me, along with many others, to New Guinea, where we were made to do coolie labour – we were treated like slaves. We were starved, beaten and killed – they didn't care if we lived or died. The *Japani* despised us because we had surrendered and they regarded us as cowards for it. They also despised us because we were dark skinned. I tell you, Pierse Sahib, I began to wonder whether I had made the wrong decision. The place was terrible. It rained and rained, we were wet for weeks. We were bitten by insects and became sick because of the terrible climate, the hard work and the lack of food. I began to ask myself why our God and our officers had abandoned us. It was a very bad time for all of us. The men were saying, we should tell the *Japani* that we have changed our mind and will now join the INA. And some did. But the *Japani* took those men, called them cowards, and mistreated them so badly that most died. We realised that we were trapped there.'

'Then I remembered what you once said to us on the hockey field, Sahib – when we were playing the Punjabis in the Army Cup and we were one goal down. Do you remember, Sahib?'

Pierse raised a quizzical eyebrow and shook his head. Prem Singh smiled.

'You said, boys, when we are losing, that is the time to play like champions, with all the confidence as if we were winning. Remember, Sahib?'

Pierse nodded. 'My father taught me that when I used to box at school. He used to say that if you behaved like a loser you will be a loser – so you must always behave like a champion.'

Prem Singh nodded understandingly. 'Yes, Pierse Sahib, I remember. So I told the men this: they must believe that we would win. I told them that, for us, just to stay alive was to win! The *Japani* wanted to destroy us but I said that we must not let them do so. We must try to stay alive so that one day, with the help of God, we could be ready to fight the *Japani* again and defeat them – and return to our families. So I started to make some rules. I said that we must avoid bringing unnecessary damage on ourselves. We would work as hard as we could for the *Japani*, we would not try to provoke them in any way, but above all we would support each other in staying alive.'

'Did it work?' asked Pierse, much moved.

'I am here, Sahib,' said Prem Singh simply. 'We were set free by the Australians at the end of 1944 and taken by ship to Australia before we were sent back here.'

Then he turned to Pierse. 'Why did you not join us at Farrer Park, Sahib?' he asked quietly. 'There were other Anglo-Indian officers there.'

Pierse was stunned by the question. It shook him deeply. He had never considered doing anything other than joining his fellow British officers in the trek to imprisonment at Changi. He recalled his conversation on the *maidan* with Sunny, and today's outburst to the Colonel: was this not his country? Was he not born in it? Why had he not joined his fellow Indians? Why had he gone with the British officers when he was not exactly one of them? He did not know how to answer Prem Singh.

'I don't know, Jemadar Sahib,' he replied truthfully. 'I had no idea that the *Japani* would try to make our people change sides. Like you, I would not have joined the INA. I could not have betrayed my Regiment. My ancestors are British; my way of life is British, it seemed correct that I should join the British officers.'

Prem Singh said nothing. He was embarrassed that he had put his officer on the spot and regretted asking the question.

'We failed all of you,' Pierse went on, 'for that I am sorry – very sorry. General Percival should have refused the *Japani* order to separate the Indian officers and men.'

'I don't think he had any choice, Pierse Sahib,' said Prem Singh. 'The *Japani* would have done it anyway.'

Anxious to change the subject, Pierse told him briefly about his imprisonment in Changi and then being sent to work on the Burma-Siam railway. He felt it inappropriate to go into any detail of the brutality of his Japanese captors as Prem Singh had said it all.

'What has happened to the rest of the boys?' he asked Prem Singh. 'Did Dina Nath survive? He was in hospital when we surrendered.'

'He joined the INA,' said Prem Singh curtly, 'and he has been dismissed from the Army without pension. You remember his cousin, Sahib, Tulsi Ram, who turned up with Chandra Sahib – they went missing after Sungei Choh?' Pierse nodded.

'Tulsi Ram was killed. The rumour is that it was Mr. Chandra who killed him as he was trying to blackmail him or desert from the INA.'

'Good Lord!' exclaimed Pierse. 'I can't believe that!'

'Mr. Chandra did a lot of bad things,' said Prem Singh angrily. 'You must be very careful of him, Sahib.'

'Why do you say that? He was my friend.'

'Pierse Sahib, his story of losing touch with the Regiment after Sungei Choh is not true. He and Tulsi Ram ran away from the attack because they were afraid. They came to Singapore before the rest of the Regiment and hid there until we appeared and they became frightened that they would be discovered. So they came back and made up a story.'

'Who told you this?' asked Pierse testily.

Prem Singh continued: 'Mr. Chandra was not really sick when he went to hospital in Singapore. He had arranged a plan with a relative who was a doctor so that he did not have to fight the *Japani*.'

'Who told you this?' demanded Pierse again, his voice carrying an edge.

Prem Singh looked Pierse in the eye then turned away, 'Dina Nath told me. Mr. Chandra recruited him in the hospital and persuaded him to join the INA. Chandra had been in contact with INA people in Singapore before the *Japani* defeated us. '

Pierse was silent. Aghast! The watch – the shopkeeper was telling the truth about a Dogra officer trying to buy a watch. Chandra had lost his. It made sense. Chandra must have been that officer. He shook his head in disbelief.

'Dina Nath told me something else, Sahib.'

'What?' asked Pierse, the blood singing in his brain, he was overwhelmed by what he had heard.

'You remember, Sahib, how Mr. Chandra was angry that you had told his family he was missing after Sungei Choh?'

'Yes, now we know why – the lying bastard!'

'He found out that his father had suffered a collapse which paralysed his arm on receiving the news, so he blamed you for it, Pierse Sahib.'

Pierse looked startled. Prem Singh continued.

'So he played a cruel joke on your father, telling him that *you* had been killed. He got a relative to send a telegram. Dina Nath overheard a conversation Mr. Chandra had with someone in Singapore.'

Pierse's rage made him shake. He could not believe that his friend would stoop so low, be so callously cruel. He jumped up. 'I'll kill that bastard, if it's the last thing I do!' he shouted. 'I'll fucking kill him!' Turning to Prem Singh, 'How many people know about this?' he demanded.

'He is a dangerous man, Sahib. Those who knew have died. Dina Nath knows, and he works for Mr. Chandra now. He is tied to Mr. Chandra, who has given him land and money. You must be careful.'

'How do you know?'

'Dina Nath is my nephew, Sahib. He told me in strict confidence as he too is afraid that one day Mr. Chandra may kill him to keep his secret safe. By telling me, he knows that I will avenge his death if anything happens.'

'Does the Colonel Sahib know?'

'No. And why should he believe this story, Sahib, there is no proof. *Kismet* may resolve all these problems. Mr. Chandra is on trial because he was a leader of the INA. He will probably be executed and the death of Tulsi Ram and the cowardly trick he played on you will be avenged. But until then he remains dangerous as his family has plenty of money to pay *goondas* and thugs to do their dirty work for them.'

* * *

In the weeks that followed, Pierse's mind was in turmoil and his frustration increased. He now wanted to be out of the Army as quickly as possible so that he could go and see Ellen and then settle his score with Chandra. Perversely, however, the Army's grip on him tightened and he found himself busier than ever training officers and men, being sent on training courses and, at the Colonel's request, building up the Regimental hockey team. Kenny wrote to him soon after the farewell at Howrah, to tell him more about Ellen. She was teaching 4th Standard children, her husband, Alec Taylor, taught history and English – and, Kenny warned, was a good boxer. Pierse smiled at this last bit. Kenny obviously thought that he was heading for a confrontation, whereas he had gone over and over in his mind how he could engineer a meeting with Ellen without her husband knowing about it. It was not that he feared a confrontation with Alec Taylor. He feared that a confrontation, if it led to violence, would completely alienate Ellen from him.

He did think about writing to Ellen and drafted a couple of letters but did not send them. No, this must be done face to face. He wanted her to see him, he wanted to look into her eyes and gauge her reaction to what he had to say. If she still loved him but was hiding behind duty, he would do everything he could to get her back. Their first meeting had to be calm and rational – God knows there would be enough emotion between the two of them anyway. It must be very finely judged, very delicately done. If she told him, truthfully, that she no longer loved him, or loved Taylor more and chose not to return to him he would have no choice but to accept it, though his natural instinct was to fight for her.

Of one thing he was sure. Chandra was the cause of his losing Ellen and would be made to pay for it. If the Viceroy cheated him of his revenge by sending Chandra to a firing squad or to be hanged, he would make public the full story of this dishonourable man. Perhaps The Statesman, following the INA trials so closely, would print the truth: that this was not a patriot; this was a coward who had dishonoured his Regiment, deliberately harmed his friends and murdered his soldiers.

* * *

Just before Christmas they held a party in the mess to mark Farrell's departure from the Regiment. Pierse felt that despite the attempts on his part to re-forge their friendship: long chats, reminisces, the drinking and high-jinks in the mess, there was a distance between them now. He told Farrell, in confidence, of his conversation with Prem Singh and of Chandra's treachery. Farrell was shocked, but had offered no words of advice or comfort. His view was that Chandra would be lucky to emerge with his life from the INA trials. The Government in London and the Army High Command wanted blood, and would have it.

'The war was a disaster for all of us, Ed. Best forget about it and look to the future. This is a time of change and we have to seize the moment. The Army doesn't want us because we embarrassed them by surrendering. So sod them! I'm off to carve a fortune for myself before the country gets turned on its head.'

And he went off to his jute mill in Dum Dum to start afresh.

CHAPTER 9

Heroes and Traitors

The Red Fort, the *Lal Quila*, past symbol of the Mughal Empire in Delhi, glowed hotly in the November sunlight. It had played its part in India's history over three centuries and within its walls were trapped the ghosts of innumerable deaths, cruelties and sadnesses caused by greed, jealousy and the lust for power. The Union Flag flew from its ramparts, as it had done following the crushing of the sepoy mutiny of 1857, a provocative yet potent symbol of Britain's Imperial hold over India. Imprisoned in this fastness were the leaders of the Indian National Army awaiting their trials for treason against the King Emperor, the shy, stuttering King George VI. They were locked in cells built into the fort's outer wall, which heated fiercely in the sun, like tandoori ovens.

In one of the gaunt barracks of grey brick and stone within the fort's perimeter, in a room whose drabness and austerity was far removed from the ornately carved state rooms of the Mughal Emperors, Anil Chandra nervously awaited a summons to a meeting with 'the powers that be'. The room was small, cold and dim, the shutters drawn, the sun's light and warmth and the sounds of Old Delhi did not penetrate here. The furniture consisted of a utilitarian table and a few hard chairs –

nothing else. It was ironic that not far away in the Emperors' magnificent private audience chamber, the Diwan-i-Khass, was engraved those immortal lines: *'If there be a paradise on earth, it is this, it is this, it is this.'* For Chandra it had been a private hell. He had not been told what the interview was about but could guess that the legal process was coming to one of its critical stages; the word on the grapevine was that some of the courts martial of INA leaders were about to begin. He sat as still as he could, trying to control his fear and conceal it from the British sergeant guarding him, who sat near the door.

Chandra's lawyer, a young, sleek Punjabi barrister of allegedly good reputation and family, Ahmed Farooqui, lately of Gray's Inn in London, and hired at great expense by his father, sat sucking on a cigarette, also tense and nervous. Chandra regarded Farooqui silently and scornfully. As a lawyer, useless! His main value had been as a conduit, a highly paid messenger boy, between Chandra, his family and his supporters in the Indian National Congress. Through him Chandra had learned of the efforts his father was making to secure his freedom or, at very least, the most lenient sentence possible. In turn Chandra transmitted instructions and information via Farooqui to his father. The threat of the death penalty or, if they were lucky, transportation for life to the penal colony on the Andaman Islands was all too real for the dozen or so top INA men; the British were determined to make an example of them to the rest of the armed forces and to the people of India. Farooqui, with his English public school accent and imperious manner only seemed to irritate the senior British Army officers who were in charge of the investigations and turn them against Chandra. He seemed to think he was operating in the Inns of Court in London where an Indian barrister was regarded as an exotic peacock and afforded a fair and patient hearing by his peers. Here, among the hard-bitten Army officers he was regarded as being just another Indian, a damn native, and cocky with it.

Chandra had come to know very well the foibles of his captors. Since being captured in Singapore after the Japanese surrendered in August, three months ago, his life had been filled with round after round of interrogations by two intelligence officers barely able to keep their contempt in check. Why did you do it they asked? Did you not agree to serve the British Indian Army? Where was your loyalty to your King and country, to your Regiment? Did you become a traitor to save your skin? Did you do it because you are a coward? Did you have dealings personally with either Rash Behari Bose or Subash Chandra Bose? Did you have a leading part in the Indian National Army? Did you fight against British troops? Did you kill British soldiers? Did you! Did you! Did you!

He had played a straight bat to all of it.

In the last years of the war his doubts had been growing about the Japanese ability to sustain and win the war once the Americans had become involved. However, he had not foreseen the collapse coming quite so quickly after the unimaginable atom bomb explosions in Japan. Earlier, when the Japanese and the INA were defeated at Kohima and Imphal in their thrust towards India, and were then forced into retreat across Burma, he had concluded that the game was up. But he had thought it could take another year or two for the Japanese to surrender. Though he hated them, he conceded that they were brave buggers who fought to the last man.

He remained convinced that his decision to join the INA had been the right one. It was better than suffering, and very probably not surviving, years of Japanese captivity. He saw at first-hand the way they treated their prisoners like sub-human cowards, to be dealt with mercilessly and without pity. In the beginning he had felt a small stirring of nationalist pride at witnessing the humiliation of the British at the hands of their oriental captors. But it soon became all too apparent that the Japanese held their Indian allies in similar contempt and treated them indifferently. He had exchanged one set of Imperialists for another, this time for a more ruthless bunch of bastards. What is it about people from small islands – the Japanese and the British – that they feel they can only survive and prosper by conquest and by expanding their territory. Their island isolation makes them arrogant; they consider themselves to be superior – but is this because they really feel inferior and have to prove their superiority? The Japanese didn't want to help liberate India, though they claimed they did. They wanted to conquer and subjugate it, steal its wealth and oppress its people, just as they were doing in Malaya, just as they had done in China. Their claim that they wanted to 'help their Asiatic Brothers overthrow the foreign yoke' was just lies and propaganda. He now hoped that the British, with their sense of fair play, would understand his position.

Other Indian officers, Shah Nawaz Khan, Gurubaksh Singh and Prem Saghal had been in the forefront of the INA leadership together with Fateh Khan, Abdul Rashid and Shinghara Singh. Some of them took to it enthusiastically, persuaded by the ideas of the charismatic Subhas Chandra Bose and genuinely believing that the Japanese were there to help them liberate their motherland from the British. They were encouraged by the Japanese and by Bose to confer on themselves 'proper' Army rank as INA commanders – Captains and Majors became Colonels and Generals. Chandra wisely resisted following suit as he just wanted to keep his head down, do as little as possible to end up in the front line units fighting the British. He wanted, above all, to survive this war and return to help his father run the family estates. As the only son, it would fall to him to carry on the business when his father was no more, and the portents for Chandra Senior were not good. Too much high living had led to deterioration in his father's health before the war, and the fit of apoplexy he had suffered when his son was reported missing in Malaya by

Pierse had robbed him of the power of his left arm. Chandra was now worried that his captivity and trial would completely finish the old man, leaving the family's business to the mercy of his many uncles if he was not around to carry it on. He would have failed his family. His father had always drummed into him, as *his* father did before him, that every generation of Chandras had a duty to add to the family's wealth. He didn't want to be the first in two centuries to fail.

* * *

Footsteps on the stone corridor outside brought the escort to take him to his interview. He and Farooqui were taken up flights of steps and into another drab corridor. There they waited until a door guarded by a sentry opened and they were ushered in to face what looked like a panel of two senior Army officers, one a red-tab, and an official dressed in a cream cotton suit and an orange tie. Overhead a ceiling fan stirred the air, but not with enough force to disturb the papers on the table. The curtains were drawn as if to keep out the questioning, prying eyes of India. As he looked around him at the other officials in the room, Chandra recognised his two intelligence officer inquisitors and also Captain 'Mac', a Scots-born officer, a colleague from the Dogras, now wearing the insignia of a Major. Mac's presence was a new development and he wondered what it meant. Chandra gave him a slight nod of recognition, but was met with a blank stare.

Chandra was dressed in Army khaki stripped of all badges and indications of rank. He and his lawyer were ushered to two chairs but he was instructed to remain standing. He was asked to identify himself, which he did, standing to attention and saying clearly, 'Lieutenant Anil Chandra, 3/17 Dogra Regiment.' Out of the corner of his eye he saw 'Mac' wince.

'I remind you of the charges against you,' said the senior

officer, a Brigadier, reading from a document. 'You are charged that you waged war against the King contrary to section 121 of the Indian Penal Code. There is a second charge of abetment to murder contrary to Section 302 of the Indian Penal Code.'

'I demand to know what this meeting is about,' Farooqui started to say...

'Be quiet!' snapped the Brigadier. 'You are here to listen to what we have concluded from the questioning of the accused and the evidence we have obtained from our enquiries. This is not a trial. You are here out of courtesy, Mr Farooqui.'

Chandra motioned to Farooqui not to respond.

'We have looked at the evidence to support the charges against you Chandra,' continued the Brigadier. 'On the charge of waging war against the King, we are satisfied that there is a case to answer that you were involved in the planning and organisation of military operations between September 1942 and April 1945. We can, however, find no evidence that you actually took part in any military operations against British or Allied forces. On the second charge of abetment to murder, the evidence is not sufficiently strong to support the charge that you were involved in the unlawful shooting of an INA member, Sepoy Tulsi Ram, for desertion. The person who made the original allegation has now withdrawn it.'

Chandra stared ahead impassively, concealing his deep sense of relief that his father had managed to 'reason' with and buy off the sepoy who had witnessed his shooting of Tulsi Ram, who was trying to blackmail him by threatening to tell the British what had really happened at Sungei Choh.

The Brigadier continued. 'Your fellow INA conspirators,' he wanted to say 'traitors', 'have told us that you were not part of the inner circle, as it were, of the INA leadership. We know that you were involved in INA affairs, but it seems that you remained on the periphery.' He looked at the official on his left then, clearing his throat, 'So, Chandra, you will be removed

from the Red Fort to a military jail and will face a formal court
martial for the act of deserting your Regiment and siding with
the enemy against the King. That is all.'

Farooqui rose to speak but Chandra again restrained him.
He nodded to the Brigadier turned and left the room.

Outside: 'Why didn't you let me speak?' protested
Farooqui.

'Don't you understand, Farooqui,' replied an exasperated
Chandra, speaking in Hindi to avoid being understood by the
sergeant of the guard, 'they are letting me off! I was facing the
death penalty! They have decided that I am just small fry and
not worth keeping imprisoned here in the Red Fort. I'll get a
regimental court martial just like the INA officers captured in
Burma – that's why a Dogra officer was there – and I'll be
cashiered from the army, forfeiting my back pay and any
allowances, just as they have done to other INA officers and
sepoys. Do you think I care about that?'

'But they must acknowledge that you also fought valiantly
for the British in Malaya before their surrender to the Japanese
– they owe you medals for that.'

'Damn the medals!' said Chandra. 'Do you realise that I will
shortly be free to go back home, help run the family business –
and, most important of all, participate in the struggle to kick the
British out of India?' Then seeing Farooqui upset, 'Look, *bhai*,
the British will take my war service into account, I am sure that
was why 'Mac' was there – the Dogra Major sitting on the
right,' he explained, seeing Farooqui's uncomprehending look.
'It will mean that I can avoid being sent to prison. The poor
fellows left behind here in the Red Fort will be executed – the
British will have their revenge, their pound of flesh. It will help
make up for the humiliation of their defeat in Malaya.'

'We will fight that!' exclaimed Farooqui. 'Nehru and Jinnah,
both of whom are excellent barristers, will take on the British.
Gandhi-ji will also help to mediate; he carries great influence

with the Viceroy and the King. And both the Indian National Congress and the Muslim League's Defence Committees can call on the help of the best legal minds in this country to protect INA patriots like you.'

'No matter how good they are or what they may do,' replied Chandra, 'the fact remains that all of us were in the INA fighting against the British. That, for the British, is an act of treason, which they cannot forgive. It is a laughable charge when you consider that we Indians do not regard the British King as our own. However, I think that if the British execute the INA leaders they will face a mutiny in the Army. So many thousands of sepoys are being cashiered or dismissed for being in the INA. Their comrades are unhappy about that because those poor men's families have suffered terribly in the years that they were away, effectively prisoners of the Japanese and not getting any pay. Now they have nothing. Our brothers in the armed forces, while not condoning the switching of sides by soldiers, will not want to see them punished too harshly now that the war has ended satisfactorily. The memories of the great mutiny of 1857 are still fresh in people's minds, Farooqui. You may remember that our people were blown from the mouths of cannons or were hanged without trial at the roadside for rising against the British. Those memories go deep within us Indians. The mood of the country has hardened after the war. Yes, some would agree that anyone who served in the INA should be punished for changing sides – but there is recognition, a belief I would say, that we were fighting for the cause of a free India – and a free India will be sympathetic to that. The INA leaders may, by their deaths, light the fire that burns the British out of India. If the Japanese can chase them out of Malaya we can chase them out of India.'

That afternoon, Chandra, his hands handcuffed behind his back, was taken in a covered truck to a military jail in the Delhi Cantonment. He sat impassively as the British soldiers escorting him heaped abuse and derision upon him. When they arrived, as he made to jump out of the truck, one of them tripped him so that he fell face first unable to break his fall with his hands. He lay dazed and bruised, his face scraped.

'The dozy Jiff bugger,' quickly exclaimed the guard who had done it, 'he slipped'. And they laughed as they hauled him to his feet. Jiff, was slang for Japanese Indian Fifth Column, the derogatory term for the INA men.

* * *

His father came to visit him in the military jail, accompanied by Basu, a Congress official dressed in white homespun cotton with a white fore and aft cap, the hallmark of the Indian National Congress. Chandra stooped and touched his father's feet in respect; he wanted to hug him but was unsure how this would be received. He noticed that his father kept his useless left hand tucked into the pocket of his *achkan*. Though they had met once before when he was allowed to visit at the Red Fort, Chandra still struggled with his emotions, watched coldly by the fair-haired British military policeman sitting in a corner of the room.

Basu was the replacement for the incompetent Farooqui. He was sent by the Indian National Congress's INA Defence Committee. He was a handsome young Bengali, clever, confident and with a very diplomatic manner which concealed a strong will. He was a political animal to his fingertips, and those nicotine-stained fingertips were always scissored around a lit cigarette. He was an Advocate, as Indian trained lawyers were called.

'I am not a famous London-trained lawyer, Chandra-ji,' he said in Hindi, introducing himself, but I have experience of handling these courts martial and I know enough about the law and the circumstances surrounding the creation of the INA to have constructed a good defence.'

'Speak in English,' ordered the guard.

'Sir,' said Basu smiling and shaking his head sympathetically, 'my English no very good. But also, as legal person for Mr Chandra, I must speak my client best way – to understand, eh? I have done legal person before – many, many times,' he emphasised this with a wide sweep of his arm. 'I am allowed to make consult in Hindi – you can ask Colonel Sahib if not believe.' The guard looked unsure. 'Go ask, Sir, go, go, I'm begging you,' urged Basu with a smile, waving his arms to usher the guard out.

'No. That's okay,' replied the guard, he didn't want to go trotting off to seek the advice of an officer only to be made a fool of in front of these natives.

'Basu looked suitably grateful, turned to Chandra and said, in Hindi, 'Arsehole! Don't worry, Chandra-ji, my English is quite fluent, Wynberg Allen School, Mussoorie and Presidency College, Calcutta. I just don't want my defence arguments conveyed to your prosecutors in advance of the court martial.'

Chandra liked this chap Basu.

'Right, to business,' said Basu. 'The Congress people especially value you for the work you did on the INA's planning. Your fellow INA officers have praised you for it and they have told me a little about your role in the planning. We want people like you, who have proved their worth as leaders, to help us with our struggle against the British. The Indian public regard you INA men as patriots for putting your lives at risk for our motherland; they will gladly follow your lead.' He looked at Chandra, who merely nodded. Basu continued. 'It will help if you tell me a little about what you did in the INA Chandra-ji. Speak in Hindi,' he inclined his head in the guard's direction.

Chandra told him, very briefly, about his involvement on the periphery of the organisation.

'You can speak truthfully to me, Chandra-ji; I need to know the facts – in confidence of course – in case the British bring them up at your court martial.'

Chandra looked hard at him. 'You want to know the truth Basu? Then ask yourself what, if anything, the INA achieved? It certainly saved the lives of thousands of surrendered Indian officers and sepoys from the brutality of the Japanese by agreeing to collaborate with them. But militarily the INA was a disaster; it utterly failed to liberate a single square inch of India from the British. Bose cleverly exploited its propaganda value – most of the reports of our exploits were overblown or blatant lies. Did you see the pictures in the papers of INA troops on Indian soil? Lies! They were actually taken in Bukit Timah in Singapore. Every minor skirmish became a 'great victory'. Bose devoted much of his time to creating Ministries for this and that – he had nobody of stature to fill the roles so filled them all himself. We Army officers mostly busied ourselves on inconsequential tasks, deciding on the language to be used, the anthems to be sung, the uniforms to be worn, the design of Azad Hind Rupees and stamps – idle, useless, pointless stuff – playing at Government! I went along with it to keep my head down. The more energetic and ambitious fellows went to Burma with their troops to try to invade India – a campaign that ended in humiliation and defeat, with many men dying of sickness and starvation. The most absurd act, for me, was the formation of a women's unit, the Rani of Jhansi Regiment, mostly made up of slender middle and upper class Tamil girls who Bose exploited for propaganda purposes and then sent to Burma to fight! Fortunately for the INA's reputation they weren't called upon to do so – though they proved to be useful and courageous in operating close to the front line to nurse the sick and wounded.'

Basu listened quietly to this outpouring, sucking ruminatively on his cigarette. 'How were you captured?' he asked.

'I was captured in Singapore when the British reappeared. I was betrayed by men who held a grudge against me. The British flew me to a holding camp at Jhingergacha, about sixty miles north east of Calcutta, before they took me to Calcutta and put me on a train to Delhi, where I was delivered to the Red Fort.'

'The British put you in the 'Black' category of INA men,' said Basu. Seeing Chandra's baffled look he explained. 'The British divide the INA prisoners into three colour-coded categories. 'Whites' they regard as simple fellows who had blindly followed their leaders. They will be returned to the ranks of their Regiments. 'Greys' are men who submitted to the pressure of their officers but who, the British believe, had also become indoctrinated with the ideas of the INA. They are being sent to special reconditioning camps before decisions are made on whether to allow them to return to their regiments. I hear that a lot are being weeded out and dismissed. Those categorised as 'Black' are men the British regard as hard-core INA, fundamentally disloyal and security risks. They will not under any circumstances be allowed to rejoin their regiments – they will be court martialled.'

Chandra digested this information. 'Look Basu, if you are asking me whether I regard myself in the Grey category rather than Black, the answer is no. I was heavily involved behind the scenes in planning and, despite my views on the effectiveness of the INA, I wouldn't want you to argue a case that shows me to have submitted to the pressure of other senior officers.'

Basu nodded, relieved. 'The result of the court martial is predictable, Chandra-ji. They will find you guilty, no question about it.' He looked for Chandra's reaction, but finding none continued, 'My aim is to minimise your punishment. We want to avoid you getting a long prison sentence, to avoid you being transported to the Andaman Islands to be removed from any contact. Do not be in any doubt that the British want to punish you, to set an example to the others.' He grinned at Chandra's sudden look of concern.

'Don't worry, Chandra-ji, they suspect that you are part of the INA leadership but they cannot prove it and your comrades are not going to say anything to incriminate you. But it does not help our Congress cause if you are locked away. We want you out there with our other leaders, speaking at public rallies, tackling the British administration, helping us to get the nation behind us in kicking the British out of our country. You are a hero!'

This was new and important information to Chandra. 'Are you saying that the Congress wants me to join them? '

'Yes. We have heard nothing but good things about you, and your father has been of such great support to us, helping us with funds to keep the struggle going. Don't you want to be part of it?'

Chandra looked at his father. In the glance that sparked between them he understood the opportunity that was being placed his way to help secure freedom for India and, in doing so, power and wealth for the family. Maybe fate was being kinder than he thought.

'So what will our defence be based on?' he asked.

'The tone should not be strident, but factual and dignified,' said Basu, rummaging in his leather bag for a sheaf of papers, smiling encouragingly at the military policeman who suddenly looked worried at what Basu might retrieve. 'We start with the assertion that the British effectively abandoned their Indian officers and men by handing them over to the Japanese at Farrer Park in Singapore on 17th February 1942, two days after the surrender.' He paused to light another cigarette, inhaling deeply and exhaling a slow and steady stream of smoke. 'As you may remember, there was one British officer there, a Lt. Colonel Hunt, and he, on behalf of General Percival, formally handed the 50,000 Indian officers and soldiers over to Major Fujiwara of the Imperial Japanese Army. The British had washed their hands of you. Fujiwara welcomed you as brothers, fellow Asians, and pledged Japanese support for the liberation of India.' Chandra nodded, he remembered. Basu continued, 'We will ask why there were no other senior ranking British officers present, only a mere Lt. Colonel? We will ask the court martial this. It is a great shame on the British. What else were all of you to do?'

'Could we not also say that we went over to the Japanese in order to try to help our British comrades by getting the Japanese to treat them better and being ready to overcome the Japanese if we got the chance?'

'No!' exclaimed Basu harshly, "if you say that, the British will laugh at you. Later on they will throw that back in your face to discredit you as a Congress-wallah. It is a weak defence, the defence of cowards! You have to make the British understand that *they* are guilty of dereliction of duty. How can *they* punish you when *they* have been responsible by abandoning you? Why did General Percival not refuse the Japanese request to separate the Indian troops from the British? Because the British didn't want you in their prisoner of war club, that's why. They didn't want Indians witnessing the humiliation of the *Burra Sahibs*.'

Chandra nodded. He admired Basu, he was a clever bugger.

'And,' continued Basu,' we will emphasise your good war record – facing the Japanese at Kota Bharu and giving them a serious setback, probably their greatest in Malaya. This was done by Indian troops, not by a British regiment. Then we will describe your part in the other battles as you retreated and, finally, describe your action against the Japanese at the defence of Singapore.'

I wasn't at that one,' said Chandra, 'I was in hospital with suspected appendicitis.'

'A more dangerous place, so far as I can gather,' replied Basu smoothly. 'You were at the mercy of the Japanese – many patients were killed by them in the hospitals. I presume that you escaped, probably in great pain?'

Chandra nodded.

'Then we come to the central issue of treason. My answer to that, an argument that I have used in these courts martial, is that you are not a free man under the British. Their King is not your king. Your loyalty may be to the Nawab of Delhi, or Lucknow, or wherever you live in India, to the dynasties that have ruled our country legitimately for centuries. How can you be charged with treason if the British have imposed their King on you? It is like saying that a captured German officer in a prison camp in England can be charged with treason against King George. Of course he can't. Hitler was still his leader, not King George! He is not a British national, neither are you! All of us are Indians; we are prisoners, captives of the British, who rule our country by force.'

* * *

The court martial did not take place for a few weeks until mid-January 1946. Basu, resourceful as ever, had successfully delayed it until the outcomes of the Red Fort trials of the first three INA leaders were known. Those trials, which the British would have liked to have held in private, away from the critical gaze of India, were widely reported in The Statesman and Hindu newspapers. They outlined the defence arguments and reported in detail the evidence of witnesses – which served only to support the case for the INA men and elevate them to heroic status with the public. The defendants, hitherto little known, became household names. The outcome of the trials was, as Basu said, predictable – the three INA leaders were found guilty of treason – but were not found guilty of murder or, except for one defendant, of abetment to murder. However, in the changing political climate, the British establishment realised that to condemn them to death or sentence them to transportation for life would be to invite nationwide unrest on an unprecedented scale, maybe even a mutiny in the armed forces. This could unleash a cataclysm, another 1857, that would drive the British, in their war-weakened state, ignominiously from their greatest Imperial possession.

A few days after the verdicts at the end of December the sentences were commuted on New Year's Day 1946 by the Commander-in-Chief, General Sir Claude Auchinleck, and the defendants were released. This caused a furore among the British, but for Basu and Chandra it was a clear sign of the likely outcome in Chandra's court martial.

And so it proved. The Judge Advocate, in his summing up to the Court Martial Board, said that Chandra had clearly acted to wage war against the King in joining the INA and in helping to plan its operations. But there were also mitigating circumstances: Chandra had a good war record, as officers from his Regiment had testified, and by all accounts was a respectable and respected Dogra officer who had set out at the beginning of the war to help his country.

They cashiered him, discharged him dishonourably from the Army – and set him free.

* * *

'Now,' said Basu as they walked outside the gates of the military establishment, 'your real work begins.'

Waiting out there with a car was a former Dogra sepoy who had served with Chandra in the INA and who had been sent by

Chandra's family to collect him and take him home. The sepoy salaamed.

'Welcome back, Chandra Sahib,' he said, but looked worried.

'What is it Dina Nath?' asked Chandra. 'This is not a time for a sad face. Basu *bhai* here says that we have much work to do.'

'It's Pierse Sahib,' said Dina Nath. 'He's back in the Regiment and he has said that he is going to find you and kill you.'

CHAPTER 10

The Turn of the Wheel

In January 1946, following the commutation of the sentences of the INA men, the political movement to get the British out of India intensified and unrest lay thick in the air. The British had all but given the Indians a pledge of independence after the war and the Indians were determined to redeem it. Millions of Indians were being de-mobbed from the Services or made redundant in war industries. They had no jobs to go to. The Congress and the Muslim League continued their pressure on the British to quit and rallies, riots and disorder were taking place around the country. Unfortunately, deep schisms were also appearing in the relationship between the Hindu-based Congress and the Muslim League as Jinnah, its leader, obdurately continued to press for a separate Muslim state.

Mohamed Ali Jinna was an unlikely advocate for a Muslim state. In dress, manner and culture he embodied the Victorian aesthete. He had gone to England to train as a barrister at the Inns of Court and had come back as an Englishman. He drank, ate pork and forsook the mosque. He was now a successful Bombay lawyer. He had rejected the idea of 'Pakistan', 'land of the pure', the creation of a separate Islamic state, when it was first proposed in 1933 by a Muslim graduate student, Rahmat

Ali. But the turning point came after the 1937 elections when Congress refused him a proportionate share of the power in those Provinces with a substantial Muslim population. He felt that he would never get a fair deal from a Congress-run India and devoted his energies to securing Pakistan.

Towards the end of February there was a mutiny in the Navy. Thousands of sailors in the Royal Indian Navy revolted, angry at their treatment by inept and bullying British officers. Dockside walls were plastered with 'Jai Hind' and 'British Quit India' slogans. The revolt spread to the cotton mills of Bombay, which came out on strike, sending excitable crowds surging on to the streets of the city. Over seven thousand sailors joined the uprising. There were riots and the crowds were fired upon by British units ordered to quell the disturbances. Over two hundred demonstrators were killed, and over a thousand injured. The mutiny was over three days later but it had shaken the Viceroy and his Government.

Morale was low among the British servicemen stationed in India. The 'Tommies' were disgruntled that it was taking so long to return them home to Blighty and demobilisation. There was outspoken resistance in the ranks to proposals to send some of them on to do duty further eastwards in Java. They just wanted to go home from this benighted country. It was feared that the misbehaviour and low morale of the British servicemen might infect the Indian troops. The Indian Army was wobbling. The British Indian Army was fed up. The Government didn't seem to have the will or the ability to keep the lid on the growing tension.

One evening, in the officers' mess, the Adjutant took Pierse aside and quietly dropped a bombshell.

'You were a friend of Chandra's, weren't you Pierse? I've heard this afternoon that he was found guilty of treason by the court martial.'

Pierse's heart beat faster. 'Has sentence been passed?'

'Yes – it's dreadful.'

'Death?' asked Pierse.

The Adjutant looked at him. 'No, it's worse than that. They've cashiered the bugger and let him go free!'

Pierse gasped. He felt the rage rise. But the Adjutant was not finished.

'He has gone off with those Congress-wallahs and we will no doubt be entertained in the newspapers to accounts of his speeches rallying the rabble and demanding that the British get out of India – just as that other INA bugger did a couple of weeks ago here in Jullundur. Those traitorous INA bastards are now national heroes – can you believe it? The whole thing makes me sick to my stomach!'

Pierse was speechless. Chandra had got away scot free. The cashiering and loss of pay would not trouble him in the slightest; his family was rolling in money. He felt despair and rage at the unfairness of it all, the bile choked in his throat.

Late that night, unable to sleep, his mind racing as he turned over the events of the past few years, he vowed he would have his revenge. Was this perhaps the 'guiding light' that Father Lawrence had spoken about in St. Xavier's? The reason for living, the goal he must attain? In his heart he knew that it was not. Ellen was his guiding light – he must find her. He decided that this could wait no longer and that he must apply for leave and go south to find her, or else quit the Army. He felt that the Regiment had changed beyond all recognition now. Almost every week saw one of his old officer colleagues leaving and new ones fresh from the Military Academy arriving to take their place. The pull of military life that he had hankered for seemed no longer to be there. It was time to move on.

The next morning he saw Jemadar Prem Singh. 'Have you heard about Mr. Chandra?' he asked.

Prem Singh looked away. At length he answered, 'Yes, Sahib.'

'From Dina Nath?'

'Sahib.' Prem Singh was uncomfortable. He too was angry at the injustice of it all. Chandra would profit from his treason and dishonour. One law for the rich. Nothing seemed to have changed in India.

'Then get a message to Dina Nath. Tell him to tell Chandra that I intend to settle my score with him.'

'He already knows,' said Prem Singh quietly. 'Be careful, Sahib. He has many eyes and ears – and many hands ready to do his dirty work for money.'

Pierse went to see the Colonel and, to the Colonel's surprise and considerable relief, told him that he now wished to accelerate his departure from the Army. He felt that he could wait no longer to go and see Ellen, to try to recover her, to rebuild his life. His discharge papers finally came through in April.

'What will you do now, Pierse Sahib?' asked Prem Singh.

'I'll have to find a job, Jemadar Sahib. But first I have some unfinished business to take care of.'

'You are not going to see Mr. Chandra, I hope, Sahib. That could be very dangerous now that he has become involved with those Congress-wallahs.'

'No, no.' Pierse was about to tell him about going to see Ellen but checked himself, realising that Prem Singh was unaware of the consequences of Chandra's cruel joke. Officers simply didn't discuss that sort of thing with the other ranks or with Viceroy's Commissioned Officers, no matter how respected. It was simply not done.

'No, I've got to go to south India to see a close friend who I've not seen since before the war.' He realised with a shock that he hadn't seen or spoken to Ellen for over five years.

The wily old Jemadar acknowledged this noncommittally. He knew all about the consequences of Chandra's action – there was a network of contacts around and outside the Regiment, many of them related by blood, so little happened that did not get back to him. He admired Pierse all the more for his stoicism. He would not have dreamt of embarrassing him by letting on that he knew about his domestic affairs.

'If I can be of service to you in any way, Pierse Sahib, please let me know.' Then, his composure slipping, 'You have been a good officer to me Pierse Sahib. The Regiment will not be the same without you.'

'I'll keep in touch Prem,' said Pierse, using the Jemadar's name familiarly for the first time.

Prem Singh, nodded, the affectionate touch had not escaped him. He felt that he would like to repay Pierse for his kindness and friendship – the best way would be to rid the world of Anil Chandra. But that was a forlorn hope. He extended his hand and shook Pierse's warmly, concealing the feeling of melancholy within him.

* * *

Pierse decided that he would not return to Calcutta but go directly to Coialla to try to see Ellen. He telephoned his parents to tell them of his plans. He could sense their disappointment and concern but they knew that he had to go south and see Ellen – though they feared the consequences of that meeting and its effect on their son. He also spoke to Kenny to tell him of his decision and to ask if he had any further news.

Kenny had debated whether to tell his brother of the encounter with Farrell – but had decided against it. Ed would have been angry at not being told Farrell was in town and in need of help. Clearly, Farrell had not said anything so he'd leave it at that.

'Remember what you promised, Ed,' said Kenny. 'No punch-ups. Just talk to her. No scenes; that sort of thing won't help.'

'Yes, of course, Kenny. I'm not a bloody fool. I've thought this through and realise that I will have to tread on eggshells when I see Ellen. Now you look after yourself with all these riots. We want you out of the police as fast as possible and into a proper job.'

Pierse had decided to travel light. 'I learned that on the Burma-Siam Railway,' he said to John the Adjutant, 'all I had was just a loincloth, my plate and mug and my trusty jack-knife – for which God bless Uncle Derek!' They gave him a farewell dinner in the mess, blessed him with fine speeches and anointed him with gallons of alcohol.

Hung-over and not feeling too well, he climbed on to the truck to take him to the railway station. A young officer hurried over. 'Captain Pierse, Sir!' he called, 'a letter for you.'

Pierse looked at it – a Calcutta postmark, from Sunny. He pocketed it to read on the train as a small group of sepoys, led by Jemadar Prem Singh bearing a garland, had assembled at the gate to see him off.

* * *

Pierse took a train south via Delhi – about the same time that Anil Chandra, dressed in homespun white cotton and surrounded by armed henchmen with Dina Nath in charge, was travelling to Calcutta to address a political rally on the *maidan*. And Farrell, stuck in a job he was thought he would hate in the jute mill in Dum Dum, was beginning to realise that he wanted to stay on in India, this glorious country, forever.

Pierse opened Sunny's letter. Sunny had learned of his decision to leave the Army and had written inviting him to come and spend a weekend on his return at the family's holiday home on the coast near Digha. He also mentioned that he had joined the Indian National Congress and had made his first speech on the *maidan*, but his father had sucked him deeper into the family empire and now he had little time for politics. He exhorted Pierse, tongue in cheek, to think about supporting the Congress in pressing the British for Independence. On a more helpful note, he had included the names and addresses of senior people in two big trading companies who would be happy to interview Pierse on his return and probably offer him a management position. Pierse detected the hand of Sunny's father here – rich and influential, he had known Pierse since he first went to St. Xavier's with Sunny and the old man, a hockey fanatic too, had come to see him play for Rangers against the big Calcutta clubs, Mohun Bagan and East Bengal.

He turned over the final page and was surprised to find a note from Suchi.

Dearest Eddie,

Sunny asked me to post his letter and doesn't know I'm writing this to you. The family has been putting pressure on me to have an arranged marriage and my Mother is not speaking to me at the moment because she is angry with me. However, against my wishes they have lined up a bridegroom and the deal has been signed so by the time I next see you I will be a married woman and will go off to live with my new husband in Dacca.

You remember the talk we had at your farewell party, when I told you that there was someone else that I wanted to marry? Ed, that someone is reading this letter. It has always been you ever since we first met as children. When I saw you at the party, I knew more than ever that this was not a schoolgirl crush. I think that you realised it too.

It has been hard to write this but I just have to tell you how I feel. I know Ellen broke your heart. I would have liked to have been able to mend it, Eddie, but caste and tradition would have been against us.

With love,

Suchi.

Pierse wondered at first if this was one of Suchi's jokes. But the recollection of his meeting with her, the glances, the hints he now understood told him otherwise. She was undeniably attractive, desirable, intelligent and fun. He had been friends with her for years, but was always aware that as a high-caste Bengali girl she was going to be married to someone of the same class and caste – a profitable alliance of two families. A childhood friendship between Suchi and a male Anglo-Indian was difficult enough – anything closer was absolutely out of the question. Her family, and his, would be horrified. It could never happen; she would be ostracised by her family and friends. He doubted that Ma and Da would be too happy if he was to marry an Indian girl.

He began to laugh, thinking about the absurdity of it all. Both he and Suchi were in search of the unattainable – the joke was that he had a slightly better chance of success. He put the letter back in his pocket and tried to forget about it but couldn't. Those lustrous eyes kept swimming round his thoughts, his head began to throb and the chill began to set in. 'Bugger,' he thought, the malaria was back.

CHAPTER 11

Coíalla Nights

'So you see, Sam, I'm in a bit of a fix,' concluded Pierse as they sat in the garden fending off the crows who were taking a deep interest in the bowl of peanuts on the table, set between the glasses of whisky. 'I want to see Ellen, but don't want her husband to know because I don't want to cause an upset.'

Father Sam thought about this. Finally, 'I'll ask Baldev to make enquiries at the school to establish Ellen's whereabouts and see if he can get a message to her. He's quite good at that sort of thing – and likes the intrigue.'

Pierse shook his head. 'No messages. I have to meet her; I have to talk to her. Don't want to scare her off.'

Father Sam stared at him with narrowed eyes while he pondered. He was quite enjoying the intrigue himself. 'I've never heard of the Taylors or seen them in church – must be RCs – or atheists! But I do know the Principal of the school very well. He's a very discreet sort of cove. I'll find out about the Taylors from him and see what can be done.'

'I don't want him to know about Ellen and me,' protested Pierse.

Father Sam nodded.

The next day Pierse insisted on accompanying Father Sam and Baldev in the car on the journey to the school. He promised to remain in the vehicle, discreetly out of sight in the car park but able to observe the comings and goings of the pupils and teachers. St Peter's School, founded by a philanthropic coffee planter, stood in large grounds. Its main building, in which the classrooms and the Principal's office were housed, was faced with white stucco, fronted by a classical portico, the school's crest emblazoned in the triangle above, with double-storied wings of classrooms extending either side, protected from the sun by long verandahs. Behind stood other large buildings in which the boarders were housed, surrounded on all sides by playing fields. Pierse watched the pupils arrive for the day, the boys in their khaki uniforms, the girls in blue gymslips and white blouses, blue ribbons in their hair. Most of the pupils were Indian, but there was a sizeable contingent of Anglo-Indian children of various hues from pink to brown. The noise built up like a late dawn chorus as children chatted or played. Presently, a bell clanged, the children converged on their classrooms and quiet descended. After twenty minutes, Father Sam emerged, striding purposefully to the car. He heaved himself in and turned to Pierse.

'She's gone!' he rasped. 'She and Taylor didn't come back from the Christmas holidays. Didn't say where they were going, didn't ask for references. Principal's pretty peeved about it.'

'But someone – one of the teachers – must know where she's gone,' said a bewildered Pierse, the penny dropping that Ellen had probably been tipped off by her family or by Pammy that he was looking for her.

'Thought of that too, old chap; asked the Principal who her friends were. Got a name, a Mrs. La Fontaine, kindergarten teacher – a widow – lives with her elderly father. Ellen and she were friendly apparently and,' he turned to Pierse with a conspiratorial wink, 'the Principal has heard through one of the other teachers that Ma La Fontaine has been forwarding letters to the Taylors!' he exclaimed gleefully.

'Where do I find Mrs. La Fontaine?'

'All in good time my boy. I've got her address. Baldev can take you there after school – she's in class just now. Don't know whether she'll tell you anything, she certainly isn't telling the Principal, but you can only do your best. The Principal is trying to find out through the schools system where the Taylors have gone; bound to be at another school – just a matter of time.'

* * *

Back at the vicarage a surprise awaited them. The police sergeant stood triumphantly on the verandah, Pierse's baggage at his feet and a constable in tow. In the sergeant's hand was a coarse jute shopping bag with Pierse's wallet and jack-knife.

Pierse excitedly went through his kit and his wallet. 'Most of it is here,' he exclaimed laughing incredulously, 'except the money, of course. How the Hell.....' he turned enquiringly to the sergeant who was grinning from ear to ear.

In halting English, the sergeant said that he had gone back from meeting Pierse and Father Sam and had detailed one of his men, in mufti, to keep watch on the *tonga* rank at the station, listening to the drivers talk, looking for anything suspicious. Nothing had transpired for a day until the observant constable – the very one here – noticed that one of the *tonga* drivers had a fountain pen in his top pocket. This was unusual – what use would an illiterate *tonga* driver have for a pen? They pulled him in to the police station, gave him the third degree, which involved beating the soles of his feet with a cane until he confessed. He was able to take them to the cheap hotel room of the man called Raju, who had attacked Pierse. Raju denied everything but a search of his room had uncovered the luggage and some of Pierse's other personal possessions. The money, unfortunately, had gone.

Raju, a known petty thief and all round thug, was also given the third degree. He eventually broke down and confessed that he had seen an opportunity to follow the sick white Sahib off the train from Delhi, beat him and steal his luggage. He had not disposed of the stolen goods as he was waiting for the police investigation to blow over.

'This sounds very far-fetched,' said Father Sam tetchily. 'It doesn't make sense, none at all. First of all, the Indians rarely attack Sahibs – though I suppose that can't entirely be relied on because of the Quit India feelings. Second, a common thief would have sold on the goods within hours – and why was he in a hotel?'

'I'd like to see this Raju again,' interjected Pierse. 'I'd like to ask him a few questions, find out a bit more about him. Is he a Congress-walla? I hope he is not one of Anil Chandra's people trying to scare me – or otherwise have me killed.'

'That is absurd,' growled Father Sam. 'This is supposed to be a local chap, how would he recognise you? And I doubt that you would have been followed all the way down here.'

The sergeant was trying to follow this conversation. He interrupted to say that the *tonga* driver had confessed to helping himself to Pierse's pen, unknown to Raju. After Raju had attacked Pierse they had thought he was too seriously injured and might die. They didn't want to be had up for murder. So, as their victim was a Christian, they took the body and dumped it in the church porch to be found by the church's servants.

'Can I see Raju?' asked Pierse.

The sergeant shook his head. 'He is in Tihar Jail Sahib. Nobody can see him just now.'

After the sergeant and constable departed, promised a

reward by Pierse when his money came through, Baldev came into the room. 'He is liar, Sahib,' he said darkly to Father Sam. 'I am not believing his story. I find out.'

Though pleased that he had recovered his possessions, Pierse remained troubled by the nagging possibility that there might have been more to it than just a street robbery. He remembered Prem Singh's warning that Chandra had eyes and ears everywhere and willing hands to do his dirty work.

* * *

That evening he was driven by Baldev to a road behind the school to find the widow La Fontaine. The car pulled up outside a small, white-washed bungalow, its corrugated roof painted brown. It was set in a colourful, well-tended garden shaded with peepul and gul mohur trees; cascades of bright pink and orange bougainvillea fringed the red-tiled verandah on which a woman was playing with a dachshund. At the sound of Pierse walking through the gate the woman looked up. She was very attractive, thought Pierse, slim, with thick curling black hair that framed a pale face – and she had beautiful green eyes.

'Excuse me,' said Pierse, I'm looking for Mrs. La Fontaine.'

'And who are you?' asked the woman coolly.

'My name's Pierse, Edwin Pierse, and I've been told that she may know where I can contact a Mr. and Mrs. Alec Taylor.'

The woman stood up, looked him over and then smiled warmly. 'I wondered when you'd come,' she said. 'I'm Marion La Fontaine.' She laughed at Pierse's surprise. 'Were you expecting someone older?'

He shook his head in confusion. She grinned. 'Come in Edwin Pierse, I've been expecting you.'

'Did the Principal tell you I was coming?' enquired Pierse.

She shook her head. 'Ellen told me about you and I guessed

that it was only a matter of time before you arrived. I expected you a lot sooner.'

Sending Baldev back to the vicarage, Pierse followed Marion La Fontaine into the bungalow, trying not to step on the dachshund, called Mitzi, who darted between their legs. This was turning out to be an eventful day.

'Tea or cold *nimbu pani*?' asked Mrs La Fontaine.

'I'd prefer a whisky,' said Pierse half jokingly.

She arched her eyebrows, smiled, 'Of course. In that case I'll get Daddy in from the garden – he does all the gardening, you know, now that he's retired. You'll have to speak loudly to him, he's a little hard of hearing – all those years of noisy machines in the textile mill he managed.' Pierse noticed that she had a dimple in her right cheek when she smiled.

When she went off to summon her father, Pierse took in the room: teak furniture, lacy antimacassars covering the tops of the cushions, vases filled with fresh flowers, upright piano against one wall – presumably deaf Dad didn't play, but the charming Mrs. La Fontaine did. Photographs of relatives stood on top of the piano, a brightly coloured picture of the Sacred Heart over the door with a glowing little red glass oil lamp in front of it – almost a staple of Roman Catholic Anglo-Indian houses – and two large, framed photographs on the wall. One an older woman, he guessed she might be Mrs. La Fontaine's late mother, the resemblance was there; the other a good-looking, smiling young man, sandy haired, in army uniform – presumably the late Mr La Fontaine. Pierse went up close but couldn't make out the regiment, but the pip on his shoulder indicated that he was a Second Lieutenant.

'My late husband,' said Mrs. La Fontaine unnecessarily as she came back in from the garden. 'Daddy will be along in a few minutes, he has to get cleaned up.' She went to a sideboard and got out a bottle of whisky and a couple of glasses.

'What happened?' asked Pierse, indicating the late Mr La Fontaine.

'He was with the Chindits, never came back from Burma. Ambushed by the Japanese in '43,' she said evenly. 'Such a waste; Neil was only twenty five. We hadn't been married long.' She filled the glasses with whisky, gave him one of them, raised the other, nodded in salute and took a sip.

'You know that I'm looking for Ellen?' asked Pierse.

She nodded. 'Yes, she told me the whole story. Terrible tragedy.'

'Did she think so?'

'What do you think?'

'I won't beat about the bush Mrs. La Fontaine...'

'Please, Edwin, call me Marion.'

'Marion, everyone calls me Ed – or Pierse.' He smiled. 'I need to know where she is, I need to talk to her,' he said calmly, he didn't want to sound as if he was pleading.

She looked at him and smiled. 'Ellen doesn't want to be found by you. You can understand why.'

Just then, into the room came the Dad, a surprisingly tall and robust man. He introduced himself simply as Andrew.

'She tells everybody I'm going deaf,' said Andrew amiably in a voice that was slightly too loud, 'but you don't need to shout, I can hear most things and lip read quite well; had to, to be able to have a conversation in that bloody mill.' He helped himself to a whisky.

'Ed was Ellen's fiancé before the war, he's trying to find her, Daddy,' said Marion by way of explanation.

'Ah!' said Andrew. 'So you're the chap. Don't think she wants you to find her.'

'When she heard that you were back from the war and not killed, as she had been told, it was an enormous shock for her,' said Marion kindly.

'I know,' acknowledged Pierse. 'I understand why she got

married. I just want to talk to her now I'm back. Maybe we can put things right – I don't know. I just can't leave it like that – unfinished.'

'She was very distressed when she heard that you were safe after the war – no, I'll rephrase that, it came out wrong.' The laugh tinkled. 'She was distressed that she had taken the decision to marry thinking you were dead. She knew how upset you would be when you found out.'

'Do you know where she is?' asked Pierse bluntly.

Marion hesitated, looked at her father then bowed her head. 'Yes. But I can't tell you, I really can't. I promised Ellen.'

'Not even to right a wrong?' asked Pierse, his voice rising, his frustration showing. She looked startled by his tone and he realised that he had upset her. 'I'm sorry,' he said, 'I didn't mean to. But I only got through the war, imprisonment and bad times because I believed that Ellen and I would be together after it. You can't begin to imagine my disappointment at not being able to see her.'

'I well understand disappointment,' Marion retorted, stung by his tone. 'I waved goodbye to my husband and never saw him again. His body was never found. The last person who saw Neil saw him being used for bayonet practice by the Japanese. Yes, I understand disappointment – I live it every day.'

Before Pierse could answer, her father leant over and patted his daughter on the arm.

'Marion,' he said quietly, 'don't upset yourself. Poor Pierse here has to have an answer.'

She stood up. 'Sorry Mr Pierse. We shouldn't be quarrelling. Ellen didn't want you to find her because she doesn't want to destroy her marriage. Her husband, Alec, has been very good to her. She is afraid of what might happen if you found her.'

'I just want to talk to her, to see her once more and to find out if there is any chance for me. If she doesn't want to come back to me I'll have to understand and accept it.' His eyes were prickling with tears and he hated himself for losing control of his emotions, he didn't want to have to grovel to this young woman.

'Look,' she said, softening, 'let me think about it for a while – it's a difficult decision to make and I don't want to betray my friend's confidence or be responsible for breaking up her marriage. Let's talk about it again.'

Pierse stood up to take his leave, bitterly disappointed, holding down his frustration.

'Tell you what Pierse,' said Dad Andrew, 'come and have dinner with us tomorrow evening. We don't get many visitors here these days, and I'd like to know a bit about the war – I'm sure you would too Marion.'

Marion smiled at Pierse. 'Will you?' she asked somewhat coquettishly, touching his arm.

* * *

Father Sam puffed on his cigar and listened reflectively to Pierse's tale of the meeting as they sat in the garden having their after dinner drinks. 'If I'd known the husband was a Chindit I would have gone and seen her, talked about Burma. Didn't know the chap, wasn't in my unit. The story of his death doesn't surprise me at all – they were cruelty incarnate, the Japanese. Different culture, I suppose.' He waved his fingers in the air at Pierse, each of them shortened at the first joint by his Japanese torturers, 'All for giving them a two-fingered V-sign. Makes it harder to do now,' he grinned and did one, 'but still effective.'

'What shall I do Sam?' asked Pierse. 'She won't tell me Ellen's whereabouts, it is torturing me.'

Father Sam raised his eyebrows at the word. 'Look Pierse, you are going to have to play her like a fish on the line. Delicately but firmly try to reel her in. You may not succeed, but at least you will have had a damn good try.'

'Softly, softly, catchee monkey, eh?'
'That's the one.'

* * *

Pierse turned up at Mrs La Fontaine's the next evening with a bouquet of flowers, a box of cakes from the local baker and a generously donated bottle of Father Sam's scotch. Dinner was a convivial success. The food was good, the conversation wide-ranging. Pierse told them about the war in Malaya and his subsequent captivity, leaving out the gruesome bits. He mentioned that Father Sam had also served in the Chindits, Chaplain to the troops trying to cut off the enemy's supply lines in Burma. He conveyed an invitation from Father Sam for Marion and Andrew to visit him – which was enthusiastically accepted.

Marion talked of her husband, Neil, who, to Pierse's surprise, had been a professional musician – a clarinettist in a hotel swing band in England – before being sent to war in India. Marion had met him in Bangalore where she was teaching, they had shared a common love of music. After dinner she played the piano and sang 'There'll be bluebirds over the white cliffs of Dover,' and 'Danny Boy' – her father's favourite she explained, because he was Irish.

'And where does the La Fontaine come from?' asked Pierse.

'Neil's family were originally French, they came to England from France in the 1600s to escape persecution by the Catholics – they were French Protestants, Huguenots. They settled in London. The irony is that Neil converted to Catholicism before we got married.'

As midnight drew near, Andrew declared that he was tired after trying so hard to keep up with the conversation. He said that he was off to bed and would leave Marion and Pierse, 'you young people', to talk. Pierse wondered who was playing who like a fish.

They sat out on the dim verandah on a cane sofa, drinking

whisky and soda. Clouds chased a faint moon, the pinpricks of stars bejewelled the sky, veiled and then revealed in the passing whisper of a breeze. There was a scent of jasmine in the air. Marion asked Pierse why he had been reported as killed in action.

'It was someone's idea of a joke,' Pierse replied, 'a very calculated and cruel joke which, as you can see, has had quite an effect.'

'Do you know who did it?' asked Marion.

Pierse hesitated then told her the tale of Anil Chandra. She was shocked.

'The worst of it all,' said Pierse bitterly, 'is that this INA turncoat is now apparently to be an Indian National Congress politician and will stand to profit when the British eventually leave India.'

'Do you think they will go?' she asked.

'Oh yes; and quite soon. The regiments are shedding their British officers in anticipation – the Indianisation of the regiments had already started before the war – and the British Government has people working on the plans for the withdrawal. A three-man mission arrived from England in March to draw up plans for a new state which Indians would operate. I don't know what the future will hold for people like us – we Anglo-Indians.'

'Neil and I were planning to go back to England after the war,' she said sadly. 'That's all gone now.'

'Can I talk about Ellen?' asked Pierse tentatively.

She smiled, 'Yes, of course. Only don't press me to tell you where she's gone. I'm still thinking about that.'

'How was she?' asked Pierse. I haven't seen her for over five years. Have you any photographs of her?'

Marion shook her head, 'She is very well, very attractive, she...' turning to look Pierse in the eye, 'she knows that she made a big mistake, you know. She talked about you a lot.'

'When did she find out? About me being alive?'

'She got a telegram from her parents – they must have heard from yours. And a couple of months later a friend of hers in Calcutta wrote to say that you were looking for her.'

'Pammy,' Pierse thought. 'So what happened then?'

'She felt that she couldn't see you and was worried about the effect on Alec – and I think that Alec was worried too. So they decided to leave Coialla in the Christmas holidays and tell no one about it.'

'Except you?'

Marion nodded. 'She trusted me and she needed someone to forward her letters – she didn't want people to know where she and Alec were going.'

'Is she unhappy?'

'She's happily married to Alec, they are a devoted couple. But she is also very hurt – she is very upset that what she did, and did in good faith, has had such terrible consequences. She once said that she felt she had been disloyal.' Laying her arm on Pierse's, 'You mustn't get your hopes up, Ed. She's married now. You need to accept that she's gone and get on with finding your own happiness.'

Pierse could feel her fingers caress his bare forearm. She continued.

'There are lots of us damaged by the war – me too. We have to pick up the pieces and try to make new lives.'

Pierse didn't answer.

She slid her arm round his shoulder, pulled him to her and kissed him. He sat there, surprised, but not resisting. Who was reeling who in?

'Come,' she said, taking his hand and rising from the sofa, they walked across the verandah and she opened a door into her bedroom.

She kissed him passionately in the dark. He found himself responding. Then conscience got the better of him.

'I can't Marion. I mustn't. It would be betraying Ellen.'

'And where do you think she is just now?' she asked quietly.

* * *

He walked back to the vicarage in the early hours, guilty, elated and confused. She had been sweet, understanding and passionate. Pierse felt that some part of him had been set free. Oh God, this was becoming tangled and difficult. Marion wanted him – they needed each other, she had said, and he had enjoyed making love to her – it was his first time. Yet Suchi too had said that *she* loved him – he had put that to the back of his mind as a schoolgirl crush and because of the impossibility of it all, because of the great upset that it would cause in both families. But, thinking about it, he had grown up with Suchi and knew her well, she was lovely, intelligent and yes, he knew that he had always had feelings for her. And yet.... and yet: the one woman he had given his heart to could not – perhaps would not – give hers to him in return.

Father Sam, amused, surveyed him over the breakfast table. He had become engrossed in Pierse's life, liked him, enjoyed his company and didn't really want him to leave.

'Enjoyed the evening?' he teased. 'I heard you coming in at 2 o'clock – so you must have had a good time. Did you get what you wanted out of the merry widow?'

Pierse grinned. 'She was very accommodating Sam but, unfortunately, didn't give me Ellen's address. I'll have to go and see her again this evening – taking her to the pictures.'

'Is the softly-softly approach working?'

'Too early to tell.'

From the look on Pierse's face, Father Sam's instincts made him wonder who was catching whom.

* * *

The days clocked by; they went to the pictures, met for dinner, went on weekends to the hills, Pierse even met her friends. He was slowly being pulled apart. He was becoming more deeply involved with Marion, yet he tried hard to remain detached, to force himself to realise that this was a game of wills. Marion wanted him, but he craved information about Ellen's whereabouts. He struggled to remain true to the 'guiding light', the sense of purpose that Father Lawrence in St Xavier's had told him to find. For Pierse, that guiding light was Ellen – but should he now abandon it?

One Saturday morning at the vicarage, Father Sam, accompanied by Baldev, came to him. 'Baldev has some news, Pierse.'

'Oh?'

'You know that he didn't believe the story the police sergeant gave us about your luggage so he has been nosing about the town, asking questions. He found out that the man Raju, is not in jail and never has been. He does not even live in Coialla.' He watched for Pierse's reaction and was rewarded by a look of incomprehension and surprise. 'So last night Baldev had what he might call an 'off duty chat' with our police sergeant – you and I would call it outright thuggery. Baldev can be very persuasive. Anyway, the fellow confessed that there was more to your attack than he told us.'

'What do you mean?'

'The man Raju *had* followed you off the train and saw his opportunity when you were clearly unwell with the malaria. It looks like the police sergeant and Raju – if that's his name, which I doubt – were in on this together. It is not clear whether they were operating a bit of a scam of their own, preying on vulnerable travellers new in town, or whether they were acting under orders from someone else. The sergeant's job was to make sure that any police investigation went nowhere. But when Baldev became a little too insistent and started turning up at the police *thana* every day, he panicked and decided to retrieve your goods, keeping the money of course, then return them with a cock-and-bull story so that you were happy and the matter would end there – especially when you were told that they had arrested the people responsible.'

'It did,' replied Pierse, 'I thought that the matter was done.'

'But Baldev wasn't convinced. There was something too pat about the sergeant turning up with most of your stuff. So he did a bit of investigating of his own.'

Baldev stepped forward and handed Pierse a wad of notes. 'Your money, Pierse Sahib; I made the sergeant give it up – and a bit more Sahib, for hurting you.'

'I can't take anything extra!' protested Pierse.

'Oh! Then we'll put it in the church poor box,' said Father Sam with a disarming smile.

Pierse laughed, 'That's thievery!'

'Smiting the Pharisees old lad,' replied Father Sam amiably.

'What has happened to the sergeant? Has he been arrested? Won't Baldev get into trouble for assaulting him?'

'Baldev let him go – with a warning,' replied Father Sam. 'You know, Baldev has friends around the place, ex-sepoys like him, who make any action by the police unlikely.'

Pierse shook his head in wonderment and thanked Baldev effusively.

'Pierse,' said Father Sam kindly, 'you've been here nearly a month. Now you've got your possessions back are you planning to stay on in Coialla or move back home to Calcutta? Your people will be getting anxious about you.'

Pierse understood that Father Sam was, in his own subtle way, forcing the issue. Baldev's news had been unsettling – it was possible that Chandra knew where he was and his life could be in danger. Time to move on.

'You're right, Sam,' he said guiltily, 'I've more than outstayed my welcome and imposed on your very kind generosity for long enough. I'd better move on tomorrow. I've got an Aunt, my mother's sister, up in the hills in Munnar, in the Western Ghats. Her husband, Bertie, is the manager of a tea factory. I used to spend summers there and they wrote to me in Cal inviting me to come and stay with them for a while. I might just do that as it is close by – and then go back home.'

Later that morning, Pierse and Marion were in the botanical garden, picnicking under the shade of a rain tree while the dachshund rooted around in the shrubbery. They sat on a *dhurrie*, eating their lunch and drinking cold beer.

'Marion, there's something I need to say.'

'Yes?' she turned to him expectantly.

'I'm leaving Coialla tomorrow.'

She looked thunderstruck. 'Why?'

'I came down here to find Ellen. I've drawn a blank so it's time to look elsewhere.' He had rehearsed the words carefully.

She was furious. 'You bastard,' she shrieked, 'you've used me. All this lovey-dovey stuff – you didn't mean any of it!' She jumped up.

'That's not true, and you know it. If anything it was you who strung me along – remember? You needed time to think about whether to disclose her address to me. Has it really needed all this time?'

'But....I....us,' she was in tears. 'I thought that we had an understanding – I thought that you had feelings for me!' She was sobbing. Pierse stood there awkwardly. She turned towards him, 'I really thought you cared for me,' she wept, 'you've just taken advantage of me.'

'Marion,' he said, 'I do care for you. I have been so happy with you. I was honest with you in saying that I had to find

Ellen, to know where I stood with her. You knew that. Why did you not tell me where she was; or why didn't you say that you would never let me know her whereabouts.'

'I gave her my word!'

'Then you should have said at the beginning that you had no intention of telling me. That would have been honest.'

They drove back to her bungalow in silence. A stony-faced Marion looked pointedly out of the window, clutching the dog close to her. Pierse ached to comfort her, to be friends again, to tell her that if Ellen rejected him he would like to come back to her, but he just sat silently, lost in his thoughts.

She jumped out of the car and made straight for the front door, not looking at him, not saying 'goodbye'. She had hoped that Pierse would realise that his pursuit of Ellen was pointless and likely to fail. She found herself unexpectedly being attracted to him, she felt she already knew him well from what Ellen had confided to her about him. It had seemed a chance for the two of them, both torn by war, to make a new beginning – he seemed just right – even Ellen had jokingly said so. She had hesitated over giving him Ellen's address because she was afraid that once he had got it he would leave. Now he was leaving anyway and he mistrusted her.

* * *

That evening Pierse sat in the vicarage garden for the last time with Father Sam.

'It has been a wild goose chase, Sam,' said Pierse wearily. 'It's left me feeling even more depressed. The stupid thing is that I really like Marion La Fontaine and, if Ellen...'

'No woman wants to be second best in a man's affections, Pierse. She saw a chance for happiness with you and I suppose she wanted to keep you to herself. What will you do now?'

'I'll have to go back to Cal before too long and start looking for a job. I really should have put the feelers out before I left the Army but I've been distracted by my search. Do you think I'm stupid to pursue it Sam?'

Father Sam shrugged. 'It's a driving force, a bit like religion, I suppose. You believe in it so you do it, even though your rational self may say otherwise. I just hope it works out successfully for you, though, as a clergyman, I can't condone splitting up marriages.' He laughed, his paunch shaking with the effort.

They sat in contemplative silence, listening to the crickets in the garden borders and the sounds of the town – the constantly honking horns and the tinny, sharp and loud amplified devotional music coming from the park.

'I can't thank you enough Sam for taking me in and looking after me so generously,' said Pierse.

Father Sam looked at him. 'You know, Pierse, I've really enjoyed your company; oh, and all the shenanigans with the widow La Fontaine!' He laughed. 'I hope you will find your way down here again. I wouldn't like to lose touch with you – so do write. By the way, I heard on the radio this evening that the British Cabinet Mission has presented a plan for a unified India and Jinna, the Muslim League fellow, he has been agitating up to now for a separate Mohammedan state, has accepted the plan – looks like the end of the Raj is nigh. God Save the King – and God save all of us!' They clinked glasses.

The next morning they were saying their goodbyes when Baldev came into the room. 'Letter for Pierse Sahib,' he said, 'La Fontaine driver bring it.'

Father Sam and Pierse looked at each other in surprise as Pierse took the envelope from Baldev.

'Let's hope the merry widow has relented,' said Father Sam.

Pierse read the letter and laughed mirthlessly.

CHAPTER 12

The Rough Road to Power

Sitting in the shade by the swimming pool, eating a breakfast of *halva puris* and coffee after a morning's visit to the temple, Anil Chandra relaxed with his father. It had been over a month since the trial and Chandra Senior had insisted that his son spend time recuperating from his ordeals – the war, the INA and his incarceration – before girding himself up to support the Indian National Congress in their struggle with the British. Father and son had taken this time to get to know each other better. The father, his health failing, was anxious to pass on to his son the secrets and skills of running the family business – and also to begin casting around for a suitable bride for him. Gone was the 'dominant father, subservient son' relationship of old. The once wayward young man had turned out to be tougher, more resilient and more cunning that his father had expected and it delighted him. The Gods had indeed been kind and had turned a thorny path into one potentially strewn with roses.

'We have a chance to be in at the start of a great opportunity when the British leave,' said Chandra Senior to his son. 'Not only can we take over British owned land and companies at cheap prices, but we can also help to be part of the discussions and decisions that shape the new India. It is a chance for you, my son, to gain power and prestige – and with that will come wealth and influence.' He smiled benignly. 'Vishnu and Shiva have guided your path. They have tempered you in the fires of hell. You have been chosen by them to found a great dynasty for the Chandra family.'

Anil Chandra was used to his father's rhetoric. But he agreed with the sentiments. It was a heaven-sent opportunity and he meant to grab it with both hands.

'But you must also be careful,' continued his father. 'There are many out there who will try to stop you, to push you aside in their own scramble for power.'

Chandra agreed. His first concerns were of Pierse; he now regretted his moment of stupidity and carelessness that had turned a close friend into a devilish enemy. He did not underestimate the danger – it was too horribly real. But he had planned for that too, and Dina Nath led a team of bodyguards, most of them armed and well paid Delhi *goondas,* to ensure that he did not come to any harm. Tomorrow there was a big rally in the Punjab, and he, Chandra, was to make his debut as one of the speakers. The Congress officials had wisely decided to try him out on a smallish gathering so that he could practice his oratory.

'You are a hero,' Basu had said with a flick of his cigarette. 'Remember, whatever you say to the crowd, they will applaud you. Just be passionate, Chandra-ji. They will respond to passion.'

* * *

The next evening he sat on a brightly illuminated bamboo platform that was swathed in Congress flags, before a crowd of around four thousand people, awaiting his turn to speak. Two Congress-wallahs had already done their stuff, working themselves into a frenzy, gesticulating wildly and making gratuitously insulting remarks about the British. It had all gone down well with the crowd. It was now Chandra's turn and he was nervous. He didn't feel that he was able to replicate the hysteria of the first two – that was simply not in his nature. He knew his short speech off by heart – he had asked Basu to help with it, in the end Basu had written most of it.

They were announcing him and there was a welcoming roar from the crowd. He got to his feet, feeling awkward in the white homespun kurtha and pyjamas, nervous also that the slightly too big white fore-and-aft Congress cap might sail off his head and into the crowd in the faintest waft of a breeze. The man who had announced him, a local leader, garlanded him with marigolds and jasmine and ushered him forward to stand in front of the microphones. The view from there was, if anything, more intimidating. A sea of squatting people applauding and shouting – the whites of their clothes reflected starkly in the harsh light of the petromax lamps strung up round the *maidan* that was the venue for the meeting. As he stood there, his palms together in a respectful *namaste*, he could smell the crowd, a strong almost pungent animal smell mingled with the metallic smell of dust – these were country people and it was the hot season.

The cheering died down and the crowd looked expectantly up at him. He spoke Basu's words – startled at first by the amplified and unfamiliar sound of his own voice echoing from the tinny loudspeakers. He began quietly, slowly building up the volume, as Basu had tutored him. It was all basic stuff: I'm Anil Chandra, an officer in the Indian National Army. I sacrificed everything to fight for freedom. I abandoned the defeated army of the British *sarkar* to fight with the *Japani* to liberate our motherland. After the war the British imprisoned me and mistreated me – because they feared people like me who were fighting to throw them out. We must all join together and kick the British out of our country so that we Indians can take control over our own destiny. You should not be afraid, even though it will be hard; no struggle is easy. But we will win in the end – the British are already a defeated people. He concluded with some stirring words from Subhas Chandra Bose, the founder of the INA and shouted 'Jai Hind' and 'Chalo Delhi' – the INA slogans. They cheered enthusiastically. He waved at them, relieved it was over. The next speaker came on.

Speaker after speaker said essentially the same thing. The emotion built up and then, suddenly, the meeting was over and they played religious music over the Tannoy. The organisers of the meeting congratulated him – they seemed in awe of him because he was an INA man.

Over the next few weeks he made a number of speeches at small-town Congress rallies; he had become used to the format, more sure of himself now. But that was it! Nothing more seemed to be happening. No invitations from the Congress hierarchy to participate in their decision making or to join their committees. He was getting frustrated at being an INA turn, something of an oddity to entertain the crowd – a warm up act. He spoke of his frustration to Basu and to his father. Both urged him to be patient. His father, more pragmatic, began pulling strings and greasing palms.

Basu telephoned him one evening in great excitement. 'Chandra-ji,' he shouted, 'you have been chosen to speak at a big rally here in Delhi. It is a very important one with many Congress leaders of national fame. And the main speaker there will be Jawaharlal Nehru – our Congress No.1!'

This was the opportunity Chandra had been waiting for, to mix with the senior Congress people and to make himself known to them, to have them hear him speak. He decided that he would work carefully on his speech so that they could see that he was not just a soldier but also a man of intelligence – an ideal combination for them to have running India when the British left.

* * *

The huge Delhi *maidan* held an enormous crowd, all eager to be part of the making of history as the nation slowly moved towards freedom. They had been drawn by the chance to see their Congress heroes in the flesh and to hear their stirring words. People could sense that the time had come for India to shake off the foreign rulers who had dominated them for so long. They looked forward to an India where they would be in charge – maybe where the taxes would not be so high and where people did not have to bow and scrape to the *laat sahibs* and their imperious memsahibs.

Behind the rostrum there was a crowd of Congress leaders and officials, all waiting expectantly. Chandra was there, Basu at his side. The excitement rose and rippled through the crowd as the star attraction, Jawaharlal Nehru, appeared wearing well-tailored homespun with his trademark rose in his buttonhole and a white Congress cap on his well-barbered head. He was dapper and handsome, elegant, clever and sophisticated, with huge drive and self-discipline and an insatiable hunger for power. Born into a wealthy Kashmiri family, he was educated in England – at Harrow and Cambridge – and had trained as a Barrister at the Inns of Court in London. Gandhi was his mentor and it was no surprise that Nehru had become the leader of the Indian National Congress and was likely to play a leading role in the free India. Chandra desperately wanted to meet him.

The speakers lined up ready to make their way on to the rostrum and Nehru came down the line to greet them. Eventually he stood before Chandra, who was introduced with the explanation that he was an 'INA hero'. Nehru just said, 'Oh,' in a matter of fact tone. His eyes narrowed – whether in contempt or indifference it was hard to say. Then he moved on. Chandra felt deflated.

When Chandra's turn came to address the crowd, he gave them the speech he had so carefully prepared to impress the Congress leaders. He spoke of the history of Indian conquest from Alexander to the Mughals and finally the British. Telling the crowd how each had given something to India but had taken far more in return. He spoke of the Japanese, declaring themselves friends of their Asiatic brothers and willing to help the INA free their motherland from the British yoke. But, Chandra, said, they too had turned out to be just another set of Imperialists intent on subjugating other nations. He concluded that the future of India must lie in Indian hands – where Indians gave to their country but didn't take from it anything other than pride. He ended, as he had learned from studying speakers at the rallies he had so far attended, on a passionate high, his voice loud and commanding his gestures forceful. He sat down to muted applause.

His was disappointed with the crowd's reaction, but he had not written this speech for the crowd. He hoped that Nehru and the Congress high-ups would be impressed – any fool could do a rabble rousing speech, for him this was not the occasion for it.

Finally, Nehru stood up to speak, waiting two or three minutes for the applause to die down as the crowd went wild. Then he spoke. It was measured, yet passionate, rousing but not hysterical. It was a masterful speech, Chandra realised, aimed cleverly at several audiences. Though Nehru spoke to the vast Delhi crowd before him, there were messages for the people of India, warnings for the Viceroy and his Government, coded warnings for the leaders of the Muslim League, whose relationship with Congress was beginning to disintegrate, and messages for the world to show that this was the man, the statesman, they would have to deal with, to do business with, when India was finally free.

As they milled around in the tented pavilion behind the rostrum after the rally, Chandra felt despondent. There was so much more to politics than he realised and getting entry to the inner circle was going to be extremely difficult, if not impossible. He poured out his concerns to Basu, saying that he feared that he was not cut out for politics after hearing Nehru's mastery of his audience.

'He is a trained barrister,' Basu replied, 'he has had lots of experience in making speeches and he has been part of the struggle for many years – going to prison several times for making provocative anti-British speeches. You are a soldier – he couldn't do what you were trained for. It takes time, and practice Chandra-ji. Imagine you are speaking to your sepoys – speak from the heart.'

'This is not a debate in St Stephen's College,' said a voice. Chandra turned to find a kindly looking man, who had been standing behind him listening to the conversation with some amusement. He introduced himself as Rajendra Prasad. 'Remember, Mr Chandra, this is not a debate, not a history lesson. It is a struggle for the heart of India.' With a smile he was gone.

The next day a telephone call came through from an official in the Indian National Congress head office. Dr Prasad wanted Chandra on a committee to plan for the transition of power from the British. He had heard of Chandra's planning abilities from INA colleagues and he had been impressed by Chandra's intellectually thoughtful speech. Chandra put down the telephone, scarcely able to speak. He turned to his father, and dropped down to touch his feet. This was what they had hoped for, and more. For the first time in many years he felt intense excitement and contentment. God was good. He would begin work the next day.

* * *

In July, Chandra attended a meeting of the All India Congress Committee which had gathered to decide whether to approve the Cripps Cabinet Mission proposals. Jinna and his Muslim League colleagues had agreed to them, albeit with much reluctance. Cripps proposed an All-India Union which would preserve a unified India, within which there would be three Provinces, each with its own provincial government. One province would encompass Bombay, Madras, Orissa and the United and Central Provinces – overwhelmingly Hindu. The second would cover Punjab, Sind, Baluchistan and the North West Frontier Province –predominantly Muslim areas. The third would cover Bengal and Assam – where the religious groupings were mixed, though there was a slight predominance of Muslims. The key attraction for the Congress Committee was that the proposals preserved a unified India rather than the breakaway Muslim state being canvassed by Mr Jinna.

It was not difficult for Congress to give its formal approval to the Cripps' proposals. To cheers, an elated Nehru somewhat dismissively, and dangerously Chandra thought, given the fragility of the Muslim League's own position, told the meeting that once the Congress party was in control at the centre, which was assured because of the overwhelming majority of the Hindu population, it would act as it pleased. The meeting roared its approval, but Chandra wondered whether Nehru had unwisely disclosed his hand too soon. He turned to Basu.

'He's gone and killed it at a stroke!' he cried. 'Once Jinna hears what he has just said he will know that he is right not to trust us.'

Events were to prove him correct. Nehru's remarks, which he amplified at a press conference a few days later, confirmed Congress' duplicity in Jinna's mind. Later that July, the Muslim League withdrew its approval of the Cripps proposals and Jinna called upon Muslims in India 'to take charge of your destiny'. The rift between the two parties was now irreparable. Communal violence between Hindus and Muslims, which had erupted sporadically in the first half of the year, as Jinna's preference for a separate Muslim state became widely known, now intensified. All over India there were flare-ups that resulted in rioting, rapes, beatings and killings. Weapons were being stockpiled and old grievances which had festered over the years were being settled under cover of the communal violence. It seemed as if Viceroy Wavell and his government, indeed the Raj as a whole, weakened and tired as it was by the recent war, had neither the will nor the ability to keep the peace in India.

The Muslim League decided that the 16th of August 1946 would be designated Direct Action Day. Congress leaders, intent on countering Jinna's call, went all over India to bolster their Hindu supporters. Chandra, being an INA man, a colleague of the late Subhas Chandra Bose, the INA's Bengali leader, was asked to go to Calcutta to help rally the party's supporters there and to find out the strength of local support for the Muslim League's Action Day.

The request threw Chandra into some confusion. Calcutta was Pierse's home town and he didn't want to be walking into danger by going there. He confided in Basu.

'You'll have to go,' said Basu, 'but as it is not for another two weeks, why not send one of your men to check up on this Pierse and make sure that he is closely followed so that you know exactly where he is at any time.'

Chandra thought this a good idea and despatched Dina Nath, the only one of his bodyguard who knew what Pierse looked like, to reconnoitre the situation. After waiting anxiously for news for a few days, Chandra received Dina Nath's telephone call.

'Chandra Sahib he is not in Calcutta, but is working in South India. So everything should be safe for your visit here. But I have taken no chances and the *pan-wallah* who runs the shop opposite the gate of Pierse Sahib's house has been paid to let me know if he should return home.'

With this reassurance, Chandra, accompanied by Basu and the team of *goonda* bodyguards, went to Calcutta. Basu had arranged for Chandra to stay at the crumbling mansion of an eminent Bengali family off the Chitpur Road.

'It is better not to stay at one of the big hotels like the Grand or the Great Eastern Chandra-ji as the wrong people may find out. In any case, they are full of troops, mostly Americans but also British, and you could be in danger of harm if they find out you were an INA man.'

Chandra arrived three days before the Day of Action and spoke at a series of low key rallies in and around Calcutta. It was decided that Congress would not attempt to mount its own rally on the day itself for fear of sparking violence. Bengal's Prime Minister, Shaheed Suhrawady, a Muslim and a politician for whom corruption was a way of life, ordered the 16th of August to be a public holiday to ensure a large Muslim turnout for the marches and public meetings to be held in support of the Muslim League's demand for a separate Muslim state.

'I'm going to their rally,' Chandra said to Basu.

'Are you mad?' exploded Basu. 'A Hindu in a Muslim crowd! If they find you out you will be killed!'

'It's the only way to tell what the common people think about the idea of a separate Muslim state,' replied Chandra. 'I know what the Muslim League leaders think, but do they have popular support? The Bengal PM has been forced to call a holiday to ensure a good turn-out – maybe people aren't that keen.'

Seeing that Basu remained unconvinced, 'Don't worry Basu, I won't be wearing Congress *khadi*, and I won't be stupid enough to try to disguise myself as a Mullah. I'll just go in shirt and trousers...'

'Looking for all the world like the Hindu Delhi-wallah you are,' retorted Basu. 'And are you planning to take those *goondas* with you to protect you? They will look even more out of place!'

'No. Just Dina Nath.'

'The two of you against a mob? If they find out you are not Muslims, which they will do very easily – you don't look Muslim, you can't speak Bengali, and if they become suspicious they just have to remove your trousers. You will be murdered. This is foolish, I can't allow it.'

'I'm going,' said Chandra firmly. 'Congress wanted me to find out how much support there is for a Pakistan – this is the best way to do it. Oh, and I need you to come along too as you can understand Bengali and can tell me what people are saying in the crowd.'

'No, never,' said Basu, and meant it.

* * *

Chandra and Dina Nath, pistols uncomfortably concealed beneath their shirts, mingled on the edges of the crowd on the *maidan* before the Ochterlony Monument, where the main rally was being held. Chandra had insisted that they rub a little ash into the centre of their foreheads to give the impression that they were devout Muslims and this was proof of their daily obeisance – the mark left by foreheads rubbing against prayer mats. The crowd was edgy. The speakers, including the Bengal PM, were provocative, inciting the crowd, raising the mood to one of outrage that Congress was trying to deny them a Muslim homeland. As the noisy crowd surged and eddied, Chandra decided that he had seen enough and tapped Dina Nath on the arm – a pre-arranged signal to retreat. They moved, with some difficulty, towards the outer edges of the crowd.

'Why are you leaving?' asked a man belligerently, 'the speeches are not over yet.'

Chandra put his hand to his mouth and retched. The man jumped back. Dina Nath took hold of Chandra's arm and with an apologetic look at the man steered Chandra away.

'That was too close,' said Chandra as they walked away, still pretending to be ill. They had nearly reached Chowringhee when there was a roar and a yelling mob of young men brandishing sticks and knives came bursting out of the crowd and straight at them.

Chandra and Dina Nath looked horror-struck. Chandra reached beneath his shirt for his pistol and looked around for cover but there was none. Then, to his surprise, Dina Nath raised his fist and began shouting, 'Kill the Hindus,' and urged Chandra to run with the mob. Chandra realised that the mob was not heading for them but for the shops and pavements of Chowringhee in search of Hindu victims.

The killings began. Muslim gangs roamed the streets that evening, murdering any Hindu that they encountered. There were no police or troops to be seen. Chandra and Dina Nath slowly made their way back to the car that they had parked in one of the roads off Chowringhee. Reaching it, they drove south, it was impossible to go home through the centre of the city, moving away from the carnage, anxious to put some distance between them and the mob. But the riots and the killings were everywhere, the chants of mobs punctuated by the screams of their victims. They realised that to keep driving was to invite the attention of the blood thirsty gangs who roamed the streets.

'Stop the car here,' Chandra ordered when they reached Lower Circular Road. They abandoned the car and leapt the wall into the Christian cemetery opposite the Mullick Bazaar and crouched there, feeling they were safe. But they had been seen.

It started as a low, excited buzz that filled the lanes, grew into individual urgent, angry voices which suddenly united in a screaming hysterical hatred. With yells of 'Pakistan *zindabad*, Hindustan *murdabad*' (Long live Pakistan, death to Hindustan) a mob surged out of Mullick Bazaar. Chandra heard the shouting and pounding of feet as the mob charged their hiding place. He and Dina Nath ran back from the shelter of the wall towards the shadowy cover of the gravestones as the mob vaulted the wall and came in search of them screaming hatred, the flashing blades of knives caught briefly in the street light. There must have been about thirty men. They spotted Chandra's white clothes in the gloom and ran towards him. He wondered whether to try and face them down but quickly pulled out his pistol. The leaders of the charge checked for an instant but were pushed on by those behind stumbling over the graves. Chandra fired at the leading runner. The explosion from the .45 Webley startled the mob and the leader jerked backwards, his guts blown from the large exit wound spattering those behind. They stalled, uncertain. Then Dina Nath produced his pistol and shot one of the others – the rest turned tail and ran, scrambling over the wall. Chandra's instinct was to run deeper into the dark graveyard, but Dina Nath did the opposite. He pursued the mob, firing twice, taking care not to hit anyone. The mob, now frantic with fear, disappeared into the lanes around the bazaar.

'Let's go now, Chandra Sahib,' he urged and they ran through the graveyard unable to see clearly where they were going, tripping over the gravestones, kicking over vases of flowers, and stumbling over uneven ground till they reached the perimeter wall at the other end, scrambled over it – and into another mob.

There was something different about this lot. Then Chandra noticed that a few were wearing the *tilak*, the vermilion and sandalwood paste mark on the forehead that signified a Hindu.

'We are Hindus!' shouted Chandra. He spat into his hand and wiped the ash mark from his forehead.

The mob seemed unconvinced and advanced, weapons aloft.

'Look!' shouted Dina Nath, 'those cut-cocks the other side tried to murder us!'

Chandra reached inside his shirt and pulled the sacred thread he wore to the top of his collar – his other hand firmly grasping his pistol.

'Where did you get those guns,' the leader of the mob demanded.

'We are soldiers – Dogras,' shouted Dina Nath. 'This is Chandra Sahib, he was in the INA with Subhas Chandra Bose.'

At the revered name, the mob lowered its weapons.

'You are safe now,' the leader said. 'Would you stay with us in case the Muslims attack again? Those pistols could be useful.'

The rioting continued in the city through the night. In the light of morning Calcutta rose and seemingly went about its business though corpses lay in the streets where they had been butchered. Troops appeared and Chandra and Dina Nath were able to recover the car and drive home.

But the trouble was far from over. The riots intensified in the north of the city and Hindu mobs now took vengeance on their Muslim neighbours, buildings and shanties were set on fire, bloody and blackened corpses littered the alleyways and the grey vultures slowly circled around the pillars of black smoke in search of the kills. The rioting, looting, raping and killing went on for another five days before the army finally restored order, bringing in tanks to back up the troops – over a hundred rioters were killed. But over four thousand were dead from the actions of the mobs and a further ten thousand were wounded. In the blood and fire of Calcutta the Cripps proposals died too.

* * *

Basu made sure that Chandra's escapade, suitably embellished,

got to the ears of the Congress leadership. On his return to
Delhi he was feted and commended for his courage and
resourcefulness. It was said that the great Nehru himself had
remarked that the Congress could do with more men of action
like Chandra, rather than the paper warriors he was
surrounded with. Promotion was swift and Chandra was
asked to take a senior role in what was planned to become the
Home Ministry, under Vallabhbhai Patel, a senior Congress
leader, when Congress took over the government of India. The
Home Ministry would look after India's police, security and
information services. With promotion and greater
responsibility came patronage and there was a stream of suitors
to his office, offering favours in return for opportunities. His
work intensified – meetings, discussions, plans, appointments
and speeches around the country.

On the 2nd of September, Nehru was sworn in by the
Viceroy as the Prime Minister of an interim government.
Communal disturbances continued to be reported in Bombay,
Agra and, worst of all, in East Bengal – in Dacca Muslim mobs
went on the rampage and there were pogroms in the rural
areas. The newly pregnant Suchi and her new husband fled
back to the relative safety of Calcutta. The Viceroy coaxed
Jinnah to take part in the interim government, but he simply
used his position to pursue the cause of Pakistan. The country
was in chaos.

Chandra, his brief now clear, worked with Congress
colleagues on planning the new government of India. The
British were anxious to break the stalemate between the
Muslim League and the Congress and Chandra heard rumours
that they were planning to remove Viceroy Wavell and put in
a replacement able to come in and resolve the deadlock and
broker a deal over Indian independence.

In late December, Chandra was asked to go to Calcutta
again to make a series of speeches in that city – considered by

Congress to be a vitally important base to keep under their influence.

'This time,' he said to Basu,' as a member of the interim government, I am going to stay in the Grand Hotel, not in some north Calcutta back street in a crumbling mansion with pigeons sleeping in the ceilings and bird shit on the floors.'

'Of course, Chandra-ji,' agreed Basu. 'Now there is national prestige to consider.'

'And get the local police to assure my safety,' said Chandra. 'I don't want anyone, Pierse, Muslims, British troops, anyone who has a grudge against me, to be able to get near me.'

Basu understood. Their roles had been reversed – but he was not unhappy with the position. He had been Chandra's mentor, but now he served on Chandra's staff – and Chandra was a generous boss, wide open to his influence.

CHAPTER 13

Tea – the pause that refreshes

The rickety bus bumped and groaned its way round the hill tracks, the constant lurching, the twists and turns of the road and the clouds of exhaust fumes making the passengers nauseous. At least it was getting cooler the higher up they went and the oppressive trees and bushes that hemmed in the sides of the road gave way to lantana, ferns and vistas of hills covered in jade green tea plantations – ordered carpets of tea bushes, beautifully manicured, dipping down to turquoise streams in the valley below. At last the small hill town of Munnar came into view, the end of the journey, and the passengers began their scramble to pull baggage out from under the seats, rearrange their clothing and push forward to try to be first off the bus.

Pierse's leg ached from being jammed against the seat in front of him. He followed his fellow passengers off the bus and gathered with them around the back of it as the driver and his assistant unloaded the luggage piled on the roof. The bystanders at the small shops and tea stalls surrounding the bus terminus sipped their tea and smoked their *beedies*, watching the unfolding scene with interest. It was a piece of theatre that they witnessed several times a day, every day, but it never ceased to fascinate them.

An oldish man approached Pierse. He was neatly dressed in a white shirt and beige trousers.

'Pierse Sahib?' he enquired raising his right hand to his forehead in a salaam. Pierse nodded, he was the only non-Indian among the passengers. 'I am Balaram, Murray Sahib's driver. Car is over there Sahib,' he indicated a dark coloured Austin car. 'Which your luggage?'

By now a crowd of coolies and general hangers-on was squabbling over the piles of luggage that had come down from the bus's roof, in the hope of being handsomely paid by the passengers for hefting their bags a few yards to the next mode of transport to take them to their homes or hotels. Pierse indicated his bag and Balaram moved in and angrily waved off the coolies contemplating it, picked it up and staggered to the car, Pierse following.

They wound their way further up the hills to a familiar neat, white-washed bungalow, the green paint on its tin roof peeling, the walls mellow in the evening sun, its garden supercharged with a riot of colour. It hadn't changed much, thought Pierse, since he and Kenny were last here as teenagers during their holidays about a dozen years ago. Two big Alsatians bounded out of the front door, barking wildly, followed by Auntie Gwen, an older, rounder version of Pierse's mother, her sister. She shouted at the dogs to rein them in and enveloped her nephew in a rib-cracking hug.

'Bertie'll be back soon,' she said by way of welcome, 'I told him not to come home without a decent bottle of scotch from the club for you. Balaram,' she said addressing the driver, 'go and pick up Murray Sahib, and remind him to get the whisky from the club.'

'Sorry for the short notice of my visit, Auntie,' apologised Pierse, 'last minute decision, I felt I should come and see you as I was close by in Coialla.'

'We got the telegram this morning,' Auntie Gwen laughed. 'And since when have you required an invitation to visit us, eh? Eddie, son, you know you are always welcome here at anytime.' She examined at him closely. 'You've changed, Eddie, a little thinner, more......... more .....mature – but then, I haven't seen you for years and you're a big boy now!' She giggled, hugging him again.

He loved Auntie Gwen and her husband Uncle Bertie. They had married after a whirlwind romance when Uncle Bertie met her while he was on leave in Calcutta. Everyone said it wouldn't last; Gwen was too much the city girl, loved the dances and shows, whereas Bertie, his real name wasn't Albert but Robert, a Scotsman and engineer, was much older than her, with a deep, some said unhealthy interest in his tea factory machinery. Taking Gwen off to a one-horse town like Munnar was madness.

But here they were, nearly twenty five years later, apparently happy as anything. The marriage had produced two children, Alex and Fiona, both now grown up and no longer living in Munnar. Pierse knew that Alex was working for an engineering company in Madras, following in his father's footsteps. The headstrong Fiona had become a nurse in order to escape the pestering of the bachelor tea planters, so desperate for female company, Pierse's mother had said.

'I've telephoned Fiona,' said Auntie Gwen, as if reading his mind, 'she's working in the Naval Hospital in Cochin. I've asked if she and David, her fiancé, can come up for the weekend. He's English, a Navy Lieutenant,' she added, 'very nice boy.'

As Pierse sat sipping a cold beer in the comfortable sitting room with its teak and cane furniture and hunting trophies on the walls, catching up on the family news with Auntie Gwen, the car returned and through the door came Uncle Bertie dressed, as always, in a white shirt and khaki shorts, with white knee-length socks. His bald head and ruddy face framed a wide grin despite the pipe clenched between his teeth. He triumphantly brandished a bottle of scotch.

'Hello Edwin,' he said, shaking hands vigorously. He always called Pierse by his full Christian name – nobody else did. 'Managed to get you some malt whisky,' he laughed. 'The Club Steward was a bit reluctant to part with it – stocks are low after everyone drank themselves silly when we heard the war had ended. I told him that you had returned from the war – and from the dead – and that if anyone deserved a damned good malt whisky, you did! This one's for you, with his compliments.'

They chatted over dinner and late into the night as the scotch sank slowly down the bottle. Uncle Bertie and Auntie Gwen wanted to know all about his time in Malaya. Pierse skimmed the surface, the war was over and there was little to be gained by re-living its horrors for his gentle hosts – they might not believe him anyway. They told him of their life and their children. Uncle Bertie was now the manager of the Madhumala tea factory, one of the biggest in the area and his fame was assured as he had invented an important piece of machinery to improve the tea process.

'What will you do,' Pierse asked them, 'when the British go – as looks likely?'

'I hope that the British will leave India with a sensible government,' said Uncle Bertie contemplatively, his Scots burr mixed in nicely with the rolling intonation of the local language, Malayalam, which he spoke fluently. 'They can't cling on; but I hope that they don't leave chaos behind. I,' he looked across at Gwen and checked himself, 'we – intend to stay here. I've got a small stake in Finlays, so we are okay for money, and we bought this house. Finlays are happy for me to stay on until I want to stop.' Finlay Muir and Company was the major owner of the tea estates around Munnar and had been since the late 1800s.

'Why would we want to go back to Britain?' Auntie Gwen added. 'I don't know the country and Bertie says he escaped it a long time ago. This is a paradise for both of us. Bertie has Scotland's cold climate at night, when you most need it to be cool, and I get India's warmth during the day to keep my garden growing. All our friends are here, there's plenty of shooting too. And whenever I get fidgety for the bright lights, we go down to Cochin for a few days – and get to see Fiona into the bargain.'

'You've come at the wrong time Edwin,' said Uncle Bertie, with mock seriousness. Pierse looked surprised. 'The monsoon – it's due any moment now,' he tapped his watch, 'it's June, remember?'

'Oh, I remember the monsoon from our holidays here,' grinned Pierse, 'it shan't keep me from exploring the place.' He wondered though how he would react to the torrential rain. Would it bring back uncomfortable memories of the rain-soaked battles in Malaya or, worse, would it trigger memories of his barbaric time as prisoner of the Japs at Songkurai Camp on the Burma-Siam Railway. The camp was surrounded by trees and thick jungle, almost always in the shade and during the monsoon the incessant rain heaped misery upon misery. 'Death Valley' they called it during the monsoon. He sometimes had nightmares about the war, and that camp in particular. Small things could trigger bad flashbacks.

Uncle Bertie suddenly jumped up. 'Come along Edwin, I've got something to show you.'

'What? Now?' Auntie Gwen remonstrated.

But Uncle Bertie was already heading for the front door, picking up a torch as he went. He led the way to a shed at the side of the bungalow, unlocked the padlock and threw open the door. In the light of the torch Pierse could see a tarpaulin covered mound which Uncle Bertie uncovered with a crackling flourish.

'Well, Edwin, what do you think of that,' he exclaimed proudly.

'It's a motorcycle,' replied Pierse cautiously, 'ex-army dispatch riders' too by the look of it.'

'That's right, got it at an army surplus sale. They are selling a lot of kit very cheaply now they no longer need it. This is a BSA M20, 500 cc, side valve,' said Uncle Bertie enthusiastically – this meant little to Pierse but he smiled at Uncle Bertie's enthusiasm for anything mechanical. 'Tuned it myself, it's ready to go. Want to have a try?'

Pierse demurred. 'I can ride – sort of,' he said, 'but not with half a bottle of scotch inside me, in the dark on strange hilly roads. Tomorrow morning perhaps.'

'Nonsense!' said Uncle Bertie who was already straddling the bike and kicking down the starter pedal. The machine burst into life. 'Climb on the back,' he ordered and, with a reluctant Pierse astride, took off down the drive and into the road with only the motorcycle's headlight to illuminate the way. Dark shapes flew past as Uncle Bertie swung the bike this way and that round the bends in the rough road. Pierse clung on tight, tucking in close behind Uncle Bertie to avoid the bitingly cold wind and sparks from his pipe as they wound their way up the mountain. His initial fear gave way to resignation and then, slowly, to a sense of dare-devil enjoyment as the bike was expertly steered up the hills and all the way home by an exultant Uncle Bertie.

'*Hic itur ad astra,*' shouted Uncle Bertie.

'What?'

'It's Latin for 'you can see the stars from here'. Look at the stars!'

They glittered like scattered diamonds over blue-black velvet – millions of them, bright but empty other worlds looking down on two drunken fools on an old motorcycle in the darkness of the Kannan Devan Hills.

'You bloody idiot, Bertie, you could have both been killed,' said Auntie Gwen on their return, but the twitching corners of her mouth suggested amusement.

'Have you done this too?' asked Pierse suspiciously of her. She laughed uproariously, yes, she had – they had – often. Uncle Bertie didn't seem to be such a dry old stick after all.

* * *

The monsoon broke the next afternoon. Strong winds rushed up the valley and the rain tumbled out of black, boiling clouds, hard and heavy, rattling like pebbles on the tin roof and flowing like a curtain round the verandahs to drench the flower beds, then trickling down the drive and into the road to join the other rivulets cascading down the hill. Pierse was equipped for it. He had gone down that morning at Auntie Gwen's insistence, wobbling on the unfamiliar motorcycle, to the Munnar Supply Association, the shop run by the tea planters, to purchase an oilcloth mac and a planters' broad brimmed hat. He stared at the rain for a while – remembering the terrible past. He decided that he must venture out, challenge the rain and prove to himself that he was master over his fears.

The motorcycle throbbed up the road, splashing the reddish muddy water over his legs, sliding a little in the ruts. He rode carefully, steadily, hat brim pulled down to keep the rain out of his eyes, until he reached Top Station. There he dismounted and walked to the road's edge, watching the monsoon sweep over the hills and valleys, the rain pooling at his feet. The Western Ghats, where Munnar lay, was one of the first places in India to feel the monsoon's caress as it came in over the Arabian Sea every June. Those scudding clouds would soon be on their way across the country to rain on Father Sam, Baldev and Marion, and then make their way up India to rattle the front door of his home in Calcutta and turn its streets into rivers. He wondered how many days it would take for that to happen – two or three perhaps. He shouted a wish into the sky, 'God bless you Mum and Da – and Kenny – you randy pig!' He laughed at the absurdity of it, but he felt good. Then he whispered as an afterthought, 'and you, Ellen, wherever you are.'

In the days that followed, Pierse travelled the roads around Munnar, mostly alone on the motorbike, but sometimes, when the weather was dry, with the servant boy, Kunnu, on the pillion. Kunnu was the son of Balaram, the driver. He was about thirteen years' old, dark skinned and wiry, with curly hair. He had appointed himself as a sort of groom, a keeper of the motorcycle, and would set to work cleaning and polishing it every time Pierse returned. According to Uncle Bertie, he could turn out to be a good mechanic and was already let loose to fix small problems on the bike. He spoke a little English, and Pierse amused himself by getting Kunnu to teach him Malayalam words and phrases. He took him up to the hill above Christ Church, the stone-built, very English church where the planters, those who were still capable of standing after a hard Saturday night's drinking in the Club, went to worship the God who had made this paradise in which they lived and worked.

Pierse liked to sit by the tomb of Mrs May, right on the hill's summit, and take in the view. Years ago Aunt Gwen had told him the story of Eleanor May, the new young bride of a planter in the 1800s who had stood on this spot and was so enraptured by the view that she turned to her husband and said that when she died she would like to be buried there. Two days later cholera granted her wish. Time had added the graves of other planters and their wives and children and the church had been grafted on to the graveyard. Pierse liked to sit there and admire the view that Mrs May had loved – and just keep her company. He wondered what would happen to the tombs and the church when the British eventually left India to its very different Gods.

He went to dinner with Bertie and Gwen at the High Range Club, the planters' club, where Uncle Bertie was a member. It was a weekend, and the place was filled with tea planters who had come in from their estates to drink and meet their colleagues and friends. Some of the older ones, grizzled men with weather-beaten faces, made more and more taciturn by their lonely lives, sat silently in the heavy teak chairs in their private smokescreens of cigar or pipe smoke, reading newspapers or journals held in strong red hands, burra pegs of whisky or gin close at hand. They sat in convivial isolation – exactly how they liked to be. Those with families sat at table with their wives, dressed in the latest fashions copied by the local tailor, and sometimes accompanied by their spoiled children, home from boarding school, eating dinner, taking a break from estate life. The younger planters were clustered round the bar, drinking hard, their laughter and animated conversation becoming more raucous and boisterous as the evening went on. Many had passed this way over the years: the hats of past club members who had departed for Blighty or lay buried in Munnar's red soil were inscribed with their names and years of service in white paint and hung over the bar as a reminder.

Pierse spent an alcoholic evening talking to the young planters and playing billiards with them – not allowed to pay for any of his drinks by his generous hosts. He promised to drive up to see their tea estates – they were starved of company and always welcomed the chance to talk to visitors. A number of Munnar's young planters had gone to war and some had not returned. The elderly planters left behind grumbled about the big increase in their work as a consequence. A few younger men had filled some of the vacancies, but Munnar, because of its isolation was not a popular posting.

* * *

That weekend Fiona arrived with David, her fiancé. She had grown tall, like the other Pierse women, her brown hair cut in a bob. Pierse could see why the tea planters had been so keen on her.

'I had to get away, Ed,' she said laughing, 'there was the danger of offending so many of them if you went out with one of them. It was becoming too complicated – some of the chaps chasing after me had known me as a child in nappies, for God's sake!'

Fiancé David, an Oxford University educated Englishman who was, in civilian life, a school teacher in the Surrey Hills, was hoping to return to England with Fiona when he was demobbed from the navy.

'Are you going to leave all of this?' asked Pierse teasingly of Fiona.

'It will be a wrench, Ed, it's a big step,' she said seriously. 'I'm trying to persuade David to try teaching over here for a bit but I don't think I'll succeed. Maybe our time in India has finally come to an end.'

She was naturally very interested in Pierse's experiences in prison camp, asking him how the prisoners had fared without medicines and proper medical equipment. He didn't really want to talk about his experiences in the Burma-Siam Railway camp at Songkurai but Fiona was insistent.

'Please tell me, Ed. I'm interested. Maybe there are things that we could learn.'

Reluctantly, not wanting to appear uncooperative or offend her, Pierse told her.

'We lost a lot of men in the Burma-Siam jungle because of disease – malaria, dysentery, malnutrition – and through overwork and torture. We were fed little and worked hard; the hours were long and the guards cruel. Beatings and torture were routine and you tried to stay out of trouble because a cut or, worse, a broken limb because of an accident or a beating, could be a death sentence. There were no proper medicines and the doctors did what they could with very little. The worst of it was cholera. We got it so badly, I think, because the constant rain made the latrines overflow and we were stepping in the filth, carrying it around on our feet. Hundreds died very quickly in our camp, about thirty each day. We had nothing to treat them with. The doctors tried their best but all they had was aspirin, quinine and mercurochrome so it was no use. The men died where they lay, usually went within a day or two. We had to drag the bodies out and cremate them on a bonfire which we kept going day and night. It was unsettling to see friends you had eaten breakfast with being cremated at dinner time.'

'How did you survive?'

'I was lucky, I suppose. I decided early on that I had to make sure that I came home – for Ellen,' he said lamely. The family knew about Ellen and had diplomatically avoided mentioning her. 'I thought I was in trouble when I got a tropical ulcer on my leg. It was so easy to get them as we were wearing shorts or loin cloths – 'Jap happys' we called them – while we worked on building the railway, and you were always scraping or cutting your legs on the rocks or the sharp grasses and they became infected because of the rain, dirt or flies. There was no soap or antiseptic of course and, as we were all suffering from malnutrition by then, our bodies couldn't heal. The ulcers were very painful and often got to the point where they became so infected that they ate into the bone; the only hope was to have your leg amputated or you would die of gangrene.'

'Amputated without anaesthetic?' asked Fiona incredulously.

'Oh yes. They held you down and did it – it was like the

olden days. Unfortunately, most didn't survive the shock of the operation in their weakened state, or gangrene set in anyway.'

'And what happened to you?' asked Auntie Gwen, who was listening intently, running her finger down the long scar on Pierse's leg.

'Luck again, Aunt,' he said nonchalantly. 'There were some Eurasians in the camp, mixed Malay and European. They had become friendly with me when they found out I was Anglo-Indian. When I got the ulcer, and it was clear that I was in trouble because it became infected, they got some maggots from the latrine and cleansed them, kept them in clean surroundings for a few days. Then they opened up my ulcer with this penknife,' he produced Uncle Derek's penknife from his pocket, 'which they sterilised by boiling the blade. They scraped as much of the dead flesh as they could out of the ulcer, put the maggots in and bandaged it loosely.'

Fiona shuddered, speechless.

'It was extremely painful, but I didn't think that I was going to survive anyway; the Eurasians had said that this had been used by natives as a cure so I had to take a chance. After a few days, they opened the bandage – the smell from the maggots was appalling, it made us all throw up. But, you know, the wound was clean. Those maggots had eaten all the dead flesh and the hole in my leg was pink. I kept it bandaged and only washed it with boiled water, with a little salt in it, which wasn't pleasant. But it healed.'

'Did they do this for the other patients?' asked Fiona.

'No. The doctors wouldn't hear of it. They thought it was too horrible and too risky. Native mumbo jumbo, they said. I suppose the thought of using maggots from the latrine was too awful. They just kept sawing the legs off – and the chaps just kept hopping on to the funeral pyre.' He smiled at the bad joke.

Uncle Bertie, who had listened in silence, leant over, patted Pierse on the shoulder and continued puffing on his pipe.

* * *

Later that evening after Uncle Bertie and Aunt Gwen had gone to bed, he sat talking with Fiona and David. She suddenly turned to him and said, 'The prison camp on the Railway, you didn't want to talk about it. Why?'

'It stirs up very painful memories – things that I just want to forget. Things that people who weren't there would find it hard to believe. They'd think I was making it up.'

'I believe you, Ed. Tell me.'

He contemplated this in silence for a while as she looked expectantly at him. She reached out and took his hand.

'Tell me.'

'I have never ever felt so alone in my life even though I was surrounded by people. Whether you lived or died was a matter of chance – the whole of nature, as well as those cruel Jap bastards, was conspiring against you. Too many were unlucky. Everyone's preoccupation was trying to stay alive. I really don't want to talk about it or think about it – it is too upsetting.'

'Have you spoken to anyone about your time there?'

He shook his head.

'Not even your Mum and Dad – or Kenny?'

'No. It would upset them too much.'

'You need to talk about it, Ed, to someone, anyone. Talking could help.'

He sat there gazing down the valley. Then, lowering his gaze to the floor, he began.

'The Japs told us that we were being sent to the hills to do some light work on the railway to get our health back,' he said uncertainly, swallowing hard. 'I was suffering with a bad case of dysentery so someone suggested my name. They thought I would be useful, bring some experience because Da was in the railway.' He stopped and looked at her; she nodded and gently squeezed his hand.

'In April '43 we were loaded on to covered railway freight wagons in Singapore, really packed in, we could just about sit down. Some chaps thought they were off on a holiday and had packed gramophones and records, books, cooking pots – that sort of thing, though why they believed the Japs I don't know. The five day journey was a nightmare in those baking wagons and many of us were suffering with dysentery – so the wagons quickly became unpleasant. There was no water and we rarely stopped for food and to stretch our legs. Some of the chaps didn't make it. Are you sure you really want to hear this Fiona?'

She nodded.

Pierse continued. 'We reached a place called Ban Pong in southern Siam and thought we had arrived. But there our troubles really began. They said that we were to march the one hundred and fifty miles to our camp on a road parallel to a railway track. They could have put us on a train if they had wanted to.'

David shook his head. 'The cruel, cruel bastards,' he said.

'I lost count of the number of days that the march took. Men just fell by the roadside unable to go on. We had to leave them there. Of course we had to chuck away all the stuff we had brought as we couldn't carry it – the Jap guards helped themselves to much of it. When we eventually reached our camp at Songkurai the rain was bucketing down, but the huts were roofless and we had to set about building them. We got them done in a couple of days and were packed in at night, shoulder to shoulder. The work of building the railway was hard, very hard. We didn't have proper tools and the Japs drove us ferociously to meet their deadlines. It would have been just about tolerable if we were fit, but we didn't have proper food – just a small portion of rice with vegetables, usually chickpeas, or fish, which we ate standing in the rain. I managed to barter my watch with a local villager for a regular supply of ducks' eggs to keep me going. We worked on Tokyo time. So work started at 3 am and did not end until after nightfall. Many of us were sick and, because we couldn't work as hard as expected, the beatings increased. People just collapsed at work or were beaten by the guards and died. Sorry Fiona,' said Pierse looking distressed. 'I don't want to say anymore. Sorry.'

'When did you get back to Singapore?' she insisted, determined that he should unburden himself.

'It was in December '43. This time we travelled by train to Ban Pong and were put on another train. We didn't know where we were heading; some thought Indo-China and another prison camp. So it was with relief that we recognised the familiar landscape of Malaya. When we arrived back at Changi POW camp they were shocked. One thousand six hundred men had left in April but just over a hundred returned in December. Most of us who came back were in a very bad way – walking skeletons, just about.'

Pierse couldn't continue, abruptly stood up, said a curt 'Goodnight' and went to his room.

Fiona and David sat there in an uncomfortable silence, embarrassed that their prurience had upset Pierse.

* * *

In the days that followed, Pierse took up the invitations from the other planters and went to see them at their work: supervising the early morning muster of the workers before they went off to their various jobs; watching the dextrous picking of the tea leaves by slyly flirtatious hill-women; the weighing and transportation of the bundles to the factories. They showed him how ground was cleared and manured for new planting – they told him that it took eight years for a tea bush to mature. He visited the workers' lines to inspect them for cleanliness, saw the school where the workers' children were given a basic education and the hospital and dispensary where they were treated for illness. He observed the planters presiding over the monthly pay distribution and arbitrating in disputes. The biggest part of the work, they said, was that of managing the large numbers of workers. They employed one and a quarter workers for every acre of land, which meant a force of hundreds for some of the bigger estates. The planters lived well, looked after by a team of servants, supervised by their wives if they were married or, if not, by a senior servant – a sort of major domo, who 'adjusted the accounts' as one of the planters delicately put it, so that he made a good living too. In the evenings and at weekends they repaired to the convivial bar and dining room at the High Range Club to drink and to yarn.

Bertie took him round his tea factory, proudly showing him the process for turning the fresh-picked tea leaves into the finished article, with machines to dry them, roll them, sieve them, grade them and pack them. An amused Pierse noticed that Uncle Bertie strolled about his machines like a general inspecting his tanks and artillery, patting them here, stroking them there; making a little adjustment or two. The workers snapped to attention when he spoke to them, but it was out of respect, not fear, and they wobbled their heads, wreathed in smiles when he moved on.

But above all, Pierse rode the motorcycle into the hills, the far Anaimalais, the elephant hills, and the Nilgiris, sometimes leaving it concealed in the bushes while he continued trekking on foot, often in the rain. He saw the neelakurinji bloom – the elusive blue flower that had given its name to the Nilgiris, the 'blue hills'. It only bloomed once every twelve years – so seeing it was a rare privilege – it turned the slopes into carpets of startling blue. He walked for miles, lost in the unspoilt beauty of the hills and jungles and the ordered world of the manicured estates – thinking, always thinking. He felt that he was slowly purging his mind of the burden of the war, of horrific imprisonment, and of the terrible disappointment of losing Ellen. His thoughts began to turn away from the past and towards his future.

He thought about the country. He knew so little about India, its mountains, plains, deserts and the lush tropical lands around the coasts. The people were not one people, but a mix of Aryans, Dravidians, people who were the products of conquests and trade – Persians, British, Dutch, French, Portuguese, Chinese, Jews and Arabs – now intermingled to produce hybrid races. They didn't speak one language but hundreds – the north didn't understand the rolling tongues of the south and vice versa. There had been a long history of oppression by minor princes, of cruelty and suppression through caste and religion. Could anyone bring all of this together into one independent country, or did it take the iron hand of a conqueror to force the people into working for common cause. In some ways that had already happened – the Quit India movement had caught the popular imagination in 1942 because the people wanted to be rid of their British invaders. But when the British were gone, what then? Was there a place for people like him, Anglo-Indians, in a new India? Would he have to become more Indian to survive, to blend in? If not, would India be generous in allowing all her people to retain their faiths, languages and cultures and yet be counted together as 'Indians'?

And if he decided not to stay in India but to go to Britain, to a country his parents called home, but which neither they nor he had ever seen except in the pages of books and newspapers and in films. Would the British accept him as one of them? Of would that country, teetering on the edge of survival after the war, reject all incomers of dubious provenance? He just didn't know.

The British would go; this was not their country, it was more their playground, their bank vault. Their roots were in Surrey, or Kent, or Yorkshire, or Wales. But so were his – weren't they? In Wales! So why stay? But when he thought about it in the clear, bright hills with forests rolling greenly down their sides in the misty rain, his roots had long ago been transplanted from Wales and grafted on to Indian stock – and those new trees had now firmly taken hold and were flourishing in India, watered by the monsoons and warmed by an un-Welsh tropical sun. They were not the same old root stock, they were new! Original! Unique! They belonged here and would wither and die in the cold and grey of the Northern Hemisphere.

* * *

He was sitting in his room one afternoon replying to letters from his mother and from Kenny – both asking when he was returning home. Kenny's letter was full of tales of the disturbances and demonstrations in Calcutta, hardly an inviting prospect compared with Munnar. Pierse had been in Munnar for just over a month and he felt ready to move on, go back home and look for a job. He had discussed the options with Uncle Bertie, but Bertie's world was a narrow one of engineering and machines, neither of which Pierse had an inclination towards. He was interrupted by a strange car coming up the drive with Uncle Bertie in the back accompanied by two other men.

'Edwin,' called Bertie urgently, 'get the motorbike. One of the chaps has gone missing and a group of us are going down the Cochin Road to search for him.'

Auntie Gwen had come out to see what was the matter and Uncle Bertie explained that 'Sapper' Lawrence, a planter from the Devadas estate, had gone down to the plain on his motorcycle to spend yesterday, Sunday, with his current lady love but had not arrived back at the tea estate last night. The alarm had been raised when he hadn't reported for work this morning. Lady love had said that he had left her before midnight, so the police were alerted but had failed to discover his whereabouts. The planters decided to conduct their own search.

The twisty Cochin Road was a reasonably good one, it had been opened as recently as '31 but it needed to be driven with care. The impatient planters raced up and down it in their cars or motorcycles, often with the best part of a bottle of scotch or gin in them. A small mistake in the wrong place could mean going over the edge and down the *khud* below. It was thought that this is what must have happened to Sapper. The search party, planters and estate workers in trucks, men on motorcycles, met outside the gabled red brick and red tiled Munnar Supply Association building and moved off in convoy, having divided up the search area. They shouted out and shone torches down the ravines but could see nothing through the thick vegetation and there were no skid marks on the road. The rain began to fall and, as the sun set, as it did regularly in the Tropics at 6.30pm, groups began to abandon their task for the night and make their way back to the club for supper and a few whiskies.

Pierse was with Uncle Bertie and a few companions having a drink at the bar and bemoaning the fate of Sapper when the club steward interrupted them.

'They've found him!' he exclaimed. 'Some of the chaps have come back to try to get the Supply Association opened so that they can get some more equipment to lift him up from the ravine he has fallen into.'

'Is he badly hurt?' enquired Uncle Bertie.

'Don't know, but they've gone to knock up the Doc to take him back with them and I'm going to tell the police inspector.'

Drinks were hurriedly swallowed. They rushed out of the club and drove down the Cochin Road until they found the search party looking down into the ravine at the road side. The searchers had shone a powerful hunting torch into the gloom and by pure chance one of the estate workers had noticed something reflect among the leaves. As he was an agile young chap, they secured him to a rope and he bravely slithered his way down in the darkness. He called up to confirm that he had found Sapper, seriously injured and unconscious. They worked through the night to lift him out and send him to hospital.

The talk in the Club the next evening was of Sapper's poor condition; he had broken several bones and remained very ill. They also talked of the gap that his hospitalisation would leave among the already depleted ranks of planters.

'Couldn't have come at a worse time,' muttered one of them, 'we have two chaps retiring next month, with passages booked to go back to England. The company says that they can't give us immediate replacements as they have vacancies all over the show. Too many young Managers and Assistants were allowed to go off to fight. They should have declared them to be in reserved occupations and exempt from military service.'

'What!' said another, 'tea planters, a reserved occupation!' and he laughed scornfully.

'The forces drank enough of the bloody stuff to keep them going,' retorted the first.

'Finlays says it's going to train some Indian managers,' said a third. 'Imagine, Indians running the show! They won't have the authority or the leadership. The workers won't respect them.'

'Why not?' argued Pierse. 'I served with many fine Indian officers, good leaders, chaps who could think on their feet. They'd be first class managers.'

'It won't work,' said the first planter, 'they won't fit in.'

Pierse was getting irritated. 'Why won't they fit in?' he asked testily. 'They went to good schools, many of them went to university and they come from good families. Is it because their skin is dark – and they wouldn't be allowed in the club?'

'Now, now, Edwin,' said Uncle Bertie, anxious to defuse the situation.

'I'm sorry,' said Pierse, realising that he was in danger of offending his hosts.

Back home he said to Uncle Bertie, 'If the estates are so strapped for managers, perhaps I can help out for a while until Sapper is back or the replacements get here.'

'But you know nothing about being a tea planter, dear boy. And you don't speak the language. Planters need about six to eight months' training.'

'I know enough to be going on with, Uncle, I've been out with most of the chaps seeing the work they do, and there are assistants and overseers to help. Most of it is about managing the workers and I've enough experience of managing troops.'

'Hmmm,' said Uncle Bertie noncommittally. Auntie Gwen looked at Pierse and shrugged.

The next evening at dinner Uncle Bertie said casually, with a twinkle in his eye, 'I've spoken to the company today about our vacancies and they have, surprisingly, agreed that you can work temporarily as a planter for them Edwin'.

Pierse was taken aback. He stammered his thanks.

'Only as an assistant, mind, and it is temporary, but it would certainly help us out. When can you start?'

Pierse gratefully shook his hand. He realised that a lot of arm-twisting must have gone on behind the scenes. Auntie Gwen would have insisted that Bertie talk to the company. Bertie had probably conferred with the other planters and got their agreement. And the company bosses in Finlays, deferring to Bertie's reputation, had no option but to agree.

'I won't let you down Uncle,' said an elated Pierse.

Bertie looked at him for a moment, then raised his glass, 'You'll make a fine tea planter Edwin,' he grinned, 'but you'll have to go and live in Sapper's house on the Devadas Estate.'

* * *

Pierse took to the new job with enthusiasm. Sapper Lawrence's assistant at the Devadas Estate, Sansom, a newish planter in his late 30s, had been temporarily promoted to the Manager's job – he was now the *Periadorai*, the 'big man' as the local language, Malayalam, had it. Pierse was the *Chinnadorai*, the 'little man'. They got on well together. Sapper had been an eccentric man to work for, so the arrival of Pierse was something of a relief to Sansom.

The work was demanding and Pierse's day started with the 6 o'clock muster and finished at 5 o'clock in the evening. The estate was some distance away from the club so he spent more time on the estate learning the job and receiving lessons in Malayalam. At weekends he went to stay with Auntie Gwen and Uncle Bertie and went up to the club to catch up with the news and the gossip.

In September came the news of the appointment of Mr Nehru as the interim Prime Minister of a soon-to-be Indian Government. It was now not a question of whether but when the British would pull out of India. Up in Munnar, they lived in an isolated world away from the disturbances and violence taking place elsewhere in India as the factions jockeyed for power. The planters, ever vigilant, kept a close eye on their workers, ready to snuff out any spark of the communal strife that seemed to be spreading around the country.

Sapper Lawrence died after lingering for nearly two months in hospital in Cochin. His injuries had proved to be too severe. Some of the older planters went down with Uncle Bertie for his funeral and his hat was duly hung behind the bar in a bender of a wake that Sapper would have mightily enjoyed.

* * *

One weekend in October, back at Gwen and Bertie's bungalow, Uncle Bertie gave Pierse the news that his time at Devadas was coming to an end and a replacement would arrive within a few weeks. Pierse was disappointed but took the news calmly. He had hoped that Finlays would be pleased with his work and decide to make his position permanent. He had said so often enough to Sansom and Uncle Bertie.

Sensing his disappointment, Uncle Bertie said kindly, 'It was always going to be a temporary post, Edwin. To be a tea planter you have to go through an interview and proper training. I did try on your behalf, but no luck.'

'I know,' replied Pierse, 'and thank you. But I hoped that they would see that I had done my training with Sansom. He seems pleased with my work.' Auntie Gwen leaned over and squeezed him consolingly on the arm.

'Here is a letter from Finlays thanking you and terminating your appointment from mid November,' said Uncle Bertie, handing him a sealed manila envelope. Pierse took it glumly.

'Aren't you going to read it?' asked Auntie Gwen.

Pierse was about to say 'no', but something in her manner made him slit open the envelope and read the official, stilted letter from Finlays. They thanked him for helping them out and for his work at Devadas. They gave his termination date and the amount of money he was owed. The writer of the letter, the General Manager, had appended a final paragraph in his own hand. Pierse read it and looked up at Gwen and Bertie.

'You buggers, you knew about this, didn't you! They've offered me a job at Head Office in Calcutta – I'm to be a bloody Manager. And look at the pay!' Auntie Gwen and Uncle Bertie beamed.

202 ❀ THE LION AND THE CHAKRA

'They thought that you did an absolutely marvellous job, Eddie,' said Auntie Gwen.

'Sansom wanted you to stay on permanently and told them so,' added Uncle Bertie, 'but I told them that you were wasted here. Any old fool can grow tea, but the company needs bright chaps like you to help us grapple with the changes that are taking place in India. When I heard you at the club, arguing that we ought to have Indian planters I knew that you were the sort of chap we needed in Calcutta.'

* * *

Mid-November came and Pierse took a sad and tearful farewell of his Aunt and Uncle, feeling very hung-over after his farewell party at the club the night before. Someone had jokingly asked him if he was going to hang his hat behind the bar and he had replied that he didn't want to go down in history as the planter with the shortest service in the Kannan Devan Hills. Balaram drove him back to Coialla, his Aunt had insisted on it, and he spent a couple of days with Father Sam and Baldev before taking the long train journey up to Calcutta.

Back in Coialla he decided not to go and see Marion – and she had not bothered to take up the invitation to visit Father Sam. 'Let sleeping dogs lie,' he said to Father Sam.

'Surely you mean sleeping bitches,' laughed Father Sam. 'By the way, Pierse, you never did tell me what was in the note she wrote to you before you left.'

'She told me that Ellen was pregnant.'

CHAPTER 14

The Lion and the Chakra – 1947

The clatter of machinery inside the Hamilton Jute Mill made it impossible to hear the sound of the protesters outside the gates. The two gatekeepers, ex-sepoys armed only with iron-tipped bamboo *lathis*, quickly locked the gates and one of them ran into the mill to warn the managers; outside the gates stood a small but noisy crowd of demonstrators. They bore a fluttering of green Muslim League flags and crude banners proclaiming 'Congress Out' and 'Hamilton Mill – unfair to Muslims' in both English and Bengali. They chanted slogans, fists pounding the air in emphasis.

One of the leaders of the demonstration, a tall, bearded Muslim of about thirty years of age, screamed his slogans with a particular vehemence. The gatekeeper recognised him – an ex-employee who had been sacked a few days ago, by all accounts a trouble-maker. He too brandished a *lathi*, raising it high and striking the gate threateningly to mark the beat of each chant. The gatekeeper wondered whether he should tell him to stop attacking the Company's property but, sizing him up, thought better of it.

Soon the other gatekeeper emerged with a small group of people from the mill's main door. There were a couple of young European managers, a Bengali supervisor and three mill guards bearing *lathis*. One of the European managers, a stocky Englishman called Chennery, came right up to the gate, held up his hand and shouted for silence. The demonstrators chanted on until the tall Muslim held up his *lathi* to silence them.

'What is the meaning of this?' shouted Chennery.

'Jute mill is unfair to Mussulmans! Give us our jobs back!' one of the demonstrators shouted. But the tall Muslim silenced him.

Then another leader of the demonstration, a grey haired East Bengali stepped forward. 'Sir,' he said, 'you have unfairly sacked a good worker, Azim Khan,' he indicated the tall Muslim. 'You cannot do this – he has done nothing wrong. He was sacked for protesting about his treatment and the treatment of other Muslims in the factory. Give him his job back and we will go away.'

The silence while Chennery Sahib considered this was broken by the big, bespectacled Bengali supervisor standing behind him.

'Go away!' he shouted angrily. 'This man was sacked for insubordination. We will never have him back!'

Azim Khan turned and spoke excitedly to his compatriots and the chanting began again as the demonstrators rushed forward and pushed at the gates. Azim Khan raised his *lathi* and hurled abuse at the group inside the factory and then, in his rage, vaulted the gate and dashed towards the Bengali supervisor, swinging the *lathi*, intent on whacking him. Other demonstrators followed. Chennery and his group began to retreat, but the second European, coolly stepped forward and stood his ground. He advanced on the mob. They stopped.

'You – stay here!' he said pointing to Azim Khan. 'The rest of you, get back to the other side of the gates.' The voice was commanding. They hesitated, but Azim Khan nodded to them and they reluctantly complied. Groups of workers had gathered at the windows to watch.

The European strode over to Azim Khan. 'Who sacked you?' he asked.

'Farrell Sahib, it was him, Bannerjee.' He pointed to the Bengali Supervisor. 'I had done nothing wrong Sahib.'

'First, tell your people to go now if you want me to listen to what you have to say,' said Farrell. 'This is not the way to do business and threatening us will not get you back your job.' Azim Khan looked uncertain.

'If you don't, I can't help you Azim Khan,' said Farrell, lowering his voice. 'Chennery Sahib has already called for the police and you could be arrested for trespassing on the mill premises.'

Azim Khan went to the gate and spoke to the grey-haired man. He called to the demonstrators and after a short discussion they began to disperse, shouting their slogans in defiant retreat.

Taking the *lathi* away from Azim Khan, Farrell beckoned him into the gatehouse.

'Stay there till I call for you,' he said. He then went across the compound to Bannerjee and took him to his office.

'What happened, Bannerjee?' he asked.

'Mr. Farrell, he is always making trouble. Always complaining, saying we should have more Muslim workers. He is general nuisance. Then two days ago one of the men said he had stolen his food. They had argument and Azim Khan tried to beat him. You have seen, Sir, how violent he can be. The other men said they would not work with him, so I sacked him. He is bad influence, Sir.'

'Question is, Bannerjee, is he a good worker?'

'He is okay worker, Sir, but very much trouble. All workers are not liking him. When he is there, production is suffering.' Patches of sweat were gathering under Bannerjee's armpits.

'But he has been here a long time, I understand.'

Bannerjee uneasily rocked his head in acknowledgement. 'Yes, Mr Farrell, but bad influence, very bad, Sir. He will cause much trouble for the company.'

'Okay, Bannerjee, let me go and talk to him,' said Farrell wearily. He had a good idea what all of this was about.

Azim Khan confirmed that he has earned the ire of his mainly Hindu colleagues because of his strong Muslim League views. He denied stealing anyone's food.

'They got me sacked, Sahib, because I had a discussion with them and told them that we want a separate Muslim state in Bengal when the British go. They became angry with me. But the Hindus are killing our people Sahib, we cannot live together if the British go – they will kill us all.'

'Why can't you work together peacefully,' asked Farrell, 'keep your political views outside the mill.'

'Sahib, they are the trouble-makers. That Bannerjee wants to get rid of me. Now that I have gone, he will get rid of other Muslim workers one by one because there will be no one to fight for them. He wants to give all the jobs to his Congress-wallahs.'

Farrell doubted that either Azim Khan or Bannerjee was telling him the whole truth.

'Look,' he said to Azim Khan, 'I can't have people working here who are causing trouble with the other workers; we have a mill to run. Now, tell me exactly what has happened, tell me the truth – or I can't help you.'

Azim Khan considered this for a moment. 'Close the door, Sahib,' he whispered. Farrell did so.

'Sahib, what I will tell you is the truth, but if Bannerjee knows that it came from me my life could be over.' Farrell nodded. 'The truth, Sahib, is that Bannerjee is one of the Congress leaders in this area and he is trying to remove all the Muslim workers from your mill so that it is Hindus only. If you don't believe me, check your records for people who have lost their jobs in recent months – all Muslims, all by Bannerjee or his Hindu supervisor friends. Get someone to attend a meeting of the Congress-wallahs in their office near the bazaar – they are having big meeting there tomorrow night, Sahib, at 7 o'clock and you will see that I am right. Bannerjee is very influential man, Sahib, very dangerous.'

'Okay, Azim Khan,' said Farrell resignedly, 'let me look into all of this and I'll see what I can do. But if I do manage to get you your job back I want no more politics in the mill, do you understand? I suggest you go back home and give me a few days; someone will get in touch with you after that. I can't promise that you'll get your job back, but I'll look into the circumstances of your sacking and make a fair decision.'

Farrell relayed the gist of his conversations to Chennery.

'There could be something in it,' Chennery said, 'we have had a few Muslim workers go recently, and Hindus come in as replacements – no Muslims.'

'I'm going to get to the bottom of this,' replied Farrell, 'we can't have Congress agitators dictating who we employ. I think I'll go along to this Congress meeting tomorrow.'

'Are you off your head, old boy? A red-haired European will stand out from the crowd.'

'I don't intend to stay for the whole meeting, which will be for their members anyway and not open to the public. No, I'll just barge in and ask if Bannerjee is there – say we have an emergency at the factory or something like that.'

'Why not simply ask Bannerjee if he is a Congress chap?'

'Because he will know who told me, and it could put Azim Khan's life at risk.' Chennery looked sceptical at this somewhat dubious reasoning.

* * *

Farrell parked his car in the busy bazaar across the street from

the Congress office, where the meeting had been going for
about an hour. He sidestepped the hawkers and the rickshaws,
avoided as best he could the dirty water puddling in the
middle of the street, remembering his disaster at Dehra Dun,
and walked up to the shabby building, its grimy walls covered
with peeling political posters, stencilled graffiti and the red-
brown sprays of *pan* spittle, the entrance portico festooned with
squiggles of haphazard electrical wiring. He strode
purposefully through the cracked and worn entrance door,
across the mosaic floor of smashed pieces of crockery
embedded in cement, and was immediately challenged by a
young Congress official who rose quickly from a desk in the
lobby, barring his way, saying that the meeting was private.
Farrell pushed him aside, saying hotly that he had an
emergency and burst through the door of the meeting room.
The surprise of the thirty or so party faithful at this
unwarranted intrusion was nothing compared to the surprise
and shock that hit Farrell.

There on the dais was Bannerjee addressing the faithful,
clearly a Congress big-wig. But it was the garlanded and
white-clad guest of honour that caused Farrell to gasp – Anil
Chandra! Farrell hadn't seen him since remonstrating with him
in his tent before the battle for Singapore in '42. Chandra
looked startled too! Bannerjee, a look of fear on his face,
jumped off the stage and exited through a side door. The
audience turned towards Farrell, there were angry shouts and
gesticulations at his intrusion and Farrell began retreating the
way he had come.

'Sit down,' shouted Anil Chandra, 'let him be. He is a friend
of mine!' He pushed his way through the angry audience to
Farrell. 'Hello Mike,' he smiled, offering his hand, 'why the
dramatic entrance?' and steered him out of the meeting room
into the lobby.

Thinking quickly, Farrell said, 'I heard you were in the

vicinity Anil and thought I'd drop in. Had no idea that you were in the middle of a meeting. I'm sorry.'

Chandra smiled at the blatant lie. 'Why don't we have dinner tomorrow, Mike, and catch up with our news? Let's say 8 o'clock at the Grand Hotel?'

'Not the Grand,' replied Farrell, remembering his past embarrassment, 'let's make it Firpo's instead – the food's better.' He shook Chandra's hand again and left.

* * *

The large upstairs restaurant at Firpo's, with tables set around the dance floor and a small orchestra playing jazz standards, had a reputation for good, if expensive food. It was already about three-quarters full, mainly uniformed American servicemen and their local girlfriends. Over against a far wall a group of three Indian businessmen sat awkwardly at a dimly lit table sipping drinks and warily regarding the unfamiliar cutlery and napery – Chandra's bodyguards. As Farrell entered, Anil Chandra, seated alone at a prime table next to the dance floor, stood up and waved to him. Chandra was immaculately dressed in an expensive dove grey suit, white shirt and dark tie, looking every inch the prosperous businessman. Farrell felt slightly self-conscious in his creased cream cotton suit.

'I'm surprised that you're not embarrassed to be seen with an INA pariah like me,' was Chandra's smiling opening remark as they greeted each other.

'The war is in the past, Anil,' replied Farrell affably, 'it wasn't a particularly joyous experience for any of us, so best forgotten, eh? How are you? Tell me what you are doing now – I hear rumours that you are an important Congress big-wig now."

'I had the proverbial cloud with the silver lining, Mike. We

INA 'traitors' turned out to be Congress's 'freedom fighters'. They gave me a chance to show what I could do to help in the new interim Government. I must be doing something that they like because they have given me a good position in what will become a new Home Ministry when the British eventually go. I have a lot of dealings with Nehru, not so much with Gandhi-ji – he is usually off visiting a village somewhere in the back of beyond. What about you?'

'Demobbed late last year and decided to stay on in India – I like it here – so took a job in the Hamilton jute mill in Dum Dum. The British Manager, Archibald, and his Deputy, Chennery, will probably return to England when the Raj does go and I could find myself rapidly promoted to Manager.'

As they ordered drinks and examined the menu, Farrell asked how Chandra had got on with the Japanese in Singapore.

'At first they kept telling us that we were all Asian brothers together,' said Chandra, 'but this was a very thin pretence. Before long they were treating us with contempt. They would ignore us; give us very little food, that sort of thing. Some of our sepoys decided that they couldn't trust the Japanese and went back to being POWs. But then Subhas Bose arrived and the position got better. He had influence with the Japanese Government and with Hitler, you see, so the Japs took us more seriously. What about you, Mike?'

'Well, captivity at Changi was hard but not brutal at first. But then the Japs wanted all of us to sign a declaration that we wouldn't escape. We refused, of course, and there was a stand-off where they packed thousands of us into the Selarang Barracks and kept us there until we did sign. It was most unpleasant. We did have some trouble from the Sikh guards that the Japanese deployed to patrol our camp. They tried to take it out on our chaps – kicking, slapping, that sort of thing. Until one day, someone had had enough and one of the Sikhs was grabbed and shoved head-first down a field lavatory. The

Japs just laughed, they didn't punish anyone. The Sikhs were more wary and better behaved after that.'

'I did hear about that – power can sometimes bring out the worst in people,' laughed Chandra.

'And not just in the captors,' sighed Farrell. 'We had some of the old regular Army officers, still full of crusty bullshit. One chap, an artillery Major of the very old school, insisted on being saluted by the lower ranks and wanted to put fellow prisoners on a charge if they were improperly dressed, even though by then our clothes were in tatters. Another of these idiots was picked to go off to work on the Burma-Siam Railway and seriously discussed with his fellow officers whether he should pack his mess kit for dinner. Someone more worldly wise told him that when he went on the railway he wouldn't necessarily have any clothes to wear – and that there might not actually be any dinner. They were such bloody old fools.'

'But did you remain healthy?' asked Chandra. 'Did the Japs mistreat you?'

'No, they didn't mistreat me, Anil, 'but we were left malnourished. I got a bad case of rice balls...'

'Food poisoning?' asked Chandra.

'No!' Farrell laughed heartily. 'It was a condition caused by lack of vitamins because all we had to eat was rice. The skin on your scrotum peeled off and left you raw – most unpleasant, and not a subject to be talking about at dinner. We eventually cured it by getting the Japs to give us the rice husks – which contained all the vitamins.'

Chandra told him about his work with the Indian National Congress as the waiter took their order.

'Strange flag, the Congress flag,' said Farrell, 'like the orange white and green of the Italian flag laid sideways; and what is the significance of the blue spinning wheel in the centre?'

'Basu, a bright chap who works for me, jokes that the

saffron, white and green colours represent lentils, rice and vegetables – *dhall, bath and subzi,*' laughed Chandra. 'The spinning wheel is Gandhi-ji's idea – simplicity, connecting to the villages. The Congress high-ups want to keep the colours for a new flag for an independent India, especially as it embodies all of the groups who support the Quit India movement.'

'And will of course show Congress in the ascendancy!' laughed Farrell. 'But won't the Muslim League object?'

'If the Muslim League persuades the British to give them their own Muslim state they can have their own flag. Why shouldn't we have a representation of the Congress flag? We, after all, were the mainstays behind the independence movement and we represent a wide group of like-minded people. Personally, I think that the spinning wheel is a somewhat backward-looking emblem but it embodies the values of Gandhi-ji and he carries a lot of influence. Some have suggested that we change it to something more forward-looking, like a dharma chakra – which represents the wheel of life. The chakra is also the warlike discus carried by Vishnu, the Preserver.'

'The British lion run over by the chakra wheel or battered by Vishnu's discus. How appropriate,' laughed Farrell.

'More appropriate than you think, Mike. One of the incarnations of the god Vishnu is Narasimha, a man-lion, with a lion's head and a human body, who holds in his hand a chakra. According to Hindu mythology, he appeared to save the world from an arrogant demon figure. Maybe Narasimha is saving us from the arrogant British demon!' Farrell laughed politely at Chandra's barbed joke.

'But I like to think of it as embodying both – the lion and the chakra – Britain and the new India – working together to make this country prosperous and protecting it from other demons,' continued Chandra pretending to be diplomatic. Both exploded with laughter at the mealy-mouthed sentiment just uttered.

Chandra casually asked if Farrell had heard from Pierse.

'I thought you'd know his whereabouts, Anil, Home Ministry and all that!'

Chandra shook his head, as though he had no idea. Farrell gave him a sharp look; he wasn't going along with the deceit.

'Oh come on, Anil, don't bugger about. I'm sure that you know where Pierse is and that he intends to settle up with you for the wrong that you have done him.' Chandra shook his head again as though bewildered.

'Look,' said Farrell quietly, 'both of us have wronged Ed. I inadvertently put his name down to work on the Japanese Railway, foolishly believing that he would enjoy that because he came from a railway family. The Japs told us that it was light work, a holiday in the hills – of course they lied. I put his name down as a joke, but a very poor joke it turned out to be. They mistreated him, they mistreated all of them unspeakably – he came back looking like a skeleton, very ill – I couldn't recognise him when he and the few others who had survived walked through the gate at Changi after months on the railway. I was deeply ashamed at what I'd done – still am. When I finally made my peace with him at the depot in Jullundur, just before I left the army, he was very gracious about it but I don't think that we will ever recover our friendship. '

'I had no idea,' said Chandra.

'You are going to have to try to make your own peace with him – if you want to, that is.'

'I didn't do anything,' protested Chandra.

Farrell looked at him through narrowed eyes and said laconically, 'As a budding politician you must learn to lie more convincingly, Anil. You did a cruel and very shitty thing to someone who was your friend. We both did.'

* * *

They ate their way through a very good dinner talking about the political situation.

'What were you doing in Dum Dum?' asked Farrell as the plates were being cleared away.

'Rallying the Congress chaps,' replied Chandra. 'Bengal is one of those very mixed areas, Hindus and Muslims, and feelings are running high after the August riots. I am trying to improve the Congress party's organisation as we will have to face elections here in the future, and we want to be able to win them.'

'Where does Bannerjee figure in all of this?'

'He is the local party leader,' said Chandra. 'I gather that he works for your mill.'

'Not any more.' Chandra looked surprised. 'He didn't turn up for work today after he did a bunk when he saw me at your party HQ yesterday. We've sacked him.'

'Why?'

'We can't have the Congress party deciding who we should employ in the mill,' replied Farrell firmly. 'Bannerjee and his chums were getting rid of our Muslim workers and replacing them with Hindus. We can't have that.'

'Mike, this could be a bad move. If you sack Bannerjee the workers will come out on strike.'

'I'll hire new ones,' said Farrell defiantly, 'Muslims. Look Anil, Bannerjee was sacking Muslims just because they were Muslims and not because they were bad workers. We had a demonstration by sacked Muslim workers outside our gates yesterday led by a man called Azim Khan, a good worker who had been sacked for nothing by Bannerjee. I can't have that. As a member of an interim Indian Government don't you think that you should be looking after the interests of all Indian people, whatever their faith, not just those who are Hindu?'

'Bannerjee sacked Azim Khan because he was a murderer,' replied Chandra testily. 'In the August riots he was one of the ringleaders who were killing Hindus.'

'If you know that, why not tell the police.'

'Do you think they will do anything? The Chief Minister of Bengal is a Muslim and he has the police in his power. Your Hindu workers know what Azim Khan and his fellows did – that's why they don't want to work with them. Bannerjee was protecting your business.'

'I'm not having Bannerjee back,' said Farrell, 'I'm not having politics in the mill. We're there to process jute, for God's sake!'

Chandra sipped his drink thoughtfully. Then, his voice hard, he said, 'Mike, in a year or two the British will be gone. India will be ruled by the Congress party – whether or not Jinna and the Muslim League get their way. When Congress is in power we will decide who runs India. Many in the Viceroy's Government are already working with us to protect their commercial interests, though we are insisting that they should employ more Indians as managers. If you keep Bannerjee in your mill, we would be happy to have you stay on as the Manager.' He smiled.

'Blackmail, eh? You know me, Anil, stubborn as ever. A year or two is a long time, and by then I may decide that I want to go back home to Blighty anyway. Meanwhile we have a jute mill to run. So, I'm sorry Anil, but no deal. Bannerjee stays out – and if any of your Congress chaps tries to stir up trouble in the mill, out they go too.'

'It is not as simple as that, Mike,' Chandra said quietly. 'Personally, I don't care about Bannerjee. But if you sack him he loses face – and Congress loses face and the Muslim League and its murderers benefit. It may be alright for now, when the British are in power, but it will do your company no good in the long term. I'm sure that your company's Directors would not want a strike in the mill – nor would they be too happy to have a British manager there who had lied about his background.'

'What do you mean?' snapped Farrell, raising his voice, his heart racing.

'Home Ministry,' replied Chandra. 'I am able to see the information that police and others keep on people. You told Pierse and me that you went to Haileybury, the famous public school in England founded by the East India Company. I must tell you that we had our doubts when, to our surprise, you proved to have such a poor seat at polo – any upper class Englishman would have been brought up with horses, practically slept with them. I dug deeper and found records that show you went to Highbury, which I learn is a common school in the north of London. At first I thought that it was a spelling mistake, but got someone to check up and found out that it wasn't. I'm sure that your Directors would not be happy to have been deceived by you.'

Farrell stared stonily at Chandra. 'That is nothing compared to the lies that you have told, Chandra. At least I'm not a coward.' He stood up, angrily pushing the table away and rattling the cutlery and the glassware. The bodyguards rose, ready to move forward, one of them reaching under his jacket.

'Or a bloody turncoat!' he added, storming out.

CHAPTER 15

Reckoning

Chandra, bodyguards in tow, walked the few hundred yards back to the Grand Hotel, where he was staying while in Calcutta. He was angry with himself for so clumsily attempting to coerce Farrell, and angry that his stupidity had cost him another friendship. He didn't really care about Bannerjee being reinstated in the jute mill, and, if the truth be told, he found Bannerjee's revengeful policy of removing the Muslim workers offensive – Azim Khan could have been dealt with in other ways. What he ought to have done as a senior Congress and Government official was to have reprimanded or removed Bannerjee for stoking up racial hatred and his discussion with Farrell should have been about how they could put right the damage that had been done.

He decided that he would telephone Farrell in the morning and sort matters out. He resolved too that Bannerjee would be sent packing from his Congress job. An India built on racial hatred was an India that was doomed from the start. On a whim he asked Dina Nath to scout around quickly to try to see if Farrell was in the streets around Firpo's and, if so, to ask him to come and have a conciliatory drink. Dina Nath, whom Farrell would recognise from the Regiment, went off.

217

Reaching the corridor to his room, Chandra said goodnight to the bodyguards. As usual, one of them was left on guard, sitting on a chair outside; the other went off to get some sleep before taking his shift.

Chandra unlocked the door and closed it behind him. He reached for the light switch but an unseen hand clamped his mouth and something sharp prodded him in the ribs. He started to try to break free but froze when a whispered voice said, 'Struggle and you'll get hurt, Anil!' There was no mistaking who it was.

'Pierse?' he choked out but the hand tightened its grip round his mouth.

Pierse pushed him into the bathroom and kicked the door shut. He reached behind and switched on the light and Chandra saw in the mirror that he was holding a familiar opened knife in his right hand, the blade now pointed at his neck.

'Hello, Anil,' said Pierse grimly. 'Don't try any heroics – I don't want to have to hurt you or your guard outside if he tries to rescue you.'

'What do you want?' croaked Chandra, now thoroughly frightened. 'Did Farrell put you up to this?'

'Farrell? What the hell are you talking about! You know damn well why I'm here.'

'I was just having dinner with him in Firpo's.'

'I'm surprised that he wants to be seen with you. Striking another deal, were you?' said Pierse evenly; though he wondered why the hell they had been meeting but couldn't be sure that Chandra was just trying to distract him.

'How did you get into my room?'

'Half the hotel staff can get into your room. You're a difficult man to get to see, surrounded as you are by bodyguards and arse-lickers. This was the only way. Now, I'm going to turn you round and sit you on the edge of the bathtub.

If you shout or make any attempt to rush me it would be a mistake. I want some answers.' Chandra nodded fearfully.

Pierse looked at him curiously. He had not seen Chandra since before the battle for Singapore, and then only briefly. Now he looked paunchy and unfit, sweating profusely in his suit.

'Why did you tell my family that I was dead?'

'Look Ed, it was all a mistake.'

'I'll say, given that I'm standing here today.'

'No, no, it was a misunderstanding. I was angry that the letter you sent to my parents telling them I had gone missing at Sungei Choh so upset my father that he had an apoplectic fit that left him partly paralysed. I was very angry.'

'And yet, Anil, you had deceived us all. You had gone missing but it was by choice – you had done a bunk. Why blame me for something that you had done?'

'I know. I'm sorry Ed. When I found out that my father had suffered I blamed you – I know it was stupid of me but I wasn't thinking straight. I was just so fearful that your action had come so close to destroying my family. If my father had died my uncles would have helped themselves to our business and I was trapped in Malaya, powerless to stop them.'

'So you decided to pay me back?'

'No. It was not of my doing I swear to you on *Jawala Mata*! I was talking to a cousin of mine who lived in Singapore, I had hidden in their house after Sungei Choh and I lived with them again briefly after the Japanese took over. I said to him that you wouldn't have liked it if that had happened to your family. It was he who sent the message to your people. He thought that he was helping me get my own back. I assumed that he had told them you were missing – just as you had told my people. I didn't find out until after the war that he had told them you were dead. '

'Do you really expect me to believe that nonsense? You, Anil, who lied about Sungei Choh, who hid in Singapore and then turned up suitably dishevelled at our billet in Nee Soon with a fanciful story about joining with another unit, who pretended to have appendicitis so that you could get out of the battle with the Japs. You have lied all along. I thought that I knew you well. I thought that you were my friend. How could you do this to me?'

'I was frightened, Ed. I simply couldn't face another battle. I wasn't cut out to be a soldier. My nerve went at Kota Bharu when I fell into the stream and thought that I would die. My family was too heavy a burden on me.'

'You and your family are like jackals, like vultures. You prey on others to fatten yourselves. That's all you can think about – always looking for opportunities to exploit them to your benefit. Look at you. You now pretend to be a politician, but what you're really after is to line your pockets and get rich. You don't care about India. All you care about is yourself!'

Chandra's knees were knocking and he was shivering uncontrollably. 'L-look, Ed,' he begged, 'c-can I g-go and sit on the bed please, I p-promise not to call out, but I c-can't b-balance on the edge of the b-bath in my p-present state.'

Pierse looked at him. He saw a gibbering, frightened man, not the cocky Lt. Chandra of the Dogras. He remembered the times when they had been friends; doing dares – racing the ice-cream wallahs' tricycles round the parade ground or running through the hills dressed as village women – all for ridiculous bets. This cowering wretch wasn't the Chandra he had known. The desire for revenge, that strong impulse that had driven him since his return, went out of him.

Chandra saw it too.

'P-please, Ed, I b-beg of you, p-please let me sit on the b-bed.'

Pierse motioned with the knife for him to stand up and, with the other hand on the collar of his suit, escorted him towards the bed. Chandra's legs were giving way and he stumbled into the bedside table knocking the phone and sat down heavily, his face a picture of despair.

'I regret what happened, but I promise you that I didn't do it. I swear that it was not me who told your family.'

Pierse lowered the knife.

'Because of you, Anil, I lost Ellen. She was told that I was dead so she married someone else. She was everything to me. I only survived through my captivity because I was determined to get back to her. Do you know the shock you feel when you come home to find that the person you love, the reason for your existence, has gone? And gone because some malevolent bastard played a cruel trick?' His mouth was set in a snarl.

Trying to defuse the tension, Chandra said, 'I'm truly sorry, Ed,' and reached down to touch his feet in the Hindu mark of respect and contrition but Pierse swiftly stepped back and the knife went up.

'You've ruined both of our lives, Ellen's and mine. I've tried to find her but she is too ashamed to be found. Why should a cowardly bastard like you live, and prosper from your actions? What kind of an India will we build if we let people like you run it? Gandhi would be appalled.'

'If you kill me you will only ruin your own life, Ed. Please be reasonable. I will do my best to make things up to you. I will find Ellen and explain. There may still be a chance to put things right,' said Chandra agitatedly.

'Were you responsible for my being attacked in Coialla?'

Chandra hesitated, and Pierse realised that his instincts had been right. 'Why?' he asked.

'He was asked to keep an eye on you, not attack you,' said Chandra.

'Another one of your lies, eh?' retorted Pierse.

There was a knock on the door. 'Chandra Sahib, are you alright?' asked a voice.

'Get him to go away,' Pierse hissed. Chandra nodded.

'It's a routine call,' he whispered. Then, loudly, 'Yes, I am okay Govinda-ji,' he answered, 'I am in bed. Thank you.'

'Good night, Maharaj,' replied the voice, and Pierse relaxed.

* * *

The door burst open, splintering the architrave around the lock, and the bodyguard, pistol in hand, rushed in and charged Pierse. As Pierse turned to meet him, Chandra grabbed his knife arm and kicked his legs from under him and the bodyguard, followed closely by his fellow and two of the Hotel's security men, overwhelmed Pierse and threw him roughly to the floor, pinning him down, pistols at his head.

'You bastard!' spat Pierse.

Chandra rewarded him with a kick in the ribs. 'My security is very good Ed, and I have you to thank for it. When you let me sit on the bed I nudged the phone off the hook. Of course the operator realised that something was wrong as I didn't speak to her and she could probably hear our conversation – so the alert went out and my guards called out at the door. When they got the code word 'Govinda-ji' they knew that I needed help, so here they are. And you know what, Ed? I didn't think you had it in you to kill me – all that British fair play and your Catholic upbringing. Well, I'm not British or Catholic and we do things differently. I can't have you threatening my life. I haven't killed anyone in your family – so why do you want to kill me?'

He conferred in an undertone with one of the bodyguards and they hauled Pierse to his feet. One struck him suddenly and forcefully in the throat cutting off all his power of speech and leaving him choking and in agonising pain. They dragged him down the corridor and into the lift, and took him to the lane behind the hotel. In the dark, shielded from prying eyes by the large dustbins and general detritus of the hotel that guests never see, Chandra's two *goondas* began to beat him and kick him.

Pierse curled himself into a tight ball as the kicks thudded into his back and ribs and into his protecting arms and shins. Memories of Songkurai prison camp and the brutal Korean guards employed by the Japs came flooding back and he rolled around trying desperately to protect his head and his balls. The bodyguards, their first flurry of violence expended, now kicked him more calculatedly, aiming the blows to cause the maximum damage. Pierse's brain flashed white with pain as each kick went in, he tried to scream but only guttural animal sounds would come through his damaged throat. He saw Ellen's face in the flashes – she was mouthing something to him, the words soundless, he strained to make them out. But with each flash her image faded – bleached – she seemed to be in pain too. Then nothing; he lost consciousness as a vicious kick went into his spine and lifted him off the floor as one of the bodyguards tried to stop his noise.

The man then stepped back and levelled his pistol at Pierse's battered, bleeding, recumbent form and a shot rang out.

The other bodyguard looked surprised as his companion suddenly jerked away as though pulled by an invisible string and collapsed on his back, his gun clattering to the ground. He was quite dead, sightless eyes slowly rolling into his head, never to see the sun rise again above Calcutta. Dina Nath stood there in the shadows; gun in hand, the soft trail of smoke snaking from its barrel. He aimed it at the standing man who, in his terror, dropped his pistol and fell to his knees, his hands together in a supplication of mercy.

'You bastard,' shouted Dina Nath, 'what have you done to him? If you have killed him I will surely kill you! He was my officer; I will not have you dishonour a Dogra officer!' Forcing the man to lie face down, hands behind his head, Dina Nath knelt beside Pierse and checked his breathing and his pulse. Nothing! The portents didn't look good. Ordering the man to stand up he grabbed him by the scruff of his neck and ran him through the courtyard to the parked car, forced him to drive it round and together they loaded Pierse into the back seat, his blood spreading rapidly over the white cotton covers.

'Drive, *jaldhi*,' shouted Dina Nath, 'go to the Medical College Hospital in College Street and get there – quickly,' the last word was screamed at the terrified bodyguard as he banged his head with the barrel of the pistol.

* * *

Chandra waited anxiously in his hotel room for news from his men. Where the hell was Dina Nath; the security man had said that he was not in his room and the bodyguards had not returned. The hours passed and in the lonely watches of the night he became more and more agitated. He rang Basu for advice. He did not want the police involved. He began to regret giving his thugs a free hand to deal with Pierse. Then there was a knock on the door and he opened it, fiddling with the patchy repair to its lock, to find a grim, bloodstained Dina Nath. He came in and closed the door behind him.

'Where were you when we needed you – Pierse was discovered in my room!' said Chandra, his fear turning to anger.

'I had gone to look for Farrell Sahib as you asked me to. But I came across the men killing Pierse Sahib.'

'Is he dead?' asked a shocked Chandra.

'You told the men to make sure that he was not able to threaten you again. They are *goondas*, thugs, they did what you asked.'

Chandra sat down heavily. Then jumped up and ran to the

bathroom where he retched up his fine Firpo's dinner. When he returned to the room, Dina Nath had Pierse's knife in his hand, the blade closed.

'I will take this to his family,' he said. 'One other thing, I don't want to work for you anymore.'

'Where are the men?' asked Chandra sharply, pointedly ignoring what he had just said.

Dina Nath stared at him stonily. 'I shot one and the other will never work for you again, Sir.'

'What!' exclaimed Chandra, shocked and frightened. 'What about the police?'

'How can you do this to a friend Mr Chandra? He was a brother officer who saved your life in the war with the *Japani*. He did nothing wrong to you but you damaged his life. When the war ended and I heard that Pierse Sahib had survived, I decided that I would work with you – not to prevent Pierse Sahib from harming you, he would never do that – but it was to prevent you from killing him, just as you killed my cousin in Malaya.'

Chandra was taken aback but decided to go on the attack.

'I gave you land for helping me in Malaya and for agreeing to work for me. I can just as easily take it all back. Do you want that?'

Dina Nath smiled menacingly and this scared Chandra, who suddenly remembered that he was armed and had already shot one bodyguard and done something unspeakable to the other.

'My uncle, Jemadar Prem Singh, said that if I ever harmed Pierse Sahib he would kill me – and there are several others in the Regiment who would do it also. He was our officer, Sir, and a good man. I have done my duty to you and I have protected your life. There is no threat to you now from Pierse Sahib so there is no need for me to continue working for you. But if you try to take away my land and ruin my family I will not let you do it.' The threat was clear and Chandra was in no doubt that it was real. He tried to mollify Dina Nath.

'Look Dina Nath, I am very sorry about what happened to Pierse Sahib. The men should have not been so harsh – I told them to hurt him, as a warning, not to kill him. But they are just *goondas,* they are animals. Please continue to work for me. I need your help.'

'No Sir,' Dina Nath shook his head. 'I am going now to see Pierse Sahib in hospital.'

'He is alive?' exclaimed Chandra, his spirits suddenly lifted.

'I don't know.'

CHAPTER 16

A Game of Hockey

'C'mon boys! We can win this one and get into the finals of the Beighton Cup. Ragunath, you take the left wing, Dina Nath, right wing. Now, let's go!'

The pitch ran steeply downhill all the way through the tea bushes to the ravine and the river in the valley, then uphill through more tea bushes to the goal on top of a misty, high hill.

'Watch the ball. If you hit it too hard it explodes like a water balloon. God, I keep tripping on the roots of the tea bushes and falling on to the rocks – my back and ribs hurt. These damn maggots come bursting out of the soil at my feet, it's too bloody slippery.'

'The pickers are in the way Sahib. They won't move. They just keep smiling – and flirting. Move, you women!'

'Shit. Another fall, my whole body aches and I can't breathe. We are never going to get down this hill.'

'Take the motorcycle, dear fellow,' says Uncle Bertie.

'Thanks, but it will just slide uncontrollably down the slope and I'll get nowhere – I'll just crash, like Sapper.'

'Ah! But not if you fill the petrol tank with tea! Tea will give it grip.'

'Thanks – that's better uncle Bertie. Dina, Ragu – keep up,

227

228 # THE LION AND THE CHAKRA

we must play a fast passing game. Who is on our team – is Lt. Chandra with us or against us? Hey! Anil, stop lobbing grenades at us and get on with the game. Oh, Uncle Bertie, has Mrs May arrived? She said that she would come to cheer me on. We can't win if she doesn't come.'

At last the river.

'Who put that bloody train in the way? Mike! Mike! Get your train out of our way. We have to go up the hill to score a goal.'

'Sorry, old chap. Can't move the train until all the troops are accounted for,' says Farrell, waving his cricket bat cheerily. The grinning skeletons in their 'Jap happys' continue to hack at the rocks and move the rails into position.

'Shoot him, Dina Nath – shoot the bloody lot of them! Then ask my Da and Uncle Derek to get the damn train out of the valley. By the way, have you seen Mrs May? She said she would watch us from the top of the hill.'

'Ragu has got over the river,' says Dina Nath, 'but the *Japani* are shooting at him Sahib.'

'Those buggers! Why can they never play fair? Why do they always play dirty! They don't know the offside rule either, and they don't bloody care. Dina Nath you move further out to the right wing. Ragu, you run ahead and get behind them. Prem Singh, bring up the Bren gun, we'll enfilade the bastards. Okay, up the hill boys, the goal is in sight. Owwww. They've shot me, I think. I'm in pain.'

'Keep going, Sahib,' says Ragu, 'the monsoon is waiting behind the goal posts.'

'I'll help you Ed, 'says Kenny, patting his pocket. 'I've got sausages, and you know how the Japs love those.'

'I can't go on Ken, I'm hurting all over. Has Mrs May arrived?'

'Don't think so. I'll ask a policeman. Ha Ha.'

'Dribble the ball! Keep passing! Up, up, and up the hill. Try not to slip on the slope! Bugger! I've fallen again – my side hurts. C'mon, dodge the Japs. Cut them down! Swipe them with your hockey sticks, but don't raise them above the shoulder or it's a foul. '

At last, the goal is in sight.

'C'mon boys, nearly there! Play like champions! Pass it to me Ragu and I'll score. Father Lawrence, what are you doing in the goal! Move out, we have to score.'

'You can't do that,' he says, 'I'm keeping my butterflies in the netting. You'll have to wait till they've gone.'

'Perhaps I can help,' says Father Sam, touching his lighted cigar to one of the butterflies. It catches fire and flares up, setting light to the next one and that sets fire to the next. Soon the goal is filled with flashes of fire as the butterflies flame and burn to a crisp.

'Thanks, Father Sam. A friend in need – is a bloody nuisance, eh? Pass the ball to me Ragu – now!'

Father Lawrence pauses then pulls a gun out of a large book and points it, but Baldev whacks him with a *kirpan*. The netting turns to cloud. Mrs May is standing on the hill with her umbrella up.

'Ah! Mrs May, thanks for coming. You are just in time to see me scoring a goal.'

The ball is struck and flies in a cascade of water through the cloud-net. 'Goal! Goal! *Jawala Mata ki Jai*! Let's follow the ball boys, through the net and out the other side.'

Boom! Lightning flashes.

'Oh my God, I've been struck and the pain is unbelievable.'

The black clouds compress like sponges and the deluge falls. Slowly all are washed clean. The pain recedes and mist obscures the pitch. Mrs May smiles, then waves farewell.

'Bye, Mrs May.'

CHAPTER 17

Resurrection

'He's said something!' shouted Kenny excitedly, his voice echoing around the stark cement walls of the white-washed hospital room. His call brought the others running. They gathered round the bed, breathless.

'What'd he say? Did you hear? Did you catch his words?'

'It sounded something like, um, like – Bye, Mrs May! But it was so faint that I can't be certain.'

'Who is Mrs May?!' They looked at each other but nobody knew. They shrugged.

'Are you sure that he said something Kenny? You're not just imagining it, Son? He could have just sighed. He's been groaning a lot.'

Kenny looked at his father, annoyed that he was being doubted. 'Yes, I'm sure, Da. I'm absolutely, completely, irrefutably sure.'

They were tired. No, more than tired, they were exhausted husks from days and nights of their vigil round the hospital bed, all hopes dashed by the doctors – just waiting for death to call at his leisure. The nightmare had begun four nights ago when an insistent late night pounding on the door had roused the family. They found a blood-stained and incoherent Dina Nath on the doorstep. They didn't know who he was and at first thought that he had been a victim of the communal violence that was sparking all over Calcutta and was seeking refuge. Kenny had drawn his truncheon. But the man kept repeating, 'Pierse Sahib! Lieutenant Pierse Sahib! Hospital! Hospital!' and they understood that something bad had happened to Ed.

Driven by Dina Nath to the Medical College Hospital, they were totally unprepared for the sight of an unconscious, bloody and almost unrecognisable Ed, surrounded by doctors and nurses, with tubes in his arms and down his throat. The English doctor's laconic response to their obvious question, 'How is he?' had stunned them.

'He is in a very bad way, I'm afraid. He's been kicked about a bit: broken ribs and collar bone, damaged back, damaged throat, possibly a broken shin, contusions all over. He has lost a lot of blood. His pulse is very weak. He is dying.'

Those last three words, spoken as a matter of fact, shocked them to the core. Da Pierse broke down, weeping quietly into his handkerchief, Mrs Pierse stood there trying to keep her emotions in check, tears escaping down her face and dripping on to the hospital floor. All Kenny could feel was rage.

He turned to Dina Nath. 'Where are the people who did this?' he asked roughly.

Dina Nath took his arm and steered him out of the room and into the corridor.

'Think about your brother now, Sir. Don't worry about the men who did this, I have taken care of them.'

'I'm a bloody policeman, dammit! Tell me what happened or – I'll arrest you.'

Dina Nath looked him at him reassuringly. 'I'm not going anywhere, Sir. Pierse Sahib was my officer. He may not live many more minutes; you should go and stay with him.'

A chastened Kenny nodded and turned back into the room.

His mother stood by the bedside, holding Ed's hand and uttering prayers and little sobs in her grief.

'A nurse has gone to get a priest to give him the Last Sacrament,' said his father.

Kenny suppressed the desire to retort that his brother was an atheist. At this awful time poor Ed needed all the help that he could get.

Over the next four days there were visitors. The managers from Finlays, where Pierse had been working for a couple of months, Uncle Derek and Aunt Philly, Sunny, friends from the Rangers' hockey team and, surprisingly, Mike Farrell, summoned by the tireless Dina Nath. They had come to stand at his bed not knowing what to say or do. They waited for the end, but Pierse was refusing to die.

Now he had spoken! Doctor Laconic said that this was a good sign, that his brain might not have been damaged. They took turns at his bed, night and day, and watched him slowly, painfully unfold from his dark coma and come back to them piece by piece. His eyes flickered and opened, he tried to speak but his throat hurt. He took sips of water, he shouted in pain as the doctors and nurses examined him and dressed his wounds. And Ed Pierse gradually re-inhabited his damaged body. They kept him in the hospital for a month while his bones knitted and the bruises went from red and purple to yellowy green and he looked, as Kenny remarked, like an accident in a paint factory. He slowly found his feet, his leg thankfully not broken but badly cut and bruised. He had been lucky that one of his assailants had been wearing *chappals* and that his kicks had not been so damaging.

'Who is Mrs May?' asked his mother one day. Pierse looked nonplussed for a second then made the connection. He decided that she wouldn't understand the complete truth and just said that it was someone he used to talk to in Munnar.

* * *

As he convalesced at home, Farrell took to visiting him some weekends and they would sit and talk in the garden, catching up and slowly rebuilding their friendship. Farrell didn't tell him about the incident with the girl in the Grand – Kenny, touched by his unexpected visits to see his brother as he lay unconscious in hospital, had assured him that, so far as he was concerned, it was covered by Police confidentiality and would never be mentioned. Farrell had thanked Kenny stiffly, aware that there was another matter, his putting forward Pierse for the Jap railway, that Kenny would never forgive. He pondered whether to tell Pierse why he had put his name forward but decided against doing so. It would wound Pierse deeply to know that his fellow British officers regarded him as 'not one of them'. He had suffered enough already. Farrell felt deeply ashamed of himself for not standing up for his friend; putting his self-interest first.

They told each other of their last meetings with Chandra, though Farrell omitted any mention of Haileybury.

'I had a letter from him about a week after we dined in Firpo's,' said Farrell, 'want to read it?' He passed over an envelope, Pierse opened it and read:

'*Dear Mike,*

I'm sorry that our dinner had such an unfortunate ending. I regretted it immediately and sent Dina Nath, an ex-Dogra sepoy, to try to find you so that I could put matters right.

You were right to sack Bannerjee. I have also dismissed him from the local Congress party committee. I have warned the people in the local party not to stir up trouble in the jute mill or they too will be sacked. You are right; we cannot have such bigots in our new, free India.

I would humbly advise you not to re-employ Azim Khan. He is a murderer and the Hindu men in the mill would not be happy if you took him back.

234 ● THE LION AND THE CHAKRA

*I apologise for many of the things I said to you. I want to keep you
as a friend. I hope your ambition to be manager of the jute mill is
realised; you can count on me for support.*

Your friend,

Anil'

'Funny thing is,' said Farrell, 'our friend Azim Khan
disappeared a few days later. Nobody can say where he is or
what happened. The problem was sorted out for me. By the
way, has Kenny reported your attack to the police? They came
close to killing you.'

'I shouldn't have waylaid Chandra in his hotel room, so it
was my fault. I have to take the punishment – have to accept it.
Anyway, my attackers are dead. Justice done,' Pierse laughed
self-consciously.

'Would you have killed him?'

'Hell, no! I just wanted to know why he had done what he
did. That's all. I might have beaten him up and felt better about
it all but I was out-manoeuvred. Thank God for Dina Nath.'

'Where is he now?'

'He went back to his village to farm his land. He doesn't
work for Chandra anymore. He was always a good man to
have with you in a scrap. '

'No, I meant Chandra.'

'Oh. I gather that he fled back to Delhi and is still doing the
rounds as a politician. Dina Nath told me that he was quite
frightened when he heard that I was at death's door; probably
more worried about the effect on his political career if the police
got involved. Poor old Kenny is wrestling with his conscience
because Dina Nath finished off both bodyguards and I don't
think Ken can come to terms with being an upright policeman
and concealing a double murderer. He is talking about

resigning and going back to college – the parents are pleased.'

* * *

Pierse eventually limped back to work with Finlays, settling in to a not wholly unfamiliar world of tea and the administration of the company's tea estates, recruiting new Indian managers to fill the vacancies left by the war and by planters packing up and returning to England.

In Delhi, eminent men were engaged in their various ways on the complicated work of sorting out India's independence. The Raj, like the Moghul Emperors before it, liked to imagine that it brought a benign and harmonious rule over its subjects where otherwise law and order would disintegrate. Viceroy Wavell therefore continued to coax the implacable Jinna to join Nehru in the Interim Government, but Jinna was having none of it. He doggedly continued to advance his demand for a separate Muslim state: 'We shall have India divided,' he proclaimed, 'or we shall have India destroyed.' The exasperated British Government in London felt that Wavell did not have it in him to resolve the thorny issue of India's freedom and told him in January that he was being removed.

In March, Wavell's replacement, the energetic and charismatic Lord Louis Mountbatten, a cousin of the King, arrived in Delhi with his glamorous wife, Edwina. He had been given a brief to divest Britain of India by the end of June the following year – 1948. He didn't want the job, being unwilling to go down in history as the man responsible for dismantling the British Raj. After all, this was an Empire that had, improbably, begun in 1599 over the Dutch imposition of five shillings on the price of a pound of pepper, which stirred the furious British to found the East India Company and take control of the spice trade. Mountbatten had placed demand upon impossible demand on Prime Minister Attlee in the hope that he would eventually give up and turn to someone else. Instead, Attlee gave him everything he asked for. Most crucial of all, he agreed that Mountbatten could broker a solution without requiring the approval of the Cabinet in London – so desperate were the bankrupt British to withdraw from India.

Mountbatten arrived with mixed feelings at the familiar imposing Lutyens' designed red and white Barauli stone Viceroy's House in New Delhi, its floors and walls of white, green, yellow and black marble. It was here in this opulent palace that he had asked Edwina to marry him a quarter of a century earlier during a Viceroy's Ball to honour his cousin, Edward, the Prince of Wales who was on a State Visit. Mountbatten was now met by the outgoing Viceroy, the one-eyed old soldier Wavell; this was yet another of his impossible demands. Custom dictated that the outgoing and incoming Viceroys passed at sea, one leaving from the Gateway of India in Bombay, as the other arrived – saving India the embarrassment of having two such 'Gods' on its soil at the same time. But these were extraordinary times.

In his office Wavell produced a manila folder labelled 'Operation Madhouse' from his safe. This, he confessed, was the only viable plan he could arrive at for disentangling the British from India. It involved the British evacuating India province by province – women and children first, then civilians, then soldiers – until India was empty of the British. It was an absurd plan, a recipe for total chaos, a clear indication that London was right about him and his lack of political nous.

Mountbatten quickly set about meeting the principal players, Nehru, Gandhi and Jinnah, in private to gauge their feelings; he also consulted the provincial Governors. It soon became clear to him that unless the British moved urgently to grant India its independence, the country would disintegrate into civil war and chaos – the British did not have the troops or the will to hold the country together and Hindu-Muslim disturbances were on the increase. He wrote to London recommending that he radically bring forward the date for granting independence from June 1948 to within a few months time – the summer of 1947.

That April, with Jinna still refusing to budge, Nehru and Congress accepted Mountbatten's view that partition was inevitable. A sorrowful Gandhi remained opposed. In June Mountbatten announced that the 15th of August, just over two months' away, was the date on which India and Pakistan would become independent dominions.

Pierse heard from his former Dogra colleagues that Auchinleck, the Commander in Chief, had been given just four weeks to prepare a plan to divide the Army between India and Pakistan and that over thirteen thousand British officers were to be replaced. But other urgent divisions had also to take place: all of the assets and the debts had to be divided between India and Pakistan – from the cash and gold in the banks to the tables, chairs, typewriters, fans, clocks, bicycles and people in the Government Ministries. Eighty per cent of the assets were to remain in India, twenty per cent to go to Pakistan. This, naturally, led to intense arguments and innumerable petty wrangles among the bureaucrats – and double-dealing among the politicians.

And who was going to draw up the new boundaries? An owlish London lawyer, luxuriating in the cool climate of Simla, where Government moved to in the summer, gazed with many misgivings at the finely detailed map of India spread before him. A genuine former pupil of Haileybury, Cyril Radcliffe, an eminent barrister from Lincoln's Inn, was given the job by that other Old Haileyburian, Prime Minister Attlee. He had protested that he knew nothing about India; Attlee had assured him that this was, curiously, an ideal recommendation for the job – he would be free of prejudice or taint in approaching the task. Radcliffe's pencilled boundary lines when eventually expanded from the paper maps would scythe through the homes and lands separating 80 million people in the provinces of the Punjab and Bengal. Dividing all of the territory on ethnic or religious lines was impossible as, over centuries, the people of India had learned to coexist together in the towns and villages. Now, some would find that their houses lay on one side of the boundary, their fields on the other. Ancestral homes occupied for centuries would be abandoned because they lay on the wrong side of the divide. Crucially, Mountbatten made it clear to Radcliffe that he did not want his proposals announced until *after* the new dominions came into being. Lord Louis loved a good ceremonial 'do' and he did not want to spoil the elaborate Independence celebrations that had been planned! Yet the delay proved fatal to hundreds of thousands.

With the announcement that India was to be partitioned into two new states, the violence escalated dangerously. Neighbour turned on neighbour, tenant on landlord, stranger on stranger. Simmering grievances, religious rivalries, historical hurts, a desire for vengeance arising from angry reactions to newspaper or radio reports of killings and violence, or often simply a desire for booty – all were the triggers for indiscriminate killing, raping and looting. The epicentre of the violence was in the Punjab as Sikhs, Hindus and Muslims fought for possession of the territory that was being carved up in the Vice Regal Lodge and at working lunches in the Cecil Hotel in other-worldly Simla.

* * *

Pierse's family followed the events with growing concern. Some of their friends were already booking passages on the ships to London and the Anglo-Indians, fearful of the future, talked of leaving if they could acquire British citizenship and get the money together for their passages 'home'. Should the

Pierses stay or should they too go? Da Pierse declared that he was too old and too set in his ways to move to Blighty and start all over again – even if it was possible to find work at his age in war ravaged Britain. Kenny came in one day and announced that he had put in an application to the Kenya police. Pierse wasn't sure where he stood. He loved this country, he was born in it, had fought for it, spoke the language – all the things that Sunny and he had discussed on the *maidan*. He didn't want to leave it but he remained uncertain about what India would be like once the British went. Would there be a place for people like the Anglo-Indians? Would they be seen as an unwelcome reminder of a colonial past? Were they just the detritus of conquest, to be discarded in what was, after all, turning out to be an epic setback for Britain? Would the mobs turn on a defenceless minority, just like they were turning on each other, to revenge the hurt of three centuries?

He was sitting with Mike Farrell one evening in the first week of August; they were having a quick drink with a somewhat downcast Kenny before setting off to have dinner in one of the restaurants on Park Street.

'Cheer up, Ken,' said Pierse, 'there are plenty more fish in the sea.'

Kenny glared at him morosely. 'It's not bloody fish I'm after, is it!'

Farrell looked quizzically at Pierse.

'Kenny met this girl, Mike, very, very beautiful; she is a stenographer for Jardines. She was interested in Ken – must have been the uniform Ken, can't think of anything else,' he laughed, punching his brother's arm affectionately.

'So where's the problem?' asked Farrell.

'She turned out to be a bloody *mama ko poocho*', muttered Kenny disgustedly.

'Don't understand,' said Farrell.

'Mike, she didn't make a move without consulting her

mother – the constant chaperone – everything was *mama ko poocho*, ask my Mama!' Pierse hooted with laughter and Mike smiled.

'Rather cramped your style, didn't it Ken!'

'I'll say,' sighed Kenny, somewhat recovering his spirits. 'She was so damn beautiful that I suppose Mama wanted to make sure that nobody had their wicked way with her until the ring was on her finger. It was not much fun taking her out with her Ma in tow. If her mother carries on like that her lovely daughter'll die an old maid.' He downed his drink and rose, 'I'm off to have a drink with some chums; I might get lucky.'

'Why not come with us,' suggested Farrell.

'What! And have two *Papa ko poochos* of my own? No thank you.'

The rain was slowly tailing off and Pierse and Farrell checked their watches.

'Time for a quick *chota peg?*' enquired Pierse, Farrell nodded. He went to pour another drink, when a telegram arrived.

'It's for you Ed,' said his mother anxiously.

Pierse looked surprised. He took the envelope, opened it and exclaimed sharply. He handed the telegram to his mother and Farrell. It read:

'ELLEN IN JOSEPHINE CONVENT LAHORE STOP URGENT YOU GO IMMEDIATELY AS RAIL AND ROADS CROWDED WITH REFUGEES STOP WILL MEET YOU WITH CAR AT JULLUNDUR STATION STOP TELEGRAPH ARRIVAL STOP ANIL CHANDRA'

'What now?' asked his mother, looking fearful, 'don't go Eddie, it's a trap. He can't be trusted.'

'I'm going,' replied Pierse firmly, his heart thumping, his hands tingling – he suddenly felt indescribably happy. 'Can Da get me a booking on the first train to Delhi tomorrow?'

'You can't go, son,' Mrs Pierse clutched his arm. 'She has a husband, it will be his duty to look after her – they may want to remain in Lahore. Don't spoil it for her. It is not your responsibility – and you can't trust Chandra after what he did to you!'

'I just want to see her Ma, before the new border makes it impossible. I have to see her...' She saw the pleading in his eyes.

'How will you handle Taylor?' asked Farrell, 'you won't have much time there with the borders about to go up. And there's a child now.'

'I don't know!' said an exasperated Pierse. 'I'll say that I have come to offer my services to escort them home to India if they wish. Something like that. I'll think of something. I just want five minutes alone with Ellen – is that too much to ask?'

'Please don't go Eddie,' Mrs Pierse begged. 'You don't know whether Chandra is lying or not. How did he find her? He doesn't say. She's married, she has a baby – you can't turn back the clock. Be sensible.'

'I have to go Ma. I just have to go. If it is one of Chandra's tricks I will kill him this time. But I have to go – before I lose the chance forever.'

'But it is dangerous; people are being robbed and killed in the crowds that are moving each way in the Punjab. There's mayhem there. You've already come back from the dead twice – the third time could be unlucky.'

'He's gone beyond the third time, Mrs Pierse,' Farrell chuckled. 'In Malaya the Grim Reaper was fobbed off so many times that we must be in double figures by now.'

Kenny stood at the door listening to the conversation.

'Why don't I go Ed,' he said. 'Ellen knows me, Taylor won't feel threatened – I can just say that I happened to be in Lahore and can ask them if they want to remain or be escorted back to India. I can get a chance to talk to Ellen.'

Pierse shook his head. 'No, Kenny. *I* have to go; *I* have to see Ellen – don't you understand?'

'We'll have to be careful that we don't look mob-handed, like a kidnap party. That would frighten Ellen off,' mused Farrell.

'We?' exclaimed Pierse.

'Yes, we! I'm coming too.' Farrell's face creased into a wide grin. 'Don't worry Mrs Pierse, I'll look after Ed, make sure he's okay and that Chandra doesn't try any tricks. What fun,' he laughed, 'the Allsorts together again!'

CHAPTER 18

The Road to Paradise

Reaching Jullundur, Farrell and Pierse got off the train with their kitbags and pushed their way with difficulty out of the crowded station building. There in the bustling station courtyard stood Anil Chandra, dressed in a smart shirt and slacks, accompanied by two white-clad Congress people. He was engaged in a furious argument in Urdu with a yellow turbaned Punjabi bearing an extravagant moustache; the obvious object of their discussion was the somewhat old-fashioned and careworn maroon Chevrolet car that was being pointed to, fingers jabbing in time to the cadences of their speech, like two fencers with invisible swords. Chandra didn't see Pierse and Farrell approach.

'Want us to do the bastard over?' asked an amused Farrell.

Chandra spun round. He raised his arms in exaggerated welcome and shouted, 'Chaps, how nice to see you again! Welcome once more to Jullundur, home of the Dogras where, I imagine, I am *persona non grata* now. Meet the biggest bloody rogue in the place, Kochar – who can't find me a decent car and is trying to rob me blind over this one!' They shook hands – as though nothing in the recent past mattered – Pierse was too excited to care anyway.

'I'm sorry chaps, but this car is not what I expected, and the people here say that they have no others to sell or lend. There are thousands and thousands crossing what they expect will be the new border that comes into force next week on the 15th of August – Muslims going from here to what they believe will become Pakistan, Hindus coming the other way. Transport is scarce – people are paying huge sums of money to buy anything that will take them the one hundred or so miles to Lahore. The trains are erratic and when they do run they are overcrowded or too dangerous as there is the risk that they will be waylaid and the passengers attacked – killed even. So I'm sorry, but this bloody Chevvy Sedan, which is about fifteen years old and which, I am unreliably informed by this rogue here, used to belong to some minor Maharajah, is all we have got.'

'Will it get us there?' asked a now anxious Pierse as he viewed the battered and rusting body and the scratched and split leather seats with stuffing sprouting out of them.

'He says that it will,' replied Chandra. He turned to the car's owner and in Urdu said threateningly that if the car broke down he would come back and ensure that his business was shut down. The owner, now confronted by two more potential adversaries, became unctuously creepy and assured them in the name of all the Gods that the car would function perfectly well.

They set off, with Chandra driving, to take the Grand Trunk Road to Amritsar, a short section of the fabled 'long walk' that stretched like a necklace from Calcutta, in the Bay of Bengal, across the shoulder of India to Peshawar on the North West Frontier. They had hardly gone a few miles and exchanged a few stilted pleasantries before the cloud of dust ahead revealed the main road and its verges for a hundred yards each side crowded with thousands of families, Muslims going west, Hindus and Sikhs coming east, fleeing their homes, carrying everything they could, driving their livestock, anxious to be on the right side as quickly as possible – though nobody as yet knew exactly where the border would lie even though Independence was only a few days away. The crowds travelled on foot, on horseback, bullock carts, lorries, cars and buses, all jostling for space amongst a cacophony of shouted conversations, swearing, urgently honking horns, the cracking of whips and the cries of children and animals. Above them circled the birds of prey for there were already pickings for them as the sick, young, frail and the elderly fell by the wayside exhausted, thirsty and dying while the human tide rolled on. Progress was slow because of the crush of people, vehicles and animals.

The car slowed to a crawl and Chandra honked the horn and weaved in and out of the traffic as best he could. It was very hot, in the 90s, and the dust blew through the open windows, settling in their hair and on their faces, coating everything – it was like Singapore during the fighting all over again. The monsoon, usually so reliable, was late this year and there was no sign of the cooling rain, no gathering of clouds, not the faintest hint of a promise of fresher, wetter weather. Their clothes were soon running with sweat as the heat was convected by the metal body of the car and added to by its straining engine. It was not going to be the quick dash in three or four hours that Pierse and Farrell had envisaged.

'It will get better when night falls,' said Chandra, 'then hopefully people will get off the road to camp and we can make faster progress.'

'Why have you come with us Anil?' asked Pierse.

'Look Piersey, I parted on bad terms with you when we last met – and with you too Mike. For all of that I apologise most profusely. I know that you hold me responsible for your separation from Ellen – though I assure you it was not my fault. I am really very sorry that my bodyguards beat you so badly;

they were supposed to scare you off not hurt you. I want to put matters right. I owe it to you. I've been an idiot, deserting my closest friends.'

'But you're a *Burra Sahib* in Government now,' said Farrell slyly. 'How have they let you come on this trip so close to the Independence Day? And without bodyguards,' he winked at Pierse.

'Long story Mike. I said that I would go and do a reconnaissance for them and report back on the refugee situation. They are getting garbled reports – so this will give a better picture. We have had stories of killings and rape, and suggestions that the police and troops have been joining in too. There is also a worry that some ex-sepoys are planning to use their army knowledge to derail trains and attack the passengers. I scouted around for Congress once before during the Calcutta killings last August. It may be that we have to deploy more units of the Army here to maintain order, and ensure that they don't take sides – so we may have to bring in the Gurkhas. As for the bodyguards,' he laughed, 'what better than two battle-hardened Dogra officers!'

Pierse and Farrell exchanged old-fashioned looks.

'How did you find out that Ellen was in Lahore?' asked Pierse. 'Do you know in which school her husband, Alec Taylor, is working? He can't be working in a convent.'

'Secret police sources, eh?' chuckled Farrell.

'No, no. It was purely by chance,' protested Chandra. 'My father's friend brought his family back from Lahore for safety and the young daughter, Jaya, showed a photograph of some of the convent girls with the teachers, taken just before she left. One of the teachers looked familiar and I recognised her as Ellen – I had met her in Jullundur with you before the war Piersey, and she is distinctively tall. I asked Jaya if she knew her name but she didn't – Jaya is only six and Ellen wasn't her class teacher.'

'But how can you be sure it was her?' asked Pierse, his concern growing.

'If you fish around in the bag on the back seat you'll find the photo,' replied Chandra.

Pierse rummaged through the bag and found an envelope in which there was a small photograph of a school group, probably taken with a pupil's Brownie camera. He inhaled sharply. Even after all these years Ellen was unmistakeable. His hands shook and his heart raced.

'Are you sure you haven't doctored the photograph Anil?' asked a mischievous Farrell.

Pierse looked closely at the photograph, comparing the shadows, looking for clues. He handed it to Farrell, who also examined it closely.

'Did you get your chaps to check that it is Ellen and that she is still there? I hope that we are not going there simply on the evidence of this photograph!' said Pierse sharply.

'With all the chaos around it has not been possible to check, Ed. Look, I know that it's a hard thing to ask after all that has happened,' said Chandra quietly, 'but please try to trust me. I want to put matters right between us. This is all we have to go on – if she's there, we'll find her. If she's gone elsewhere then maybe somebody can tell us where.'

'And Taylor?'

'I don't know anything about him. We'll have to ask at the convent to find out where they live.'

'How long ago was the photograph taken?' asked Pierse anxiously. 'Will she still be there at the convent?'

'I can't guarantee that,' replied Chandra, 'the photograph was taken about a month ago. She was there then. She might have left – many are leaving Lahore because they don't want to live in a Muslim-dominated Pakistan – but as you can see from this road, getting out isn't easy and the trains are so packed that people are having to travel on the roof.'

Pierse's mind raced, this was his best chance yet, though it was an uncertain one. And if he found her, how was he was going to be able to get Ellen alone to talk to her. He and Farrell had discussed several possibilities while on the train, some bordering on the criminal. Whatever happened, they would have to move quickly.

They took turns to drive, carefully nursing the aged car, and reached Amritsar, the holy place of the Sikhs, shortly after sunset. After a quick dinner in that crowded city, packed with refugees and seething with an undercurrent of violence, they set off once again to drive the thirty or so miles to Lahore. It was just as crowded at night and twice as dangerous in the darkness in the feeble light of the headlights and the kerosene lanterns carried by some in the crowd. They made very slow progress.

'You know,' said Chandra, 'not many months ago, the rich people would drive from Amritsar to Lahore just to have their breakfast.'

'Not now they won't,' Pierse retorted, 'not once they have to cross a new border.'

'And might have to drop their trousers,' laughed Chandra.

'Watch out!' shouted Farrell, who was driving, and the car squealed to a standstill as three blue-turbaned Sikhs, swords drawn, ran out from the cover of a bullock cart and blocked the road ahead of them clearly intent on robbery or mayhem. A car was rich pickings and Muslims fleeing to Pakistan were fair game, especially under cover of the night. The crowd ignored them and surged on by, grateful that they were not the objects of their attention.

'I could run the car through them,' shouted Farrell, 'but the way ahead is not clear and we won't get far.' He wished now that he had been armed. Pierse was clicking open his knife.

Chandra flung open the passenger door and stepped into the road, a small blue steel automatic pistol in his hand levelled at the robbers. They didn't wait but disappeared into the crowd. He got back in.

'Drive on Mike, we'd better keep the doors tight and the windows up just in case the buggers decide to try again. Thought we might run in to trouble so brought this as protection, American, nine shot magazine.' He grinned to mask the fact that the attempted robbery had rattled him.

'Just remember to cock it next time,' snorted Farrell.

Later, when they stopped to let the engine cool down, Pierse cut some stout sticks, about a yard long, for Farrell and himself, sharpening one end of each to a point so that they could be used to club or spear. The knowledge that Chandra had a pistol made him uneasy – he wanted to be prepared.

'Ever the Boy Scout, eh, Piersey?' laughed Farrell, but he was grateful for the protection.

The night passed without further incident and they entered Lahore as a fiery orange dawn broke and illuminated the palls of smoke in parts of the Old City that tracked the places of the night's riots and killings. Some of the houses along the road had green Islamic crescents freshly painted on the gateposts to declare their allegiance and hopefully deter the mobs. They made their way slowly through the heavy traffic and dense crowds to the convent in Durand Road.

'I've always wanted to come back to Lahore – I lived here till I was eight,' said Pierse, 'especially after reading Kipling's Kim in St. Xavier's. You know, the opening paragraph, to sit, as Kim did, on the great bronze cannon, that fire breathing dragon, Zam-Zammah, outside the museum. My Ma used to tell me about it when we lived here but it meant nothing to me at the time.'

'You're not expecting a bloody municipal tour are you, Piersey?' replied Farrell sarcastically, 'the museum, Akbar's fort, then Noor Jahan's mausoleum and a mosque or two. Perhaps ending with high tea at Faletti's?'

'We're here for something far more important, more beautiful than Noor Jahan, eh Piersey,' said Chandra silkily.

'Hope she recognises you Piersey after all these years,' mocked Farrell, 'after all, you have been in the wars – so to speak!' They all laughed; relieved to have arrived at their destination.

* * *

They drew up at the convent gates, which were barred shut. Pierse hammered on them and roused the cautious *durwan* who was reluctant to open up to a battered car full of strange men until he saw the lily-skinned, freckled and ginger-haired Farrell and concluded that any Sahib wanting to come in to the convent at this hour must be important. They waited until a brisk French nun came to see them.

Apologising for disturbing her at such an early hour, Pierse stated his purpose.

'I've come to find Mrs Taylor, Sister, and possibly take her back to her home in Lucknow.'

The nun frowned as she considered this. 'I don't know of anyone 'ere called Mrs Taylor,' she replied in her heavily accented English.

Pierse's heart sank. Not again! 'Tall young woman, pretty, black hair, Anglo-Indian, Ellen Taylor and her husband Alec?' Chandra showed her the photo and pointed out Ellen.

'Ah! Ellen! Yes, but that is Ellen Lewis – zere's no 'usband 'ere.'

Pierse's heart was beating fast. 'Does she have a child with her?'

'No,' pause, 'not zat I know of.'

'Do you know where she lives Sister?'

'She is living 'ere, in zer Convent staff quarters.'

'Can I see her, Sister?'

'You've just missed 'er. She went to zer station last night to try to get a train 'ome before zer borders are put in place. Mother Superior told 'er not to go – it is very dangerous you know.....' But the nun was talking to the backs of the three, who were running to their car.

'God, I hope we're not too late,' cried a panicked Pierse as they drove towards the station as quickly as they could through streets thick with crowds. The trains were dangerous his Da had said, some had recently been ambushed and had arrived bloodstained with their passengers killed.

* * *

The first glimpse of Lahore Station, a red brick fortress with its towers, bastions, battlements and loopholes for riflemen awakened in Pierse childhood memories of cycling to it to meet his father when he finished a shift. It had deliberately been built to be defensible after the Mutiny of 1857, and Da Pierse had shown his son the iron doors in the forbidding train entrances which could be closed to seal the station against attack. The dark vaulted platforms were now filled to bursting with people trying to leave the city. A thousand voices became two thousand, three thousand, more – as they echoed and re-echoed around the ceilings. Passengers crowded every square inch of the platform floors, squatting, sitting in huddles, standing in groups, lying jammed in with their steel trunks, holdalls, baskets and bundles, fractious children, chickens and small animals – the luggage arranged like barricades around them. Some sat silent, locked in despair, all conversation exhausted, all hope receding, others engaged in loud discussions, eating and expectorating – coughing in the smoky fug of thousands of beedies and cheap cigarettes, a grey haze which drifted upwards to form a gradually thickening cloud as it was slowly compressed against the roof. Many had been waiting for days to board a train, any train, going east. The place stank of cigarettes, urine, food and stale bodies and the noisy hum of thousands of conversations was overlaid by incessant metallically echoing Tannoy announcements. Despite the bustle, there was a pervasive air of fear about as the crowd was keenly aware that they could be the target of the Muslim mobs who were hunting down any Hindus and Sikhs they could find in the city – and what better collection than this! There were armed soldiers guarding them, but their impartiality and their devotion to duty could not be relied on – would they turn against their Muslim countrymen if they attacked the Hindus? The male Sikh travellers had their *kirpans*, their swords, openly on display as a warning to deter any attack. Farrell, Chandra and Pierse anxiously scanned the crowd searching for Ellen, but couldn't spot her anywhere.

'I wonder if she left last night, I'll find out if any trains went out.' Chandra pushed his way with some difficulty towards an official in railway uniform and eventually came back with the news that one train had gone out and that it was filled to bursting with people who had already been waiting at the station for nearly a day. 'The chap says that the trains are being delayed because there have been attacks on the line and some minor derailments. I'd be surprised if she managed to get on last night's train,' he said.

'I've an idea,' said Farrell and pushed his way towards the same official and was directed further along to the ticket hall. 'I'll try and get them to make an announcement asking if Ellen Lewis can come along here,' he shouted as he shouldered and side-stepped his way through the crowd. Pierse continued to scan the waiting mass, his concern for Ellen's safety rising. Chandra suggested that he stay where he was until they saw whether anything came of Farrell's announcement, meanwhile he would work the crowd. All he had to go on was the small photograph of Ellen – but an Anglo-Indian should stand out in this crowd – and that helped.

At last the Tannoy stopped its stream of Urdu announcements and crackled with Farrell's unmistakeable English accent. 'If there is an Ellen Lewis or an Ellen Taylor from the Josephine Convent in this station, would she kindly go to the main ticket hall where a gentleman is waiting to take her back to Lucknow by car.' It was repeated twice, the words echoing round the station hall, made more indistinct because of the buzz of the crowd.

Pierse waited and waited but nothing happened. It could take time for anyone to get anywhere in this crush. After a while he decided to work his way through the mass – platform to platform – rather than stand in one place, Ellen might be anywhere. Pushing, squeezing, apologising and tripping over bundles of luggage and small children he slowly moved his way along. The sweat was pouring off him, the fear, frustration and sense of emptiness building. There was no sign of her. Maybe she had gone back to the Convent, or taken a bus, or even managed to get on last night's train. He began to feel heart-sick. As he pushed his way towards yet another platform he spotted something familiar – the distinctive robes of a nun from the convent sitting on the floor – she was giving water to a frail old Sikh woman. Maybe she could help. He struggled towards her calling out, 'Sister! Sister!'

At last she seemed to hear him above the hubbub and looked left and right to locate the sound – to find out who was calling out in English. 'Sister!' called Pierse frantically, waving his arm to attract her attention. She finally turned towards him and he stopped with a shock. 'Ellen!' he yelled, 'Ellen!'

She looked uncertain, in disbelief as though it was some sort of mad hallucination. Then she sprang up, shrugged off the crowd round her, desperately clawing, pushing and shoving and stumbled towards Pierse and flung her arms round him, sobbing and hugging him tight. The crowd was scandalised: a nun hugging and passionately kissing a young man? What madness was this? And indeed it was a kind of madness as, words unspoken, Ellen and Pierse held each other, cried together and rejoiced in finding each other again.

'She's my sister! *Mehra bahen*!' cried Pierse in Urdu, in explanation to stave off the crowd's distaste. But they were not fooled – the kisses were too passionate.

She dragged him back to collect her luggage and together, hands tightly clasped, they edged their way out of the crowded station to the forecourt reading the toll of those missing years on each others' faces, her brown eyes shiny with happiness.

'How did you know where to find me?'

'We went to the convent, the Sister told us.'

'No, no. How did you know I was in Lahore?'

'Anil Chandra found you – he saw a photograph brought back by one of the girls.'

'Chandra! The man who.....'

'Who told you about him?'

'Marion. You told her.'

'Where's.... your husband?' he asked tentatively.

'We separated nearly a year ago,' Ellen replied, caressing his face.

'I was told that you had a child.'

'Who said that?' Shocked.

'Marion La Fontaine.'

She looked down, distressed, her face reddening. 'I lost it, Eddie. I'm ashamed to say that I didn't really want it to be born. The day I found out that I was pregnant was the day that I realised that I couldn't stay married to Alec. I didn't want his child. I had made a big mistake. I wanted you back – I wanted you back so much. I told Alec that I was leaving; he was very upset and so was I – he was a good man Eddie. But it was always you. Always.'

He had tears too.

'And you're a nun now?' he asked warily.

She shook her head.

'I think that you'd better get out of that nun's outfit, people are looking at us very strangely.'

She smiled, whipped off the headdress and tossed her long black hair, which Pierse immediately caressed, savouring its touch. 'It was the Mother Superior's idea. She thought it would be safer to travel in a nun's habit as people would think twice about harming a holy person. And it would show I was Christian, not Hindu or Muslim,' she fingered the chain of the large, heavy crucifix on her chest. 'I'd change if I could – but there's nowhere here.'

They took their time to find Chandra and Farrell, laughing, hugging and catching up with snatches of their lives while they did so.

'Marion told me about you,' she said coyly. When she saw his shocked and guilty look she laughed heartily, pinching his cheek. 'She was upset that you left – because of me!' She looked pleased.

They finally found Chandra and Farrell. Both bowed with elaborate courtesy, like musketeers, on meeting Ellen.

'You must be very good friends,' she said to them, to come together all this way to get me.' They looked at each other and burst out laughing.

'I'll tell you the story some other time,' said Pierse. 'Meanwhile, let's not dilly dally, we'd better get back.'

* * *

The road back was just as crowded with refugees and their progress down it was again painfully slow. It seemed as if the whole of the Punjab was on the move. They now had to stop the car frequently to avoid the leaky radiator overheating.

Chandra cursed its owner and swore eternal damnation on him, his children and his children's children. After some hours moving at a snail's pace, Chandra became impatient.

'I think we should try the back roads that run parallel to this one. The way may be slightly longer and the roads are not as good, but we'll make more progress.'

They agreed. So he took the first turning to the left and travelled down the rough and rutted country track picking up speed. Around them in the fertile Punjab, the 'land of the five rivers', were fields of wheat, rice, sugarcane, vegetables and pulses with occasional villages, temples, mosques and gurdwaras dotted among the trees.

'Provided I turn right and generally head east or south east we should reach Amritsar or thereabouts quite quickly.'

The increased speed brought a flow of cooler air into the car and their spirits lifted. The 'lovebirds', as Mike Farrell described them, had been given the back seat and Farrell acted as navigator as Chandra wound the car round the *kutcha* tracks that skirted fields and villages, the old suspension jolting and complaining and a plume of dust rising in their wake. In some places the track was barely discernible or faded into nothing and they got themselves lost several times. By now it was late in the afternoon.

'I think it might be sensible to head west to try to pick up the Grand Trunk Road once again,' suggested Farrell. Chandra took the next right turn and sped up, anxious to beat the night. Rounding a curve, the wheels caught in the deep ruts made by years of steel-shod bullock cart wheels and the car jolted, then flipped over on to the driver's side, its momentum sliding it over an embankment in a scream of metal and clouds of dust, stones and splintered glass to tip nose first into a ditch, where it came to rest with a juddering crash that smashed the windscreen and rammed the engine off its mountings. They lay there bruised and in a state of shock. Chandra began to groan.

'Is everyone all right?' asked Farrell anxiously, a gash on his scalp, his face bruised from hitting the dashboard. Pierse and Ellen, who had clutched at each other as the car went over, reported that they seemed unhurt. But Chandra was in agony, his knee had hit the dashboard with force and it appeared to be seriously damaged.

As the car was on its side and at a steep angle in the ditch, they extricated themselves with difficulty. Getting the injured Chandra out without causing him further pain or injury was impossible, they kicked in what remained of the windscreen and hauled him out as quickly as possible through its frame amid fears that the leaking petrol could ignite. He was carried to the shelter of a nearby tree and laid on the ground. His right knee was now swollen and his foot seemed to be at an awkward angle, blood stained his trouser leg. The knee was either broken or dislocated and he had damaged his shin badly. Ellen pulled the kitbags out of the car's boot to provide him with a pillow.

'We've got to get him to a hospital quickly, Mike,' said Pierse.

'Agreed. But the car's kaput even if we could get it out of the ditch.' The crumpled bonnet had yawned open to reveal the mangled engine and the bottom of the ditch was covered in a pool of oil, steaming water and petrol.

'One of us will have to go for help. We passed some people tending wheat and sugar-cane fields a mile or so back, so a village can't be far away.'

'That might not help,' replied Farrell, 'we need to get him on to a motor car or lorry and take him to the hospital in Amritsar. Villages round here will only have bullock carts or horses. How far away are we from Amritsar?'

'I reckon that we are about twenty miles out of Lahore, so another ten to fifteen perhaps?'

'Look, Ed, you and Ellen stay here and look after him. I'll

strike out westwards and should cut across the GT Road. I'll try
to get some help there – the police and troops are patrolling.
With luck they may know who Anil is, so that should persuade
them. Scratch a message on the car to tell me where you have
gone if help arrives in the meantime.'

'Will you be able to find us again?'

'I'm a trained army officer dammit! And with luck I should
stumble across a village or two and get our bearings. With even
more luck, they may have motor transport.'

'Perhaps I should go,' suggested Pierse, 'my Urdu is better
than yours and you've bashed your face.'

Farrell laughed. 'Having just found Ellen after all these
years I'm not letting you leave her. No, you stay here; I'll be
back as quickly as I can.' He picked up one of the *lathis* that
Pierse had made earlier, said his goodbyes and strode off across
the fields towards the setting sun, trying to look nonchalant.

Pierse cut some saplings and he and Ellen splinted
Chandra's leg, tearing rags from their spare clothes. He silently
cursed Chandra for his recklessness in crashing the car and
leaving them stranded.

'We have no food and very little water,' he said quietly to
Ellen, 'and a bottle of scotch that Mike brought – we should use
that to try and anaesthetise Anil against the pain.'

'I've got a few sandwiches and some parathas in my case,'
replied Ellen, 'Mother Superior insisted that I pack them for my
train journey. We could eat those if we get really hungry.'

'I'm sorry, darling,' said Pierse, taking her hand, 'we've got
you into such a mess.'

She looked at him and smiled warmly. 'Mike will come
back with help; we'll be okay. It will give us a chance to catch
up.'

They watched over Anil Chandra, who lay ashen faced and
in great pain, disconnected from the world. Pierse gave him
several large slugs of whisky and he slowly drifted off into a

fitful doze. The shadows were lengthening and the insects and flies began to torment them, drawn by the smell of Chandra's blood. The heat and the humidity were not alleviated by even the faintest breeze and soon they were soaked in perspiration. Pierse cursed Chandra over and over in his mind for putting Ellen in this predicament. But Ellen seemed to be relaxed and at ease, looking after Chandra and talking to Pierse when Chandra dozed off. She was just happy to be back with Pierse, but he was anxious for her – she was a new responsibility for him after all these years of taking care of himself in difficult situations.

The twilight was slowly overtaking them and leaching the colour out of the land, turning browns and greens into dull shadows, the last cawings of crows were being given over to the hum of insects and the chirping of crickets. Soon it would be dark and they had no torches or lamps, only Chandra's box of matches. Pierse began gathering twigs with which to make a fire, but out of the corner of his eye he caught a movement and his skin prickled. He glanced round casually while talking to Ellen, checking the jungle around him and reaching for his *lathi*. He remembered that Chandra had brought an automatic pistol with him, it must be somewhere in the car – it certainly wasn't on him. He stood up to go and get it but figures slipped silently out of the shadows. He looked round quickly, there were at least five men, each carrying some sort of *lathi* or sharp implement, and they were slowly converging from all directions. These were not the actions of friendly people.

Pierse hailed them in Urdu. 'Can you help us brothers?' he called. 'Our car has crashed and we have an injured man here. He urgently needs to go to a doctor.' Ellen looked startled at the sudden appearance of the men and stood up too.

They came closer. Pierse could see that one of them carried an ancient *tulwar* – the distinctive curved sword of North India

– another carried a billhook, and one, his brows set in a scowl, carried an ex-army bayonet.

'Stay behind me,' he whispered to Ellen. To the men, 'What is your purpose? Have you come to help us? You,' he said, pointing with his *lathi* to the man with the bayonet, 'are you an ex-sepoy? The two of us,' indicating Chandra and himself, 'are army officers and this lady, my sister, is a holy nun.' Ellen was still wearing her nun's habit, but without the headdress.

The men came closer, their weapons held ready. Pierse stepped forward boldly and raised his *lathi* in response. They are looking to the man with the *tulwar* for their signal, he thought, and he determined that he would attack him first and try to take the *tulwar* off him and use it, and the advantage of length that it gave him, to defend himself and Ellen.

'Bugger, bugger, bugger,' he mouthed, 'all because of this stupid sod, Chandra.' He was fearful – not just for his own life but for that of Ellen's. His joy at finding her had turned to despair.

'What do you want!' he shouted and moved aggressively towards the man with the *tulwar,* his blood coursing and anger rising.

The man suddenly looked up from gazing at Chandra lying against the tree. 'Is that Lt. Chandra of the INA?' he asked.

Pierse was stunned. He nodded, confused, but still kept his eyes on the men around him.

The man with the *tulwar* lowered it and indicated to the others to do the same with their weapons.

'I saw Lt. Chandra in Singapore, when we all joined the Azad Hind Fauj; he came to talk to us. And I went last year to hear him speak in the Congress meeting near Jullundur. He is a freedom fighter!' He looked at Pierse, then knelt beside Chandra and looked at him closely. 'Chandra Sir, are you alright?'

Chandra mumbled that he was not – he was, if truth be told, a little too drunk by now to speak with any coherence.

The man rose, turned to one of his companions and told him to fetch a cart from the village. He bowed slightly to Ellen and smiling at Pierse said:

'I was in the 1/14th Punjabis Sir, fighting in Malaya, so was my cousin,' he indicated the scowling man with the bayonet.

'Mr Chandra and I were also in Malaya, 3/17th Dogras,' Pierse replied, 'I was captured by the *Japani* and imprisoned in Changi.'

'I am Nawaz Khan,' said the man, 'I am sorry if we frightened you but with all the killing going on by the Hindus and Sikhs in this area we have to be careful of strangers. Come, sir, we will take you to our village tonight and we will try to get Mr Chandra to a doctor tomorrow.'

'Look Nawaz Khan, one of our companions, also a Dogra officer, has gone for help. If he comes back and finds us gone he will not know what has happened to us. He will probably come back with an army or police lorry so we need to leave him a message to say where we have gone. I'll scratch it on the car.' Pierse was hedging his bets, trying to frighten the men, still not sure of their intentions. Nawaz Khan was unflustered.

'Leave a message, Sir. Say that we are going to Gurgaon village. If you like, I can ask one of my men to stay here for a few hours in case someone comes.'

* * *

The cart arrived, drawn by a bullock. They loaded Chandra on to it together with their baggage. Despite going back to the car for the rest of their kit, Pierse could not locate the automatic pistol in the dark and didn't want to try too hard in case he aroused their curiosity. He held Ellen's hand, squeezing it gently from time to time to keep her spirits up, and kept a watchful eye on their companions, urging them ahead of him as they walked the mile or so to the village, unable to get his bearings in the dark, the path lit only by a solitary kerosene lantern.

In the village they were shown to an empty hut with a thatched roof and a beaten earth floor. As they entered, the scowling man stepped forward and grabbed Ellen's arm roughly and tried to pull her away, shouting in broken English, 'You go with womans, you go with womans!'

Ellen, startled and frightened, struggled unsuccessfully to shake herself free of his grip, but an enraged Pierse seized the man's other arm and pushed him furiously against the hut wall, breaking his grip and heavily banging his head. The shaken and angry man fished under his shirt for his bayonet and Pierse raised his *lathi* to spear him but Nawaz Khan intervened, having hurriedly placed Chandra on the floor and run back. He admonished the scowling man who replied angrily in rapid Urdu and waved his bayonet threateningly. Nawaz Khan roughly pushed him away, indicating that he should leave; he turned apologetically to Pierse and Ellen.

'He is wanting you to go to women's hut, Miss. He thinks you will be private there and women will look after you.'

'I am supposed to be your guest,' replied Ellen evenly, 'if he wanted me to go elsewhere why did he not ask me politely.'

Nawaz Khan nodded sympathetically. 'Of course, Miss. He is sick man, from the war. He was with the *Japani* in Burma and suffered much. Then he was cashiered from Regiment, so he is not happy. He will not make trouble again. I will see to it.'

A young woman, face veiled in her sari, brought a meagre dish of *sattu* with a couple of chillies and a raw onion to accompany it, a brass pitcher of water and an oil lamp, peering curiously at these strange guests. An elderly man, who seemed to be the village healer, uncovered Chandra's injured leg and examined it carefully. He then indicated to Pierse to hold him down. Seizing hold of the leg just under the knee, he pulled it and twisted. He did so three or four times, all the while Chandra screamed and shouted out in pain and Ellen tried to comfort him. The treatment seemed unduly harsh and Pierse put his hand out to stop the man from hurting Chandra further, but he gave one last tug, there was a satisfying click, and the knee seemed to go back into its joint. Chandra lay there gasping and exhausted as the pain refused to subside to bearable levels. The man dressed the injured knee and the swollen shin with a pounded mixture of herbs; they replaced the splints and made Chandra as comfortable as they could.

* * *

As they lay in the dark listening to Chandra groan, Pierse held Ellen close and quietly told her of his fears that the villagers, especially the scowling man, could not be trusted. His attempt to separate Ellen from them had rattled Pierse – he distrusted their motives.

'Should we try to steal away in the night?' he asked her.

'We can't leave Anil on his own,' she replied, 'and we won't know where we are going in the dark. They haven't harmed us so far Eddie, I think they surrounded us because they are frightened of strangers. They could easily have robbed us or harmed us already – and done it on the roadside, away from their village.'

'But the chap with the bayonet – he appears deranged and seems to have some sort of grudge against us, possibly because we are officers and he was cashiered for his part in the INA.'

'I think Nawaz Khan will ensure that he does us no harm. And they seem to have a lot of respect for Anil.'

'Anil is not the friend he pretends to be,' whispered Pierse. 'Don't forget that he is responsible for lying about my death. He is not to be trusted.'

'But he has made amends and brought us together Eddie. And we can't leave him – he's defenceless.'

He knew she was right – so he decided not to tell her that only a few months ago Chandra had nearly had him killed.

'Where the bloody hell is Farrell,' he fumed. 'He should have found something by now.' Pierse had scratched a large message across the roof of the car where Farrell could not have missed it and one of the men had been left behind with a lantern for a couple of hours in case he returned. Pierse opened his knife and kept it close by together with his sharpened *lathi*. He remained watchful despite his exhaustion at not having slept much on the road the night before, listening to the gentle slap of bare feet on the ground outside – the villagers had mounted a guard over them, whether to keep them safe or to prevent them from leaving he couldn't tell.

Ellen shared his fears but she was determined not to show them as she knew that it would only add to his worries. She was just glad to be with him and she placed her trust in him. If they were robbed, so be it. That was not the end of the world. If they were attacked – and it didn't bear thinking about – at least she would do what she could alongside Ed. She was strong and fit. She snuggled up to him and held him tight. She wanted to make love to him, to make up for all the lost years – but that would have to wait. They remained watchful and Chandra slept only occasionally, his pain keeping him awake as the whisky had mysteriously disappeared.

Dawn came and with the first faint lightening of the sky the village burst into a cacophony of crowing roosters, rasping crows, birdsong from the thickets, anxious cattle calling out to be milked, peevish pi-dogs quarrelling. Murmured voices were followed by the hawking of throats and blowing of noses, the clash of cooking pots and the smell of the wood and dung fires. Pierse, peering through the entrance to the hut, watched the comings and goings until the people disappeared and the voices seemed to trail off; then, loud and clear, he heard a villager utter the Muslim call to prayer, though there didn't appear to be a recognisable mosque among the huts. After prayers, Nawaz Khan came to them.

'Are you better Sir?' he enquired of Chandra, who nodded and thanked him. 'We will take you to the GT Road soon Sir. There you will be able to get a lorry or car to take you to hospital. We have no doctor or hospital here.'

'Any news of our friend, Mr Farrell?' asked Pierse. Nawaz Khan shook his head.

'Can you come outside for a moment Sir?' Nawaz Khan asked Pierse, 'I need to talk to you about something.'

Pierse looked at him sceptically. He had no intention of being separated from Ellen or lured into a possible ambush.

'You can say what you want to say in here,' he said, sounding affable, his hand tight around the handle of his *lathi*. Nawaz Khan considered this for a moment and nodded agreement.

'It is embarrassing, Sir. We are poor villagers and you are rich people. We have shared our food with you and helped Mr Chandra. Could you spare us some money before you go?'

'Of course, Nawaz Khan,' said Chandra suddenly, 'we are only too happy to pay you for your trouble. 'He carefully reached into his pocket and pulled out his wallet, then extracted a handful of Rupee notes and passed them over. The sum would have equalled a villager's earnings for a year. Nawaz Khan took the money but looked anxious. 'What is it?' asked Chandra.

'Mr Chandra, Sir, my cousin wanted to rob all of you last night – only because he is mad and we are so poor Sir,' he added hastily. 'I told him that he couldn't do that to you after all that you have done for our country. But we are poor Sir and it will help me to take him for treatment if you give me some more money,' he said, looking embarrassed and wringing his hands.

Chandra drew out some more and handed it over. 'I think that that is enough, Nawaz Khan. After all, I will need money to pay the hospital.'

'Thank you, Sir,' said Nawaz Khan gratefully. 'We will be ready to go in about half an hour so please get ready.'

* * *

They loaded Chandra on to the bullock cart and, with the same five men in tow, the scowling ex-sepoy with the bayonet kept close by Nawaz Khan's side to avoid trouble, they travelled through a maze of rutted paths between the fields in what the villagers claimed to be the direction of the Grand Trunk Road. Having walked for about an hour, they could at last see above the horizon the clouds of dust raised by the crowds migrating up and down the great road. In another half hour they could hear the distant honking of horns and the roar and clatter of engines. Finally, they were in sight of the road itself with its parallel tides of human misery. The small procession halted.

'What's the matter?' enquired Pierse.

'We are going no further,' said the ex-sepoy who had been carrying the bayonet, which he suddenly produced from beneath his dhoti. The others produced the weapons that they had been carrying the night before and surrounded Pierse, Ellen and Chandra – who was sitting on the bullock cart.

'What treachery is this?' Chandra shouted.

'I'm sorry, Sir,' said a seemingly abject Nawaz Khan, 'but in return for giving you help you must give us all your money and goods. We are very poor, Sir, you are very rich. You can always get more.'

'You bastards,' exclaimed Pierse, but something sharp prodded him in the back and he knew that it was futile to try to resist. If money was all they wanted then that was okay as he could now easily get to the GT Road and find help to get them back to Amritsar.

They were searched and stripped of all their cash, watches, Ellen's gold rings and Uncle Derek's knife. They even took their shoes, leaving them barefoot and making it difficult for them to go quickly for help across the rough fields. Then, placing Chandra on the ground, they rearranged the baggage on the bullock cart and began returning the way they had come. The ex-sepoy became engaged in a furious and animated discussion with his colleagues and glances were cast behind at Pierse, Ellen and Chandra. Something was up. Nawaz Khan and the villagers shook their heads vehemently, and plucked at the ex-sepoy's shirt as he suddenly turned and came back towards Pierse, anger, resentment and menace written on his face, the bayonet held threateningly before him. His companions, clearly wanting no part of this, continued on their way, casting anxious backward glances.

Pierse, who had been relieved of his *lathi*, watched the approaching ex-sepoy warily. He whispered to Ellen, 'Run, run for the GT Road. I'll deal with him.'

She shook her head and remained by his side. Anil Chandra levered himself upright, grimacing with pain, feeling helpless in the face of the impending attack.

'Both of you run,' he urged, 'I don't think it is me he wants to harm. Go, go now!'

Pierse looked around for something to use as a weapon, but there was nothing close by. He stepped boldly towards the advancing ex-sepoy, hoping to intimidate him. But the man came on, his mouth set in a snarl, muttering imprecations, beads of nervous sweat shiny on his forehead; he seemed clearly bent on doing them harm. Nawaz Khan and the villagers stopped and anxiously turned to watch, unable or unwilling to intervene. The man was now a few feet away and suddenly darted forward with a shout. Before Pierse could stop her, Ellen stepped forward to protect him. The fiercely jabbed bayonet struck her in the chest and with a sharp cry and an exhalation of breath she went down, collapsing head first on to the track – to lie motionless, a small stream of blood wriggling its way from under her through the dusty earth.

The ex-sepoy hesitated, shocked at what he had done, this wasn't his intended victim. It was that fatal fraction of a second that Pierse in his anguish knew too well. In his rage and grief he grabbed the man's bayonet arm and pulled it forward, thrusting his knee savagely into the elbow and wrenching the joint against its natural movement. The man cried out as the joint parted and the bayonet fell from his hand as he was forced to the ground. He struggled to rise but Pierse fell on him, his knees crushing the breath out of the man's body and cracking his ribs. He tore at his face, gouged his eyes, punched his throat and barehanded sought to destroy him for what he had done to Ellen. A shadow loomed above. Pierse glanced up to find that Chandra was holding a large stone in both hands. Uncertain of his motive he rose sharply to meet this new threat.

'Watch out Ed!' shouted Chandra. Pierse followed his gaze to see Nawaz Khan and another of the villagers, weapons aloft, screaming with rage, running towards them to rescue their kinsman from further harm.

'Stop!' Chandra shouted, 'don't come any closer or I'll kill him!' He raised the stone threateningly, ready to crush the ex-sepoy's head. Nawaz Khan and his comrade checked, and halted. Pierse picked up the bayonet and advanced towards them, sidestepping the figures lying comatose in the track.

'Put down your weapons!' shouted Chandra, 'throw them towards us.' They hesitated.

'Do it now or I'll kill him,' Chandra yelled.

Nawaz Khan looked undecided; he muttered something to his companion. Then they turned and ran back to the now fast disappearing bullock cart, leaving the ex-sepoy to the mercy of Chandra.

Pierse rushed to Ellen and slowly, gently, turned her over, recoiling at the blood puddled under her. She was unconscious, the colour gone from her face, forehead bloodied from hitting the ground. Her chest, where the bayonet had struck her, was heavily bloodstained and her right hand was pierced between thumb and forefinger and bleeding badly – she had probably raised it to defend herself. Pierse scrabbled about to unbutton her nun's habit and find the wound to put pressure on it and staunch the bleeding. The slippery blood made the task difficult and, when he finally succeeded, he could not locate the wound among her bloodied underclothes. He searched frantically: puzzlement turned to hesitation, hesitation to realisation – and realisation to incredulity. He checked the folds of her habit again, then examined her hand with its stigmata-like wound pulsing blood through his and her fingers. He ripped off his shirt to bind her palm. He couldn't feel a pulse, she didn't appear to breathe. He gently patted her face. Nothing!

'Ellen! Ellen!' he whispered urgently. Her head rolled back, a sigh escaped her lips as he pulled her up. Her eyelids flickered and barely opened. Pierse began to smile, then to laugh, a harsh, hysterical, animal sound of pain mixed with relief. Ellen, barely conscious, looked at his him, puzzled. The blood from her forehead began to trickle down her face. Pierse pulled her towards him and held her close.

'What's the matter? How is she!' said Chandra anxiously, continuing to hold the stone above the now still ex-sepoy's head.

'It's a bloody miracle,' cried Pierse, laughing and sobbing at the same time as he gently cradled Ellen, 'even if I, the world's biggest damned atheist, say so! Look Anil!' he shouted, holding up the bloodied nun's crucifix that hung from the chain on her chest. 'Look! The bayonet went through her hand and struck the crucifix, the point wedged in the metal legs of Christ – see how they have been cut and buckled – and her hand held it there so that it couldn't glance off and kill her! It's a miracle!' He shook his head in wonderment. 'All this blood is from her hand!' He kissed her cheek, 'My darling girl, you're okay, you're okay! It's a good thing they were too superstitious to pinch your crucifix. And you saved my life, you brave, stupid, lovely girl!'

Ellen slowly came round, dully wiping at her face with her good hand to keep the blood from her eyes. She whimpered with the pain from her hand, head and chest and she was still groggy and faint from the shock and loss of blood. Pierse rebound her hand and cut a strip of cloth off her habit with the bayonet to bind her head.

'It hurts Eddie,' she gasped, 'it hurts so badly. Will I die?' He shook his head.

'The bayonet went through your hand – that's the worst of it, and you cracked your head as you fell. We need to get you to a doctor quickly to stop your hand bleeding.'

She noticed the ex-sepoy, beaten to a bloody pulp and now unconscious. The sight made her heave. 'Is *he* dead?' she asked fearfully as Pierse wiped the sick from her mouth.

'No – not yet,' said Pierse savagely, 'but you must try to get up. We have to go from this place.' He slowly helped her to her feet, holding her close to stop her falling.

'What do we do now?' asked Chandra, his legs trembling with the pain and effort of standing.

'We've got to get to the GT Road quickly to find help,' replied Pierse. 'Those villagers will regroup and try to recover chummy here. Nawaz Khan is no fool. He retreated, but this is his kinsman and they know that we officers won't kill him in cold blood, especially now that Ellen is alive. They are probably watching us now and working out ways to get him back – and they won't want to leave any witnesses.'

Chandra agreed. 'They will try to surround us as they did yesterday, so we should quickly move closer to the GT Road and other people.'

'What do we do with him?' asked Pierse. 'He is a useful hostage, we could take him with us, but that could make matters worse as they will definitely attack us to rescue him.'

'I think we should leave him here,' said Chandra. 'He seems to be in a very bad way, and we can't carry him. They will want to get him back quickly to the village and I wonder whether they would have the guts to try to attack us again – you have the bayonet and we can use it to try to cut some *lathis*.'

'No time for that. Let's go.'

Pierse supported Chandra with one arm, Ellen stumbled along clutched in the other. The journey, in bare feet, was slow and painful as Chandra could only move by hopping on his good leg; the sapping heat left them breathless and perspiring. Ellen's wounds began to bleed again. They barely progressed fifteen yards.

'I'll have to leave you here Anil,' gasped an exhausted Pierse, 'while Ellen and I go for help.'

'No. I'll stay with Anil,' pleaded Ellen, who just wanted to lie down and rest as the landscape shimmered and swayed around her. 'Please! You go Eddie.'

'I'm not leaving you,' replied Pierse tersely. He looked around and moved Chandra into the shade of a scrubby tree. He handed the bayonet to him. 'If they come back while we're gone,' he said apologetically.

Chandra looked at him and nodded. Pierse quickly turned away.

'Come on,' he grabbed the reluctant Ellen tightly under her arm and pulled her towards the GT Road. 'You must go, darling, you must go or they'll kill us all!'

Treading painfully across the fields in their city-soft bare feet they reached the outskirts of the crowds going east and began to push their way through it to try to get to the road and its vehicles. The mass of people, carts and animals and its accompanying pungent smell moved like a sluggishly flowing river with a strong undercurrent that carried them with it as they tried to force their way upstream towards the road. Tired and exhausted families had camped in the fields, unable to go on for the moment, sitting there with the blank expressions of people who have endured too much. There were corpses to negotiate; some barely buried in a thin cover of earth others sheeted and lying there in the path of the crowd, left by their loved ones as their desperate migration continued. They lay fly-blown, bloated and festering in the heat and would soon be watered by the monsoon rain; grotesque giant seeds that would set down the roots of hatred, the fruits of which would be harvested for generations to come.

Nothing on the road was moving at great speed because of the crush and Pierse tried to hail trucks and cars but they wouldn't stop, the drivers pointedly staring blankly ahead, anxious to keep up their grinding momentum and get as far away as possible from Lahore or Amritsar. They were certainly not going to stop for a barefoot and half naked madman and a woman bandaged and covered in blood. Pierse and Ellen were in despair, Ellen could barely remain upright – they were exhausted. They spotted an army convoy going west and Pierse pulled Ellen with him and stood in its path. He shouted hoarsely, desperately, his voice cracking in his parched throat as he tried to flag them down. The leading lorry sounded its horn insistently, its driver and passenger yelling and gesticulating to Pierse to clear out of the way but he and Ellen, holding hands, stood their ground. With squealing brakes and curses from the driver, his hand now jammed furiously on the horn, the lorry shuddered to a halt and an angry Indian officer vaulted out of the passenger door.

'Good God!' exclaimed Pierse.

Jemadar Prem Singh was equally surprised. He was on a patrol to prevent robbery and killings among the refugees.

Pierse quickly told him the story of their robbery and of the urgent need to recover the injured Anil Chandra. Prem Singh looked shocked at their condition, he shouted at the sepoys to help Ellen and Pierse into the back of the lorry where Pierse was recognised by several of the sepoys who threw him bewildered and hesitant salutes, while one of them set about dressing Ellen's wounds. Pierse directed Prem Singh across the stream of eastbound traffic to the path through which they had run, the driver hammering his horn and the sepoys waving their rifles and yelling furiously to clear a way through the crowd. There they found Anil Chandra, frightened and in pain, leaning against a tree supported by his one good leg, gripping the bayonet. Of the damaged ex-sepoy there was no trace. Chandra too was astonished to see Prem Singh, who could barely conceal his distaste at seeing the renegade officer again.

'They robbed us, those bastards,' shouted Chandra, 'and tried to kill us. Go after them!'

Prem Singh shook his head. 'We cannot get a lorry down there Mr Chandra. Be thankful that they have at least left you with your lives. We need to get Miss Ellen and you to hospital quickly.'

'They came back for that bastard,' said Chandra hysterically, 'but I hid from them and they just carried him away.'

CHAPTER 19

Freedom

The hospital in Amritsar was crowded with casualties from the bitter fighting between Hindus, Muslims and Sikhs that had erupted around the city. Injured and broken men, women and screaming children lay in the corridors awaiting attention from the harassed doctors, the corridors slushy with blood, vomit and faeces. There was a faint, sickly sweet smell of burning flesh from those who had escaped from their torched houses, scorched faces and limbs bloody and sometimes distorted. Accompanying the casualties were frightened relatives adding to the noise and the crush. Had it not been for Prem Singh and his gun-toting Dogras Ellen, Chandra and Pierse would have had to wait their turn to be seen. It was not a place in which to remain longer than was necessary – even if they could have found a hospital bed for the night.

Chandra, his leg in plaster, sat awkwardly on a chair in the hospital manager's office and awaited the arrival of a car to take him to the home of the local Congress leader. Pierse and Ellen, wounds and blistered feet patched up came to take their leave of him before being driven by the Dogras to Jullundur to board the train to Calcutta. Chandra winced when he saw the sorry state of Ellen.

'I apologise Ellen,' he said, taking hold of her good hand, tears in his eyes. 'I'm terribly sorry for putting you – for putting everybody – in so much danger by crashing the car. I thank God that we have come through it safely. I'm sorry also for all the bad things that have happened between us Piersey and I hope that we can remain friends.'

'We were lucky Anil. Very lucky!' said Pierse curtly. Then he softened slightly: 'I thank you though for helping me to find Ellen, for bringing us back together, and for your quick action in saving us from being attacked by Nawaz Khan and his lot.'

Chandra smiled weakly. He turned to Ellen.

'Ellen, my rashness nearly killed you. I will make a puja every day in thanks for the miracle that saved you. I hope that you and Ed....'

'Bloody hell!' interrupted Pierse explosively. 'How could I be so stupid! It was a great big bloody dare, wasn't it, Anil?' A grin, uncertain at first, slowly spread across Chandra's face. Ellen looked uncomprehendingly at them.

'You could easily have sent your policemen to check that the photo was indeed Ellen and they could have escorted her back from Lahore – or you could have gone yourself with a police guard.'

'When I saw Ellen's photo,' Chandra said, 'I didn't think about any of that. It was *kismet*, a divine omen – it was something we had to do – I had to do – to make amends to you Piersey, and the time was running out. I knew that you couldn't resist a challenge, so I sent the telegram. I wanted us to be back together again once more – the Allsorts.'

'We came pretty close to being killed dammit!'

'And when were you afraid of that?' Chandra smiled. 'We pulled it off Piersey, the biggest dare of all!'

'Yes, but not without cost to us,' said Pierse sharply, glancing at Ellen, 'and what about Mike? I wonder what's happened to him – I hope he is okay. It is strange that he didn't come back for us but there's so much confusion around that perhaps we shouldn't be surprised. I hope he'll turn up. The Dogras are looking for him.'

'It's a bit like the chaos of the war out there,' said Chandra, 'Mike'll turn up, you'll see. But I will also ask the police and my Congress people to try to find out where he has got to. Do you think the bugger abandoned us?'

Pierse shrugged and shook his head – but suddenly he wasn't sure.

'I really thought that *you* had abandoned me,' said Chandra.

'You know that I had to,' smiled Pierse reproachfully, 'if we were to get help. It was a chance.... Those villagers respected you and I gambled that they wouldn't harm you.'

Chandra acknowledged this, but the experience had unnerved him.

'If Ellen had been ....badly harmed,' said Pierse, looking at her, 'it would have been different. I would have gone after them.....'

Chandra nodded; Pierse would have 'gone after him' too, he reckoned.

'Anil, those things you did – in Malaya......' said Ellen hesitantly.

'Deserting the British and joining the INA, you mean?'

'Yes. I've been thinking. Those were really very brave and risky things to do to protect your family. You were taking big chances – risking your reputation, your life even.......'

Pierse looked surprised.

'It didn't seem like that at the time Ellen,' said Chandra quietly. 'It was just something I felt I had to do. I was scared of not coming back from the war, really scared Ellen. I didn't see the point of fighting the Japs – they weren't my enemy – maybe that was what decided it. I didn't want to die for a cause I didn't believe in. My family needed me more than the King Emperor did.'

They said their goodbyes and left. He had righted his wrong to Pierse by bringing Ellen back to him – his debt was cleared. They would probably never meet again. It was unspoken – it was understood.

* * *

Jemadar Prem Singh insisted that he and his men escort Pierse and Ellen to Jullundur where, after feeding them at a local hotel – Pierse didn't want to go to the Regimental Depot – and getting them kitted out at the local bazaar, he took them to the railway station and put them on the train to Calcutta.

'Prem Singh,' said Pierse feelingly as he stood at the open door of the compartment, 'it was I who said to you when I left the Regiment that if there was any way that I could help you to let me know, remember?' Prem Singh smiled. 'But instead, I am in debt to your nephew Dina Nath for my life – and to you also for the life of Ellen, and myself. How can I ever thank you enough.'

'We are brother Dogras,' said Prem Singh simply. 'We have been to hell and back Pierse Sahib, but *Jawala Mata* has been with us. I am glad that you and Mr Chandra are not at war with each other anymore. And I will try my best to find out what has happened to Farrell Sahib.' He shook Pierse's hand warmly and said a smiling goodbye to Ellen. 'I hope that God gives both of you a peaceful and happy life Miss,' adding, with a chuckle, 'and blesses you with many, many children.'

In the cool of the first class compartment, with India rushing by, they decided to make a start on that.

* * *

At midnight on the 14th of August 1947 India became free. The timing was one of ancient compromise: the astrologers had declared the 15th inauspicious because it fell on a Friday so the first stroke of midnight on the 14th, still technically a Thursday, was agreed on.

The family party at the Pierse's home in Calcutta to celebrate the safe return of Ed and Ellen paused to listen to the radio as the Union Flag of Great Britain was finally lowered on the ramparts of the Red Fort in Delhi and the new Indian tricolour was raised in its place. Chandra was right: Gandhi's spinning wheel had been replaced with the chakra – that ancient but potent symbol combining the wheel of life, the chariot wheel – despite its ancient lineage it represented the movement forward that the new India aspired to.

They heard Jawaharlal Nehru's speech, spoken in his cultivated English accent tinged with the inflexions of north India:

'Long years ago we made a tryst with destiny, and now the time comes when we shall redeem our pledge, not wholly or in full measure, but very substantially.

At the stroke of the midnight hour, when the world sleeps, India will awake to life and freedom. A moment comes, which comes but rarely in history, when we step out from the old to the new, when an age ends, and when the soul of a nation, long suppressed, finds utterance.

'We end today a period of ill fortune and India discovers herself again.'

With mixed emotions, sipping Da Pierse's best whisky, they listened in silence as the words unfolded and the future of India was vividly sketched in the ether to stir the souls of its people. At Nehru's last *'Jai Hind'* (Victory to India), Pierse silently raised his glass to Ellen and toasted her and the new India. Around them in Calcutta the ships' sirens echoed mournfully on the Hoogly River, factory hooters joined in, temple bells were rung, the horns of passing cars and lorries took up the exuberant celebration and fireworks exploded. But for the presence of one man – Gandhi – there would also have been the cries and screams of those being killed and the shouts and chants of those killing them if Hindus and Muslims had vented their fury and frustration on each other in the by-lanes and slums of Calcutta. Gandhi had come to the city to try to prevent riots rather than stay in Delhi for the pomp and celebrations – and he had miraculously succeeded, placing himself in a slum in Beliaghata, and threatening to fast unto death if its Muslim inhabitants were attacked by Hindu mobs.

* * *

'Nothing good will come of this,' said a gloomy Uncle Derek. 'We Anglos are caught here like piggy in the middle.'

'I have much to be thankful to Indians for,' said Pierse gently. 'They fought alongside me, saved my life on more than one occasion and brought Ellen back to me!' He smiled at Ellen and she squeezed his hand.

'And they stole that bloody penknife I gave you!' said Uncle Derek half jokingly.

'I've something better to keep with me now,' laughed Pierse, 'though regrettably she is not Bishop-proof! This is our country too, Uncle Derek, let's not forget that. We were born here. We are as much Indians as the various tribes, castes and people of other races who settled here over the centuries. We can choose to join in this great venture, or choose to retire from the field. It is up to us.' The words were spoken confidently, but he wondered just what lay ahead for people like him.

'But if we go to England, will they welcome us there?' asked Pierse's mother anxiously.

'They will think we are foreigners, Indians,' said Uncle

Derek bitterly. 'We are obviously not pinky-white, and we speak in a different way. It will be like having a bastard return to the fold. We're fine as cannon fodder to defend their Empire but they wouldn't want us living with them.'

'I hope that we will not be their forgotten cousins,' said Da Pierse quietly. 'Anglo-Indians like us kept the Raj going – the cogs and the levers. People like you and me, Derek, who drove the trains that moved goods and passengers round the country; people like Ma and Ellen who educated the next generation; people like Ken who kept the peace – and chaps like you, Eddie, willing to die for a country that you may never see.'

'This is just a crossroads in the passage of history Da,' replied Kenny soothingly. 'We Anglos have been around for over two hundred and fifty years and we are not going to disappear overnight. We share the same blood, the same history, as the British and of those of their countrymen who colonised America, Australia and Canada and other parts of the world. Let's not forget that the British themselves are not one race but a combination of many others who came to conquer. We are just another mix. In time as the world gets smaller and more people inter-marry, let's hope that the distinction between races will become unimportant.'

'Well, I'm not staying,' said Uncle Derek. 'It won't be long before they start to push us Anglos out of all the jobs we do and fill them with Indians. And why shouldn't they? It is their country, to them we are just pretend Englishmen – not entirely white; not entirely Indian – and they despise us because we supported the British so ardently.'

'Ed and I are staying put,' Ellen said quietly. 'We want to wait and see what happens. I know that the Hindus and Muslims are fighting each other, but no one has attacked the Christians, or the Parsees, or the Chinese here in Cal. Provided we don't try to behave like the worst kind of sahibs or memsahibs, don't try to act superior, then we should be alright.'

'Well said, Ellen,' smiled Pierse. 'Let's see what happens. Each of us will have to make up our minds where our loyalties belong.'

***

As the celebrations continued over August parts of India and Pakistan disintegrated into an orgy of unimaginable violence and killings; Sikhs, Hindus and Muslims trapped on the wrong side of the new frontiers turned on each other or fought for their lives. Worst affected was the Punjab; when the boundary line between India and Pakistan was finally announced after Independence Day it provoked, as Mountbatten had anticipated, intense fury among everyone. Up to a million people lost their lives in this most painful birth of the two nations – non-identical twins – the result of one man's obstinacy and another man's haste. The long awaited monsoon finally broke at the end of September, the killings petered out and the villagers returned to their fields. But there was a sting in the tail: the bursting monsoon brought with it severe floods and more destruction, drowning tens of thousands of refugees.

Despite the extensive searches made by Jemadar Prem Singh and his Dogras, as well as by Chandra's police, Farrell was never found. The search had to be called off as the carnage, the tide of displaced humanity and the destructive floods overwhelmed the Punjab. Men simply couldn't be spared to search for a lone Englishman when hundreds of thousands were losing their lives. They waited for word of him at the Regimental Depot in Jullundur, in the jute mill at Dum Dum – and an English butcher and his wife waited in a small suburban house in north London – but Farrell never turned up. He had, in a way, got his wish – he had been swallowed up and ended his days as 'Farrell *Sahib*' in the rich but unforgiving enigma that is India.

Chandra left Government a year later. Following Gandhi's assassination in January 1948 by a Hindu zealot, the Home Ministry was subjected to intense scrutiny and a destructive whispering campaign for failing to prevent his death. Disenchanted by the poisonous atmosphere, Chandra returned to the family business where he bribed, cheated and connived his way into a huge fortune – much to the delight of his ailing father. There was just one problem: the kick in the balls that had saved his life at Kota Bharu had done damage to his 'multiplication department'. He was destined to be the last of the Chandras.

Pierse pined for the high hills. He persuaded Finlays to let him go back to Munnar, where he worked as a tea planter and Ellen taught at a local school. They roamed the Kannan Devan, Anaimalai and Nilgiri Hills and saw the neelakurinji bloom again and again, turning the slopes a brilliant blue and marking the passage of another dozen years. Ellen declared that she never ever wanted to leave this paradise. Pierse smiled to himself; Mrs May would have approved. They never married – Taylor declined to divorce Ellen. In time the Pierses had a son. They called him Prem – which means 'love' in Hindi. He was another Boy Scout.

* * *

'I would like to see India free and strong so that she may offer herself as a willing and pure sacrifice for the betterment of the world. The individual, being pure, sacrifices himself for the family, the latter for the village, the village for the district, the district for the province, the province for the nation, the nation for all.'

Mahatma Gandhi

GLOSSARY

attap	Nipa palm, whose leaves were used for thatching
achkan	type of long jacket
babu	clerk; also a term of respect for a Bengali gentleman
bahen	sister
baksheesh	payment, often a bribe or a tip for services rendered
beedies	cheap cigarettes made of rolled tobacco leaves
bhai	brother
burra sahib	big Lord
chakra	wheel or disc.
chalo	go
chappals	slippers; sandals
charka	hand operated spinning wheel
dharma	destiny; fate

283

dhobi	washerman
dhurrie	cotton rug
Divali	Indian festival of light, celebrated with fireworks
durwan	watchman; gatekeeper
goondas	troublemakers; gangsters
hartal	stoppage of work or strike
Havildar	Indian non-commissioned officer equivalent to a sergeant
Jai Hind	Victory to India
jaldhi	quickly
Japani	Japanese
Jawala Mata	the goddess Jawala, also known as Durga, widely worshipped in the hill states
Jemadar	Viceroy's Commissioned Officer, equivalent to a Lieutenant
Jiff	derogatory term for men of the INA, derived from 'Japanese-Indian Fifth Column'
khadi	hand-woven cloth
khud	ditch

ki jai	victory to
kirpan	Sikh sword or knife
kismet	fate
kutcha	roughly made
lathi	bamboo stave, often steel-tipped
maidan	grassy open space
mali	gardener
Naik	Indian non-commissioned officer equivalent to a corporal
Namaste	greeting
nimbu pani	lime juice
paltan	platoon
pan wallah	seller of *pan* (pronounced 'parn'), the mixture of betel nut, quicklime and spices wrapped in a leaf, used as a digestive chew
patarker	firecracker
POW	prisoner of war
puchkawallas	sellers of a savory snack of potato packed into

	a crisp bubble of flour and dipped in tamarind water
raga	pattern of notes used as the basis for improvisation in Indian music
Raj	British rule
Sahib	Lord – term of respect for a gentleman
sarkar	government
sattu	dough of coarse flours of lentils and chickpeas, a staple food of the poor
sepoy	an Indian soldier, equivalent to a private
shaitan	devil
shenai	Indian clarinet-like wind instrument
thana	police station
ting-ting wallah	street vendor who advertises his wares by ringing a bell
tonga	horse drawn carriage for hire
Tuan	Malay word equivalent to Sahib
tulwar	curved North Indian sword
VCO	Viceroy's Commissioned Officer